Minnesota Architects

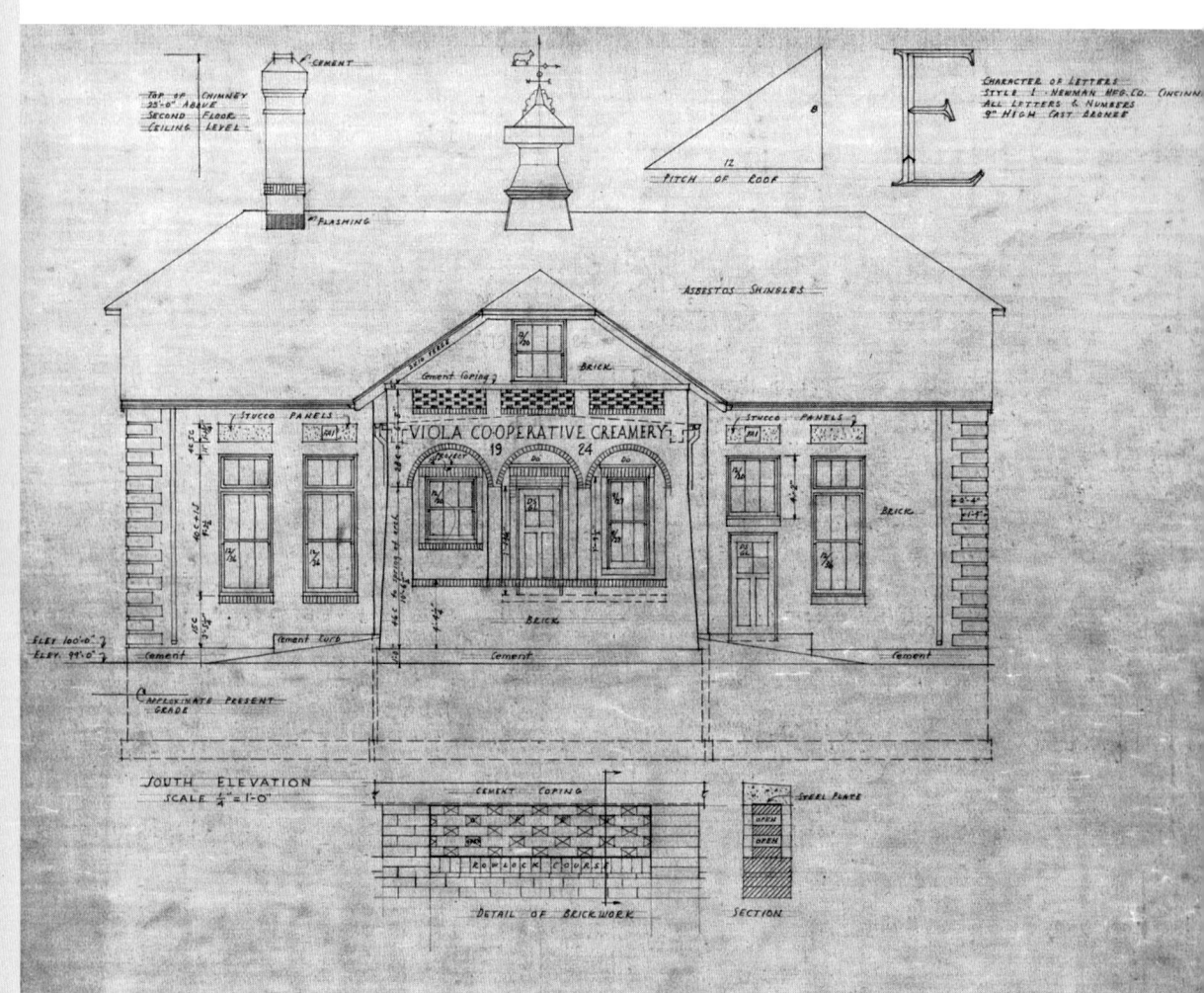

Minnesota Architects

A Biographical Dictionary

Alan K. Lathrop

University of Minnesota Press
Minneapolis · London

To Joel & Sandy —

With all best wishes & hope this book encourages a renewed interest in Minnesota's architectural history.

Every effort was made to obtain permission to reproduce material in this book. If any proper acknowledgment has not been included here, we encourage copyright holders to notify the publisher.

Copyright 2010 by Alan K. Lathrop

All rights reserved. No part of this publication may be reproduced, stored in a retrieval system, or transmitted, in any form or by any means, electronic, mechanical, photocopying, recording, or otherwise, without the prior written permission of the publisher.

Published by the University of Minnesota Press
111 Third Avenue South, Suite 290
Minneapolis, MN 55401-2520

http://www.upress.umn.edu

**Library of Congress
Cataloging-in-Publication Data**

Lathrop, Alan K., 1940–

Minnesota architects : a biographical dictionary / Alan K. Lathrop.

    p.   cm.

Includes bibliographical references.

ISBN 978-0-8166-4463-6 (hc : alk. paper)
ISBN 978-0-8166-4464-3 (pbk. : alk. paper)

1. Architects—Minnesota—Biography—Dictionaries. I. Title.

NA730.M6L38 2010
720.92'2776—dc22

                                    2009046763

Design and production by Mighty Media, Inc.
Text design by Chris Long

Printed in the United States of America on acid-free paper

The University of Minnesota is an equal-opportunity educator and employer.

20 19 18 17 16 15 14 13 12 11 10
10 9 8 7 6 5 4 3 2 1

Contents

Acknowledgments — ix

Introduction — xi

Minnesota Architects

Loren Abbett — 1
Bruce Abrahamson — 1
Slifer, Lundie, and Abrahamson — 2
Frank Abrahamson — 3
William Alban — 3
John Alden — 4
Robert Alden — 5
Charles Aldrich — 6
T. D. Allen — 6
Gerald Anderson — 7
Leon Arnal — 9
Edward Baker — 9
Carl Bard — 10
Lewis Barnett — 11
Charles Bassford — 12
Edward Bassford — 14
Lambert Bassindale — 15
John Belair — 15
Charles Bell — 16
Miriam Bend — 17
Percy Bentley — 17
Frederick Bentz — 18
George Bergmann — 19
Lloyd Bergquist — 19
Milton Bergstedt — 21
Louis Bersback — 21
George Bertrand — 22
Philip Bettenburg — 23
Merrill Birch — 24
Cyrus Bissell — 24
Christopher Boehme — 24
Bissell, Belair and Green — 25
Francis C. Boerner — 26
Septimus Bowler — 26
William T. Bray — 27
Edwin Brown — 28
James Brunet — 28
Emma Brunson — 29
Charles Buechner — 29
Carl Buetow — 30
Gerald Buctow — 31
Max Buetow — 31
Leroy Buffington — 32
Harry Carter — 33
Brooks Cavin Jr. — 34
Robert Cerny — 35
Arthur Chamberlin — 36
Rollin Chapin — 37
Cecil Chapman — 38
George Chapman — 38
Wilbur Clark — 39
Frederick Clarke — 40
Arthur Clausen — 41
Horace Cleveland — 42
Elizabeth Close — 44
Winston Close — 44
Serenus Colburn — 46
Gordon Comb — 46
E. Richard Cone — 47
Victor Cordella — 47
Frederick Corser — 48
Eugene Corwin — 49
John Coxhead — 50
Harold Crawford — 51
Ernest Croft — 52
Perry Crosier — 53
Charles Daniels — 54
Beaver Day — 54
Victor De Brauwere — 55
William Dennis — 56
Menno Detwiler — 57
Arthur Dickey — 57
Grover Dimond — 58
Grover Dimond Jr. — 59
Edward Donohue — 59
Adam Dorr — 60
William Dorr — 61

Harry Downs	61	Ernest Haley	88
Arthur Dunham	62	Joseph Haley	88
Warren Dunnell	63	Lucien Hall	89
Foster Dunwiddie	64	Richard Hammel	90
Arndt Duvall Jr.	64	Olof Hanson	91
Harold Eads	65	Collis Hardenbergh	92
Edwin Eckert	65	Gar Hargens	93
Franklin Ellerbe	66	Ernest Hartford	93
Thomas Ellerbe	66	Roy Haslund	94
Willeik Ellingsen	68	Charles Hausler	94
Harvey Ellis	68	Robert Haxby	95
George Elmslie	69	Mark Hayes	96
Arvid Elness	69	Warren Hayes	97
BRW *Incorporated*	70	William Hazel	97
Charles Elwood	70	T. P. Healy	98
Richard Faricy	71	Raymond Hermanson	98
Carleton Farnham	71	Edwin Hewitt	99
George Feick Jr.	72	I. Vernon Hill	100
Charles Ferrin	72	James Hills	101
Harry Firminger	73	James Hirsch	101
Albert Fisher	73	BWBR *Architects*	102
Nairne Fisher	74	Isaac Hodgson	103
Francis Fitzpatrick	74	Thomas Hodne	103
Mark Fitzpatrick	75	Abraham Holstead	104
Alan Fleischbein	75	Thomas Holyoke	104
LeRoy Gaarder	76	Frank Horner	106
Carl Gage	76	Lawrence Hovik	106
Augustus Gauger	77	John Howe	107
Raymond Gauger	78	Karl Humphrey Jr.	108
Frederick German	78	William Hunt	108
Cass Gilbert	79	Dorothy Ingemann	108
Victor Gilbertson	81	William Ingemann	109
Ephraim Giliuson	82	Jerome Jackson	110
Florence Glindmier	82	Silas Jacobson	111
Joel Glotter	83	John Jager	111
Carl Graffunder	83	Vincent James	112
Curtis Green	84	Magnus Jemne	113
Gene Green	84	Lemuel Jepson	115
Newton Griffith	84	Harley Johnson	115
William Grimshaw	85	Clarence Johnston	116
David Griswold	86	Harry Jones	117
Mildred Grunau	86	Roy Jones	119
Donald Haarstick	87	Edgar Joralemon	119
Charles Haglin	87	Charles Joy	120

Eino Jyring	121	Ralph Mather	152
Frank Kacmarcik	123	Sewell Mathre	153
Seeman Kaplan	123	Charles Maybury	153
Frederick Kees	124	Jefferson Maybury	155
Walter Keith	124	Harlen McClure	155
Ernest Kennedy	126	Dale McEnary	156
William Kenyon	126	Donald McLaren	156
Frank Kerr	127	Rosemary McMonigal	157
Robert Kilgore	128	Robert McNicol	157
Wesley King	129	A. Reinhold Melander	157
Frank Kinney	129	Val Michelson	158
C. LeRoy Kinports	129	William Milbrath	159
George Klein Jr.	130	Denslow Millard	160
Marvin Kline	130	William Miller	160
Augustus Knight	131	E. Townsend Mix	160
Edwin Krafft	132	Anthony Morell	162
Hermann Kretz	133	Charles Mould	162
Lowell Lamoreaux	134	Dale Mulfinger	162
Oscar Lang	135	Arthur Nichols	163
Ananias Langdon	136	James Niemeyer	164
Austin Lange	136	Carl Nystrom	164
Albert Larson	137	Didrik Omeyer	164
Stowell Leach	137	Fremont Orff	165
Charles Leonard	138	George Orff	166
Jack Liebenberg	138	Henry Orth	166
John Lindstrom	140	Edwin Overmire	167
John W. Lindstrom	140	Clayton Page	167
Peter Linhoff	141	Emmet Palmer	168
Hiram Livingston	141	Walter Pardee	168
Louis Lockwood	141	Leonard Parker	169
Franklin Long	142	Marion Parker	170
Long & Kees	143	George Pass	170
Louis Long	144	Roger Patch	171
Louis Lundgren	144	Cyril Pesek	172
Edwin Lundie	145	Gerhard Peterson	172
James MacLeod	147	Richard Peterson	173
William Macomber	147	Louis Pinault	173
Norman Madson	148	Edmund Prondzinski	174
Gottlieb Magney	148	Anthony Puck	175
John Magney	149	William Purcell	175
Michaela Mahady	149	William Purdy	177
Maurice Maine	149	Abraham Radcliffe	177
Frederick Mann	150	Edwin Radcliffe	178
Emmanuel Masqueray	151	Ralph Rapson	179

Arnold Raugland	180	Martin Thori	209
Lang and Raugland	180	Willard Thorsen	210
John Rauma	181	Olaf Thorshov	211
James Record	181	Roy Thorshov	211
Charles Reed	182	James Tillitt	211
George Ries	182	Max Toltz	212
Robert Rietow	184	*From Toltz, King and Day to TKDA*	213
Rhodes Robertson	184	Oliver Traphagen	214
Garth Rockcastle	185	Fred Traynor	215
Paul Rockey	185	Peter Truszinski	215
Fritz Rohkohl	186	Claude Turner	215
Alexander Rose	186	Wilbur Tusler	216
Olin Round	187	William Tyrie	217
David Salmela	188	Jay Tyson	218
Robert Sandberg	189	Emil Ulrici	218
Glenn Saxton	190	Albert Van Dyck	218
Albert Schippel	190	Joseph Vanderbilt	219
Charles Sedgwick	190	Service Wager	220
Donald Setter	191	Charles Wahlberg	220
Setter, Leach, and Lindstrom	192	John Wangenstein	220
Monroe Sheire	193	Wesley Wells	221
Romaine Sheire	193	Samuel Wentworth	223
Glynne Shifflet	194	Hans Wessel	223
Frederick Slifer	195	O. K. Westphal	223
Saul Smiley	196	John Wheeler	224
Claude Smith	196	Walter Wheeler	225
Julie Snow	196	Richard Whiteman	225
Kirby Snyder	197	William C. Whitney	226
Edward Sovik Jr.	198	Clarence Wigington	226
James Stageberg	199	William Willcox	228
Edward Stebbins	200	George Wirth	229
Allen Stem	201	Werner Wittkamp	229
J. Walter Stevens	202	Clark Wold	230
Charles Stinson	203	Kindy Wright	231
Sidney Stolte	203	Myrtus Wright	231
Carl Stravs	204	Phelps Wyman	233
Carl Struck	204	Albert Zschocke	233
William Sullivan	205		
Herbert Sullwold	206		
Engebret Sund	206		
Sarah Susanka	207		
James Taylor	207		
Frank Thayer	208		
Milo Thompson	209		

Acknowledgments

The author extends grateful acknowledgment to numerous persons who assisted during the compilation and preparation of this book. Naming a few and not mentioning many others is to do the unnamed a huge disservice, of course, but some people must be pointed out for the magnitude of their contributions: Todd Orjala, editor at the University of Minnesota Press, and his staff who offered advice and criticism at crucial times; Patricia Maus, curator of the Northeast History Center at the University of Minnesota–Duluth, who unstintingly and promptly provided information when requested; Heather Lawton and her staff at the Special Collections Department of the Minneapolis Public Library, some of whom have since moved on to retirement or other positions, who sought out valuable information from Minneapolis building records; Ed Kukla, former head of the above-noted Special Collections Department, now happily (I hope) retired; Barb Bezat, the author's longtime assistant in the Northwest Architectural Archives at the University of Minnesota Libraries for always providing cheerful assistance whenever it was requested; Ann Mulfort of the same department, who helpfully gave assistance in Barb's absence; Susan Roth and the staff at the State Historic Preservation Office of the Minnesota Historical Society for generously providing information when called on; Larry Millett, former architectural critic of the St. Paul *Pioneer Press*, an always dependable source of information about architects and architecture in the Twin Cities; staff members at several other repositories in the Twin Cities and outstate who took time from their busy schedules to dig out facts about architects and buildings in their locales; and the staff members of the microfilmed Newspaper Collection at the Minnesota Historical Society, a fantastic resource for tracking down the lives, activities, and fates of individuals, who were on hand to assist with the mysteries of microfilm readers and printers.

Finally, the author is deeply grateful for the devoted friendship of Josie the cat, who kept him company through many hours of writing, fact-checking, and rewriting. And, above all, for the love and strength and support and encouragement of Peggy, the world's best wife, who was always there through the good times and bad.

Introduction

The profession of architecture is almost as old as civilization. Indeed, if another infamous profession did not have a previous, if dubious, claim on the title, it might well be *the* oldest. Architects, or master builders, as they were often called in the ancient world, emerged as cities and their increasing wealth and power brought a concomitant need for the knowledge required to erect elaborate, complex buildings as symbols of their new status. Early on, urbanized civilization created a demand for temples, monuments, government buildings, and palaces, the ostentatious homes of the wealthy, in addition to engineering works such as bridges, dams, waterworks, and fortresses, all of which required a sophisticated knowledge of engineering and construction and innate artistic talent that surpassed the rudimentary expertise of rank-and-file carpenters or cottage builders. Architects became highly respected in their communities and were elevated to membership in the elite classes, sometimes combining their work as architects and builders with other top-rung governmental positions such as treasurers or advisers to the rulers, or as high priests. The monuments to their skill and ingenuity still stand today throughout Europe, the Middle East, and Asia, tributes to their anonymous creators.

While most of these individuals' names are lost to history, a scattering of them have come down to us. However, it was really not until the Middle Ages that architects became associated with their buildings and their names thus preserved for posterity. The embedding of Christianity in everyday life meant that the church was central to daily activity in every community of western Europe and this eventually led to the construction of the magnificent Gothic cathedrals in northern Europe. The men who designed the cathedrals were often priests or monks themselves and were intimately familiar with the liturgies that their buildings were designed to accommodate. They sometimes traveled from one building site to another, being so renowned in their time that their services were in high demand, and they undoubtedly did well financially because of it. Some would spend lifetimes on a single project. They were skilled craftsmen, as well as artists, although they unquestionably employed artisans on the jobs along with carpenters and stonemasons.

These buildings were unlike anything seen up to that time and were true masterpieces of craftsmanship. As cities tried to outdo each other in the quest for ever loftier and more delicate construction, the cathedrals became almost gossamer in texture, with enormous stained glass windows that made the walls thin and the interiors beautifully illuminated with a many-hued light, meant to inspire awe and wonder in the congregants. But they also became more vulnerable to collapse, as increasing heights and more glass areas meant there was less wall surface to carry the weight of the massive roofs and towers. Such innovations as flying buttresses and scissor arches were developed to shift the structural load away from the walls and distribute it more evenly. These feats of design were highly successful and resulted in structures that stand today, some eight hundred years after they were built.

The men and women who today practice "the art or science of designing and building structures," as architecture is defined in Webster's dictionary, receive a high degree of formal education and training, but this was by no means the case in centuries past. Up until the Renaissance or early modern period, training was universally attained through apprenticeships with established architects and engineers. The "science" was the first component of architecture made available for formal study, that being instruction in the techniques of construction. Later this was joined by the "art" component, or how to embellish the functional elements of buildings with ornamental elements to make them pleasing to the eye. Engineering curricula were introduced long before design curricula were, the latter, in fact, not offered by academies until late in the seventeenth century, when the Royal Academy of Architects, for example, established a course of study in Paris that emphasized design theory over building methods. A little over a century later, the Academy was succeeded by the distinguished École Nationale et Speciale des Beaux-Arts—known simply as the École des Beaux-Arts—in 1797.

In the meantime, building manuals started to appear in the seventeenth century, made widely and inexpensively available by the invention of the printing press two centuries earlier. Such manuals popularized sophisticated design and building techniques by making it possible for builders who either could not afford to or otherwise chose not to attend the academies to erect relatively complicated structures. By the late 1600s, settlers in America were bringing with them from their home countries manuals that enabled them to build fairly sophisticated structures, including houses, churches, schools, and government and commercial buildings that were much more elaborate than the log cabins and simple frame buildings we today usually associate with the colonists.

Formal training in the art of architecture did not spread to America until after the mid-1800s. Individuals who wished to avail themselves of a formal education in building design had to do so in Europe. A few schools of engineering in the United States were established prior to the Civil War, and some offered brief training in design, but there was not a single full-fledged school of architecture until 1866, when the Massachusetts Institute of Technology (MIT) opened the first one. MIT's groundbreaking lead was quickly followed by the establishment of similar schools at the University of Illinois (1870), Cornell University (1871), and Columbia University (1881). In the ensuing decades, dozens of other higher institutions followed suit.

Despite the availability of formal education in architecture after the mid-1800s, the least expensive and most accessible means for most people to gain the requisite training remained the traditional paid or unpaid apprenticeships in established offices, or employment as carpenters or contractors where one could learn the fine points of architecture literally through practice. The former, sometimes called the "English pupilage method," was the best way for young aspirants to learn drafting techniques, whereas the latter provided invaluable training in how to put together structures that, above all, would remain standing, and were functional as well.

When architects began venturing into Minnesota around the time of the Civil War, this method of education in the art and science of architecture was in common practice throughout the United

States. The first individuals arriving in the state were all trained this way; by the late 1870s, the first men with formal education were arriving. These early, formally trained architects came from eastern schools such as MIT, Cornell, Columbia, and scattered art schools. The distinction of being the first Minnesotan to have attended the prestigious École des Beaux-Arts appears to belong to Warren Dunnell, who studied there in the 1870s and came back to Minnesota to practice. In fact, only a very few men who were educated in Paris ever worked in Minnesota: Leon Arnal, Emmanuel Masqueray, Olof Hanson, Louis Pinault, Glynne Shifflet, and Edwin Hewitt, in addition to Dunnell. In the 1920s, its beaux-arts classical approach to design fell out of fashion and even fewer are known to have braved the opprobrium of peer criticism to attend the school after that. Several immigrants from eastern and central Europe were graduates of polytechnic academies and Technische Hochschulen, among them Victor Cordella, Hermann Kretz, John Jager, and perhaps George Bergmann.

The clear favorite among most Minnesota architects for undergraduate study was the University of Minnesota, after its school of architecture was established in 1912. This is probably because it was close to home for many potential students, offered first-class training, and was affordable. The University of Pennsylvania, MIT, and Harvard University were favored for graduate work because of their excellent reputations.

Early on, architects in Minnesota, as elsewhere, developed specializations. Some were known as designers of schools, others of churches, still others of large commercial buildings, while many concentrated their efforts on producing plans for private dwellings and apartment houses. The few women who ventured into the profession in the 1910s and 1920s were mainly relegated to private practices which were one- or, at best, two-person offices. Such tiny firms could only take on house design, which did not normally require more than one person's labor to create. Emma Brunson, Ethel Bartholomew, Marion Alice Parker, and Mildred Grunau are prime examples of the single-woman private practice whose chief output consisted of single-family houses.

Specialization continues down to the present time, although it is not as consistently applied as it used to be. Many firms, small and large, are quite capable of producing a wide range of buildings, especially with the advent of computer-assisted design (CAD) systems that can greatly speed up and facilitate the design process. Gone are the days of architects bending over drafting boards to draw their plans by hand.

Large companies such as Ellerbe Becket, Bentz Thompson Rietow, HGA, MS&R, and BWBR are widely known for producing large structures and, in fact, their offices are specifically and intentionally geared toward that end, having large staffs that often include engineers, and sophisticated design facilities capable of producing extremely complex buildings. Thomas Ellerbe, the scion of the firm that bears his name, once remarked that he was asked by Edwin Lundie, a colleague in St. Paul, how he, Ellerbe, could manage such a huge firm. Ellerbe responded by asking Lundie how he could get along with such a small office (of perhaps no more than two or three draftsmen, in addition to Lundie himself). The difference in architects' objectives is clearly evident in the foregoing example: Ellerbe deliberately set out to establish a practice big enough to take on major commissions from institutions such as the Mayo Clinic, Cleveland Clinic, the University of Notre Dame, and State Farm Insurance Company, while Lundie confined himself to designing prestigious and carefully crafted single-family residences that are notable for the rigorous attention to detail and high degree of design and construction quality. Both firms succeeded very well in their specialties.

Today, there are at least 350 firms of all sizes operating in Minnesota. A number of them have distinguished national and international reputations and have won literally dozens of design awards. Many are concentrated in the Twin Cities, but there are also widely recognized firms located in Duluth, St. Cloud, and Rochester, as well as other communities.

Hundreds of architects have practiced in Minnesota. Thus, it was no simple matter to select the 326 architects included in this book. Therefore, I employed a few simple criteria to help narrow the field: First, individuals must have either been born in Minnesota or worked there for at least three years. The reader will not find entries for architects from other states who set up branch offices in Minnesota, unless the principals fall under this criterion. Second, men and women were considered for inclusion if they were notable for the body of their work. Third, an effort was made to rescue from obscurity a fair sampling of architects whom time and memory had consigned to the trash heap of history, but, at the same time, for whom enough information existed to make an entry possible. Added to this is a fourth criterion, that the book must include at least a few landscape architects and contractors, especially if the latter were also architects at some point in their careers. A few engineers slipped in also, but these were by and large people whose training and competence also included architecture.

While some readers will undoubtedly be disappointed that a favorite architect was omitted, I hope that the book will nevertheless prove to be of interest and assistance to architects and architectural historians, preservationists, and the general public, and a useful resource for some years to come. As H. L. Mencken once wrote, the author has made "a reasonably honest effort to stick to the cardinal facts," while tossing in, once in a while, a personal note or two aimed at elucidating and enhancing the information presented. Unfortunately, many details of individual lives are missing or may be inaccurate either due to inadequate or incomplete records or because the author could not locate relevant information.

Finally, a note about "Notable Buildings," the list of structures that appears at the end of the biographical entries. The buildings listed are attributions and do not necessarily mean that the individual under whom the structures are listed was the only designer unless he or she was working alone at the time. This is especially true in the case of large firms or partnerships, where it is sometimes difficult, if not impossible, to determine which individual was chiefly responsible for certain designs. Thus, the lists of structures are sometimes duplicated to indicate either that the buildings were the work of more than one person or should be attributed to the firm in which the individuals were members or partners.

So, sit back and enjoy learning about the lives of Minnesota architects and overlooked or unknown facets of Minnesota history. ∎

Minnesota Architects

Loren Abbett (1912–1956)
Loren B. Abbett was born on October 11, 1912, in Worthington, Minnesota. His family moved to Duluth while he was still in grade school. After graduating from Duluth Central High School, he studied engineering at Duluth Junior College, and then entered the University of Minnesota, where he earned his bachelor's degree in architecture in 1934. Abbett worked as a draftsman and designer at Hewitt & Brown in Minneapolis for three years, and then joined Haxby & Bissell in the same capacity.

In 1938 Abbett moved to Des Moines and was employed by McBroom & Higgins as a draftsman, designer, and job captain. He returned to Minneapolis in 1940 and worked for Pesek & Shifflet (1940–41) and Magney, Tusler & Setter (1941–42) before moving to Yakima, Washington, where he entered the firm of John W. Maloney as coordinator of war construction projects. After World War II, he returned to Minneapolis and again worked at Magney, Tusler & Setter, this time as head draftsman. In 1956, he formed a partnership with David Griswold, but it ended when Abbett was tragically killed in Minneapolis on April 26, 1956.

Notable Buildings
Bankers Life Insurance Company, Des Moines, Iowa (1939)

Bruce Abrahamson (1925–2008)
Bruce Arnold Abrahamson was born in Minneapolis in 1925. He attended public schools in the city and entered the U.S. Navy after graduating from North High School in 1943. After World War II, he attended the University of Minnesota's School of Architecture and graduated with distinction in 1949. Abrahamson received a master's degree from Harvard University's Graduate School of Design the following year, and was awarded the prestigious Rotch Traveling Scholarship, enabling him to spend a year in Europe following graduation. He returned to join the firm of Skidmore, Owings and Merrill in Chicago. In 1953, Curtis Green, whom he had met while working as a student at Thorshov and Cerny in Minneapolis, asked him to enter the fledgling partnership of Hammel and Green in St. Paul. Abrahamson accepted and became a member of the firm early in 1954, which was renamed Hammel, Green and Abrahamson (HGA) in 1964 when he became a director and vice president. He remained active in HGA until he retired on January 6, 1995.

Slifer, Lundie, and Abrahamson

Fred Slifer and Frank Abrahamson began their careers as draftsmen in the office of Emmanuel Masqueray in St. Paul in the 1910s. Along with another draftsman, Edwin Lundie, they continued Masqueray's practice after his death in 1917 long enough to finish work already under way, and then closed the office. They parted company in 1919 with Slifer and Abrahamson beginning a long-term partnership and Lundie opening his own private practice.

When Slifer died in 1948, Abrahamson continued the business in partnership with E. Richard Cone, who had been in the firm since the mid-1930s. The latter left the firm about ten years later to team up with Gerhard Peterson at Northfield Architects, Inc. After that, the two men formed a partnership in 1950 in St. Paul that lasted for about twenty years. Abrahamson remained active on his own up to his retirement in the late 1960s. He died in 1974. Cone retired in early 1972 and the partnership with Peterson dissolved at about the same time.

Lundie, in the meantime, went on to manage a highly successful private practice until his death in 1972; he was the original member of a legacy reaching back more than sixty years.

Orchestra Hall, Minneapolis, 1973–74 (Bruce Abrahamson and Hardy Holtzmann Pfeiffer, New York). *Photograph 1982. Courtesy of Minnesota Historical Society.*

He taught in the School of Architecture at the University of Minnesota from 1957 to 1977.

Abrahamson died in Minneapolis on November 11, 2008.

Notable Buildings
Orchestra Hall, 1111 Nicollet Avenue, Minneapolis (1973–74) (with Hardy Holtzmann Pfeiffer, New York)

WITH CURTIS GREEN AND RICHARD HAMMEL
Colonial Church of Edina, 6200 Colonial Way, Edina (1978–79)
Science Museum of Minnesota, 10th and Wabasha Streets, St. Paul (1979–80)

Frank Abrahamson (1884–1972)
Frank August Abrahamson was born in Motley, Minnesota, on September 21, 1884. He attended the University of Pennsylvania, where he received a Bachelor of Science degree in architecture in 1911. Abrahamson was employed in the office of Emmanuel Masqueray in St. Paul and, after the latter's death in 1917, joined fellow employees Fred Slifer and Edwin Lundie in a partnership to finish the work on hand in Masqueray's office. In 1919, at the completion of the pending commissions, Slifer and Abrahamson formed their own firm, specializing in church design. Abrahamson continued to maintain the practice after Slifer died in 1948.

Abrahamson retired in 1969 and died in Webster, Wisconsin, in July 1972.

Notable Buildings

WITH FREDERICK SLIFER
Evangelical Lutheran Church of the Redeemer, 285 N. Dale Street, St. Paul (1922)
St. Casimir School, 930 Geranium Avenue E., St. Paul (1923)
Mount Olive Lutheran Church, 3045 Chicago Avenue S., Minneapolis (1925)
Hamline University Methodist Church, 1514 Englewood Avenue, St. Paul (1928)

William Alban (1873–1961)
William Linley Alban was born on April 29, 1873, in Plover, Wisconsin. He moved to St. Paul sometime before 1900 and joined the firm of Omeyer and Thori as chief draftsman. He was briefly in partnership with Thori (Thori, Alban & Fisher) and, after Thori died in February 1905, maintained a practice with James E. Fisher until the latter's death in 1910. Shortly afterward, Alban formed a partnership with Charles Hausler and then, after Hausler left to set up a practice with Percy Bentley, became a partner of George L. Lockhart. The duration of this partnership is not known, but Alban was in private practice from at least the early 1920s until 1946, when he joined Ellerbe Architects. He retired in 1954 and resumed private practice until his death in St. Paul on July 1, 1961.

Notable Buildings

ALBAN & FISHER
First Methodist Episcopal Church, Eau Claire, Wisconsin (1909–1911)

ALBAN & HAUSLER
H. W. Strickler residence, St. Anthony Park, St. Paul (1913)
St. Anthony Park Methodist Church, Como and Hillside Avenues, St. Paul (1913)
Knox Presbyterian Church, 1536 Minnehaha Avenue W., St. Paul (1913–14)

Crow Wing County Courthouse, Brainerd, 1919–20 (John Alden). *Photograph ca. 1925. Courtesy of* Minnesota Historical Society.

Gutterson residence, 2181 Doswell Avenue, St. Paul (1916)

ALBAN & LOCKHART
Armstrong School, Armstrong, Iowa (1915–16)

ALBAN
Ezekiel Lutheran Church, River Falls, Wisconsin (1926)
Pilgrim Baptist Church, 732 Central Avenue W., St. Paul (1928)

John Alden (1873–1933)
Jon Olafson was born in Offerdal, Jamtland, Sweden, on August 2, 1873. He was raised in Sweden and attended public schools there. He emigrated to the United States in March 1891, where he settled in Cottonwood County, Minnesota, with his family. Although his date of arrival is not certain, he probably arrived there in May of the same year. At some point between 1891 and 1899, he changed his name to Alden and moved to Spicer, Minnesota.

Alden's training for a career in architecture probably was in architects' offices, the usual means for attaining such training in the late nineteenth century. He first appears as a draftsman working for Omeyer and Thori in St. Paul in 1902. He moved on to Thomas Holyoke's office two years later, where he spent less than a year before joining the Great Northern Railway as a draftsman in the engineering department. From 1906 to 1912, Alden was employed as chief draftsman for J. Walter Stevens and then formed a partnership with William T. Harris, which lasted until 1918. Due to a downturn in the economy during World War I, Alden discontinued the partnership and joined the Pan Motor Company in St. Cloud as a structural and heating and ventilating engineer. It is not known how long he remained with this company, but it appears he resumed private practice in the early 1920s and continued until at least 1928.

Alden died in St. Paul on September 26, 1933, and is buried in Acacia Park Cemetery in Mendota Heights.

Notable Buildings
Great Northern Railway Depot, Wayzata (1906)
W. D. Jamieson residence, 1908 W. Selby Avenue, St. Paul (1912)
Albert P. Wallich residence, 1164 Summit Avenue, St. Paul (1914)
Crow Wing County Courthouse, Brainerd (1919–20)
St. Philips Church, Litchfield (1921)
Capitol City Masonic Lodge, 1190 W. James Avenue, St. Paul (1923)
Studebaker Garage, 850 Grand Avenue, St. Paul (1926)
Macalester Presbyterian Church, 435 S. Hamline Avenue, St. Paul (1927)

Robert Alden (1810–1877)
Robert Spencer Alden was born in Verona, New York, on September 11, 1810. When he was fourteen years of age, he moved to Genessee County, New York. It is not known what training he had or what occupations he engaged in, but he is known to have moved to St. Joseph County (South Bend), Indiana, in 1838 and worked in architecture and engineering. It is possible that he received some kind of training in New York. It is not known whether he opened his own office in Indiana or was employed by another firm.

In 1849, like thousands of others, Alden was drawn to the California gold fields and, like most of them, failed to make his fortune. He returned to Indiana and resided there until March 1856, when he moved to the fledgling settlement of St. Anthony, Minnesota, and opened an architectural office. He is, therefore, one of the earliest—if not *the* earliest—architect to arrive in Minnesota Territory. Alden began almost immediately to design buildings for St. Anthony, one of the first being the grand Winslow House hotel, which stood on the river bluff above the Falls of St. Anthony. He is credited with both designing and supervising the construction of this building.

From 1871 to 1872 Alden was associated with H. G. Howe, then briefly with Franklin Long in 1874, and Joseph Haley in 1875–76. Otherwise, Alden maintained a private practice during the years he spent in Minnesota.

Alden died in Minneapolis on May 30, 1877.

Notable Buildings
Winslow House, St. Anthony (1856) (razed 1885)
Hennepin County Courthouse, Minneapolis (1856) (razed ca. 1910)
St. Anthony of Padua Catholic Church, 813 Main Street NE, Minneapolis (1868)
Academy of Music, Minneapolis (1871) (razed 1884)
Old Main, University of Minnesota, Minneapolis (1875) (Alden & Long) (razed 1904)

University of Minnesota Armory, Minneapolis, 1895–96 (Charles Aldrich). *Photograph 1904 by Sweet. Courtesy of Minnesota Historical Society.*

Charles Aldrich (1866–1939)
Charles Ronald Aldrich was born in Utica, Michigan (near Detroit), on July 12, 1866. He attended public schools in Detroit, where the family moved in 1872. He moved to Minnesota when he was nineteen years of age and entered the University of Minnesota, taking special courses in architecture and engineering. Aldrich was employed by William Channing Whitney in Minneapolis for a time, then he set up his own practice in the mid-1890s which he maintained for the remainder of his career in Minnesota. He also served as an instructor in manual training and mechanical drawing at the University's School of Agriculture from 1888 to about 1903. In 1905, Aldrich relocated to Washington and established an office in Seattle. In 1928, he began working for the Western Washington State Fair as a construction engineer. He worked in this capacity until his death in Puyallup, Washington, on June 30, 1939.

Notable Buildings
University of Minnesota Armory, Minneapolis (1895–96)
Jones Hall, University of Minnesota, Minneapolis (1901)
Pillsbury Branch Library (now Phillips Building), 100 University Avenue SE, Minneapolis (1902)

T. D. Allen (CA. 1841–1928)
Truman Dudley Allen was born in Niagara County, New York, about 1841. Nothing is known of his education, training, and early life. He first appears in Ironton, Wisconsin, in 1870, living with his family in the home of his parents,

Blue Earth County Courthouse, Mankato, 1886–87 (T. D. Allen). *Photograph 1903 by Charles J. Hibbard. Courtesy of Minnesota Historical Society.*

Ira and Rebecca Allen. From 1880 to 1885 he worked as a carpenter in Necedah, Wisconsin, and moved in 1886 to Antigo, Wisconsin. It appears that about this time Allen decided to become an architect, and about 1886 he relocated to Minneapolis where he opened an architectural practice with Joseph Haley. After the partnership ended a few years later, he maintained a private practice. Allen specialized in courthouses, schools, and residences in the Upper Midwest.

In 1901, he moved to Spokane, Washington, and resided there for the remainder of his life. He died there on December 14, 1928.

Notable Buildings
Blue Earth County Courthouse, Mankato (1886–87)
Rock County Courthouse, Luverne (1888)
Franklin County Courthouse, Hampton, Iowa (1890–91)
Dickinson County Courthouse, Spirit Lake, Iowa (1891)
Hardin County Courthouse, Eldora, Iowa (1891–92)
Walker School, Washburn, Wisconsin (1893–94)

Gerald Anderson (1895–1971)
Gerald Alvin Anderson was born on September 8, 1895, in St. Paul. He graduated from Central High School in 1913 and attended the University of Pennsylvania, where he was awarded a bachelor's degree in architecture in 1919. While attending school, Anderson worked during the summers in the firm of Reed and Stem in St. Paul (1913–1915) and, following graduation, joined Toltz, King & Day, also in St.

Paul. In 1930 he became an associate in the firm, and a partner in 1956, when the name was changed to Toltz, King, Duvall & Anderson. Today it is known more familiarly as TKDA, architects and engineers. Anderson specialized in the design of schools and produced many, especially in the 1950s and 1960s.

He died in St. Paul on September 6, 1971.

Notable Buildings

WITH MAX TOLTZ AND BEAVER DAY
Hamm Building, 408 St. Peter Street, St. Paul (1920)
Stearns County Courthouse, St. Cloud (1921–22)
Carl Cummins residence, 2237 Princeton Avenue, St. Paul (1924)
Spink County Courthouse, Redfield, South Dakota (1925–27)
Ward County Courthouse, Minot, North Dakota (1928–30)
Aitkin County Courthouse, Aitkin (1929)

Leon Arnal (1881–1963)
One of the very few French-born architects to work in Minnesota, Leon Arnal was born in Mouret, France, on June 14, 1881. He attended grade and high schools in Marseilles, including four years at the Marseilles Fine Arts School, graduating on July 16, 1899. Upon receiving a scholarship from the city of Marseilles, he then studied at the École des Beaux-Arts in Paris for eleven years, graduating on June 20, 1910. He came to the United States and joined the faculty of the University of Pennsylvania's School of Architecture, where he was a protégé of Paul Cret. When World War I broke out, Arnal returned to France to serve in the French army, part of the time being attached as a liaison officer to the British army. He was awarded the British Military Cross for his service.

Following the war, Arnal settled in Minneapolis, where he joined the architectural firm of Magney & Tusler. During the time he was in the firm (1919–1934), he was responsible for a number of public, institutional, and private buildings. At the same time, Arnal taught architecture at the University of Minnesota, retiring in 1948. He continued to work as an artist after his retirement.

Arnal died in Minneapolis on February 23, 1963.

Notable Buildings
Memorial Stadium, University Avenue and Oak Street, University of Minnesota, Minneapolis (1921) (razed 1992) (in association with Frederick Mann, James Forsythe, and Roy Childs Jones)
Women's Club, 410 Oak Grove Street, Minneapolis (1927)
Foshay Tower (now W Minneapolis—The Factory), 9th Street and Marquette Avenue, Minneapolis (1929)
U.S. Post Office, 100 1st Street S., Minneapolis (1935)

Edward Baker (1926–2006)
Edward Frank Baker was born in Chicago, Illinois, on May 24, 1926. He and his family moved to Minneapolis in 1932, where he graduated from West High School in 1943 and went on to serve in the U.S. Navy from 1944 to 1946. Following military service, he returned to Minneapolis and entered the University of Minnesota, and received a bachelor's degree in

Foshay Tower, Minneapolis, 1929 (Leon Arnal). *Photograph ca. 1929 by Charles J. Hibbard. Courtesy of Minnesota Historical Society.*

Northstar Center, Minneapolis, 1961–62 (Edward Baker). *Photograph 1962 by Norton & Peel. Courtesy of Minnesota Historical Society.*

architecture in 1950. Baker worked in the firm of Larson and McLaren from 1950 to 1959, then established his own practice, Baker Associates, which became one of the most successful firms in the Twin Cities. He designed the first two skyways in Minneapolis in 1962, having conceived of them in 1955 while conducting a study for a series of articles in the *Minneapolis Star* newspaper. In 1964 he was joined in practice by Austin H. Lange (Baker-Lange Associates, Inc.), which dissolved in 1973. Baker continued in private practice, designing a number of prominent buildings in the Twin Cities and elsewhere, as well as becoming successful in the real estate business.

He died on June 15, 2006, in Minneapolis.

Notable Buildings
Northstar Center, 2nd Avenue S. and 7th Street, Minneapolis (1961–62)
L'Hotel Sofitel, 5600 W. 78th Street, Bloomington (1970) (with Austin Lange)
IDS Center, 80 S. 8th Street, Minneapolis (1970–74) (Baker-Lange Associates with Johnson and Burgee, New York)
TCF Building alterations, Marquette Avenue and 8th Street (1980)

Carl Bard (1886–1953)
Carl John Bard was born in New Carlisle, Indiana, in 1886. Nothing is known of his education or early employment until he appeared in Minneapolis in 1920, where he worked initially as a draftsman in the architectural firm of Bell & Kinports. From 1921 to 1931, Bard was an architect on the staff of the Builder's Exchange in Minneapolis. In 1931 he formed a partnership with Joseph Vanderbilt, which lasted until Bard retired in 1948.

Bard moved to Michigan and died on his farm near Three Oaks on February 7, 1953.

Notable Buildings
See also Joseph Vanderbilt
Trach residence, 4860 W. Lake Harriet Parkway, Minneapolis (1928)
Granada Apartments, 1456 Lagoon Avenue, Minneapolis (1929)
Greenberg residence, 3021 James Avenue S., Minneapolis (1929–30)
Linden Hills Library, 2900 W. 43rd Street, Minneapolis (1930)
St. Francis of Assisi Catholic Church, Lake St. Croix Beach (1938) (with Joseph Vanderbilt)

St. Francis of Assisi Catholic Church, Lake St. Croix Beach, 1938 (Carl Bard and Joseph Vanderbilt). *Photograph by Bob Firth*.

Lewis Barnett (1848–1936)

Lewis C. Barnett was born in Greensburg, Kentucky, on January 13, 1848. He moved with his parents to Illinois in 1864 and attended schools in Rock Island and Davenport, Iowa. He studied engineering at Iowa State College, Ames, graduating in 1870. After leaving college, Barnett entered the grain business in northern Iowa where he saw a round grain elevator and purchased the patent rights from its inventor. He moved to Minneapolis in 1881 and began constructing grain elevators, using his patented method of building.

In 1885 Barnett formed a partnership with James L. Record in a general contracting firm. Record was already experienced in building grain elevators, and the company, Barnett & Record (incorporated in 1892), went on to construct a great many of these structures throughout the Midwest. Barnett & Record also constructed other types of industrial buildings, including coal and ore docks in Duluth and Two Harbors, Minnesota, and Superior, Wisconsin. In addition to his part ownership in the construction company, Barnett served as a director of the Security National Bank of Minneapolis, continuing in that capacity after its merger with First National Bank. He retired in 1917 and resided in Duluth until the early 1930s.

Barnett died in Washington, D.C., on May 18, 1936.

Pillsbury A Mill Grain Elevators, Minneapolis, 1910, 1914, 1916 (Barnett & Record). *Photograph ca. 1912 by Charles P. Gibson. Courtesy of Minnesota Historical Society.*

Notable Buildings

BARNETT & RECORD
Cargill elevator, Duluth (1892)
Phelps-Harrington elevator, Duluth (1892)
Daisy Mill, Superior, Wisconsin (1892)
Youghioghny Coal Co. docks, West Superior, Wisconsin (1893)
Duluth & Iron Range Railway Ore Dock #6, Two Harbors (1907–09)
Pillsbury A Mill Grain Elevators, 301 Main Street SE, Minneapolis (1910, 1914, 1916)

Charles Bassford (1879–1945)
Charles Asher Bassford was born in St. Paul on November 4, 1879, the son of Edward P. Bassford, a prominent archi-

Holman Field Administration Building, St. Paul, 1938 (Charles Bassford). *Photograph ca. 1940. Courtesy of Minnesota Historical Society.*

tect in the city. Young Bassford attended public schools and worked first in his father's office from 1897 to 1912, where he appears to have obtained his training. He also worked for the firms of Reed & Stem (1906–07) and Augustus Gauger (1907–08), both in St. Paul. In 1930 Bassford was appointed city architect in St. Paul, a position he held for the rest of his life.

He died in St. Paul on September 10, 1945.

Notable Buildings
Roy Wilkins Auditorium; 5th Street near Washington Street, St. Paul (1932)

Merchants National Bank (now Brooks Building), St. Paul, 1890–92 (Edward Bassford). *Photograph ca. 1912. Courtesy of Minnesota Historical Society.*

Lowry Hotel (now Lowry Square Apartments), St. Paul, 1926 (Lambert Bassindale). *Photograph ca. 1928 by Charles P. Gibson. Courtesy of Minnesota Historical Society.*

Cleveland Junior High School, 1000 Walsh Street (1936) (with Clarence Wigington and William Godette)

Holman Field Administration Building, 644 Bayfield Street, St. Paul (1938)

Monroe Junior High School addition (now Monroe Achievement Plus Community School), 810 Palace Avenue (1938–39) (with Clarence Wigington and William Godette)

Edward Bassford (1837–1912)

Edward Payson Bassford was born on June 7, 1837, in Calais, Maine. He attended the local schools and Calais Academy, and worked as a carpenter before going to Boston to study architecture in the school of Charles Painter. Bassford served in the Forty-fourth Massachusetts Infantry during the Civil War, then returned to Maine where he opened an architectural practice with Thomas J. Sparrow in Portland. In 1866 he and his wife moved to St. Paul and he set up an office that became one of the most successful St. Paul architectural firms in the nineteenth century. Bassford's office was also a training ground for young architects who later became successful in their own right: Cass Gilbert, Augustus Gauger, Edward J. Donohue, Silas Jacobson, and Charles Bassford.

Bassford died at Osakis, Minnesota, on July 20, 1912.

Notable Buildings
Nicollet House hotel, St. Peter (ca. 1872)
Nicollet County Courthouse, St. Peter (1885)
Merchants National Bank (now Brooks Building), 366–368 Jackson Street, St. Paul (1890–92)
Redwood County Courthouse, Redwood Falls (1891)

Lambert Bassindale (1875–1945)
Lambert A. L. Bassindale was born in Racine, Wisconsin, on February 21, 1875, of English heritage. He graduated from Racine High School in 1894 and was educated at the Chicago Art Institute. He worked with Chicago and New York architects in the design of the Cook County Courthouse and City Hall, the Chicago Northwestern Terminal, and the Union Railway Terminal in Kansas City. In 1918 Bassindale came to St. Paul to work as an associate architect with Charles Frost on the St. Paul Union Depot and the Great Northern Station in Minneapolis. In 1931 he was selected as architect for the Federal Building (Post Office) and hired the Chicago firm of Holabird & Root as consultants.

Bassindale retired in 1938 and moved to Alexandria, Indiana, where he died on May 14, 1945.

Notable Buildings
Lowry Hotel (now Lowry Square Apartments), Wabasha and 4th Streets, St. Paul (1926)
St. Paul Federal Building (Post Office), 3rd and Sibley Streets, St. Paul (1931)

John Belair (1904–1976)
John Sydney Belair was born on August 6, 1904, in Minneapolis. He received a bachelor's degree in 1926 from the Extension Division of the University of Minnesota, and later attended the School of Architecture for one year (1932–33). From 1921 to 1931 he was, first, a draftsman with Croft & Boerner in Minneapolis, and then joined Ellerbe & Company as a designer and superintendent of construction. In 1931 Belair was employed by Magney & Tusler as draftsman and designer, and in 1934 he moved to Stebbins, Haxby & Bissell in the same capacity. He remained with the latter firm until 1941, when he became an employee, as did many other architects, of companies that were designing and building military installations as part of the war effort. From 1941 to 1944 he worked successively for Shanley, vanTeylingen, Great Falls, Montana; Smith, Hinchman & Grylles, Detroit, Michigan and New Brighton, Minnesota; and Metcalf-Hamilton-K.C. Bridge Company, Edmonton, Alberta.

In 1944 Belair returned to Haxby & Bissell as associate architect and then partner. He remained in the firm, which became Bissell & Belair upon Haxby's death in 1947 and later was renamed Bissel, Belair & Green, for the remainder of his career.

Belair retired in the early 1970s and died in Sun City, Arizona, on June 30, 1976.

Notable Buildings
See also Cyrus Bissell and Gene Green
Deephaven Elementary School, Deephaven (1955)
Neil A. Armstrong Senior High School, 10655 36th Avenue N., Robbinsdale (1971)

Charles Bell (1858–1932)

Charles Emlen Bell was born in McLean County, Illinois, on March 31, 1858, the youngest of Chalkley and Mary Bell's six children. He attended West Town Boarding School in Philadelphia, a Quaker institution.

Bell began his career in architecture the same way a lot of men did in the nineteenth century, in carpentry, in which he worked for seven years. He married Nellie Wickham in 1880 and in 1884 they moved to Council Bluffs, Iowa, where Bell assisted in the construction of the post office. Afterward he established a private practice as an architect. He was briefly partners with architect J. W. Allen (1887–88) and George A. Berlinghoff (1889–91), then set up his own office once again. In 1895 he and John Hackett Kent formed a partnership with offices in Council Bluffs and Helena, Montana. They won the competition to design the Montana State Capitol, which was begun in 1898, but lost the competition for the Idaho Capitol building.

At some point, Bell and Kent dissolved their partnership and Bell moved to Minneapolis, where he became a partner of Menno Detweiler in 1904. During its brief existence, Bell & Detweiler became very successful in the design of courthouses throughout the Upper Midwest. Detweiler died in 1907 and Bell practiced alone until 1908, when he joined the firm of Tyrie and Chapman. In the meantime, Bell was chosen to design the South Dakota Capitol (1907). He remained with Tyrie and Chapman until 1913, then practiced alone except for brief partnerships with Percy Bentley (1916–17) and C. LeRoy Kinports (1920).

Bell died in Minneapolis on May 10, 1932.

Koochiching County Courthouse, International Falls, 1908 (Bell, Tyrie and Chapman). *Photograph ca. 1915. Courtesy of Minnesota Historical Society.*

Notable Buildings

Deer Lodge County Courthouse, Anaconda, Montana (1897) (Bell & Kent)

Flathead County Courthouse, Kalispell, Montana (1899) (Bell & Kent)

Grant County Courthouse, Elbow Lake (1904–05) (Bell & Detweiler)

Benton County Courthouse, Vinton, Iowa (1904–05) (Bell & Detweiler)

Lawrence County Courthouse, Deadwood, South Dakota (1905–07) (Bell & Detweiler)

Martin County Courthouse, Fairmont (1907) (Bell & Detweiler)

Marshall County Courthouse, Britton, South Dakota (1907) (Bell & Detweiler)

Koochiching County Courthouse, International Falls (1908) (Bell, Tyrie and Chapman)

Brin Glass Company, 600–604 Washington Avenue N., Minneapolis (1919) (Bell)

Miriam Bend (1883–1971)

Miriam Holman Balliet was born in Excelsior, Minnesota, on February 25, 1883. She graduated from Summit School in St. Paul in 1930, attending grade and high school there, and received degrees from Sarah Lawrence College, Bronxville, New York, and the University of Minnesota in 1932 and 1936, respectively. She began working as a student draftsman in the office of William Ingemann in St. Paul in the summer of 1936, then worked for H. Ring Clauson in Chicago that fall, and the following year moved on to the office of McEnary & Krafft in Minneapolis, where she stayed until 1940. She then was employed as an artist by the Minnesota State Arts Council, and as a supervisor at the Walker Art Center. It appears that she quit working in 1941, as she is listed in St. Paul city directories after that year as the wife of Charles M. Bend, president of the Joyce Insurance Company.

Bend died in St. Paul on August 13, 1971.

Notable Buildings

No buildings attributable to Bend have been found.

Percy Bentley (1885–1968)

Percy Dwight Bentley was born in La Crosse, Wisconsin, on January 30, 1885. He graduated from Ohio Wesleyan University, Delaware, Ohio, in 1906 and the Armour (later Illinois) Institute of Technology in 1910. He worked as a draftsman with Wells I. Bennett in Chicago during the summers of 1907 through 1909. Bentley then returned to La Crosse and set up his own practice, which specialized in the design of Prairie School residences and commercial buildings. Bentley was in partnership with Otto Merman from about 1910 to 1913, and in 1914 he relinquished his practice to his partner, moved to St. Paul, and opened an office with Charles Hausler. By 1917 he was a partner of Charles Bell in Minneapolis, and then established his own office in St. Paul for more than a decade. Bentley moved to Oregon in about 1940 and practiced there for the rest of his career.

He died in Eugene, Oregon, on February 2, 1968.

Notable Buildings

WITH OTTO MERMAN

Edward C. Bartl residence, La Crosse, Wisconsin (1910)

Henry Salzer residence, La Crosse, Wisconsin (1912)

Frank and Rosa Seifert residence, St. Paul, 1914 (Percy Bentley and Charles Hausler). *Photograph ca. 1964 by Eugene Debs Becker. Courtesy of Minnesota Historical Society.*

Dr. H. H. Chase residence, La Crosse, Wisconsin (1913)

WITH CHARLES HAUSLER

Frank and Rosa Seifert residence, 975 Osceola Avenue, St. Paul (1914)

Albert Wunderlich residence, 1599 Portland Avenue, St. Paul (1915)

M. L. Fugina residence, Fountain City, Wisconsin (1916)

Sigma Alpha Epsilon fraternity house, 1815 University Avenue SE, Minneapolis (1928)

Frederick Bentz (B. 1922)
Frederick Jacob Bentz was born in McGregor, Iowa, on November 26, 1922, and attended the Eastman School of Music at the University of Rochester, New York. He served in the U.S. Army during World War II and, following military service, received a bachelor's degree in architecture from the University of Minnesota. He was employed in the office of Long and Thorshov in Minneapolis beginning in 1948 and became an associate and chief draftsman in the successor firm, Thorshov and Cerny, in 1956. In 1971 he formed a successful partnership, Bentz Thompson Rietow, in Minneapolis, with fellow employees Milo Thompson and Robert Rietow.

Bentz retired from practice in 1993.

Notable Buildings
See also Robert Rietow and Milo Thompson

Le Jeune residence, Orono, Maine (ca. 1980)

Wooddale Church, 6630 Shady Oak Road, Eden Prairie (1984–90)

Lake Harriet Band Shell, 4135 Lake Harriet Parkway W., Minneapolis (1985)

Brown Krause manor, 3600 Chicago Avenue S., Minneapolis (1996)

Beth Shalom Synagogue, Hopkins (2002)

George Bergmann (1845–1910)
George Bergmann was born in Germany in 1845, but nothing else is known of his early life and training. He arrived in St. Paul around 1880 and was employed by Augustus Gauger as a draftsman. In 1884 he formed a partnership with John F. Fisher, designing churches for Catholic parishes in central Minnesota and elsewhere. In 1898 he moved to St. Cloud to enter into business with Allen E. Hussey. The firm lasted about five years, after which Bergmann retired to his farm near Fairchild, Wisconsin.

Bergmann died in Fairchild, Wisconsin, on February 28, 1910.

Notable Buildings
St. Martin's Catholic Church, St. Martin (1887) (with John Fisher)
St. Agnes Catholic Church, Roscoe (1898) (possibly with John Fisher)
Church of St. Mary, Melrose (1898) (with A. E. Hussey)
St. Michael's Church, Spring Hill (1900–02) (with A. E. Hussey)
St. Michael's Catholic Church, Buckman (1902) (with A. E. Hussey)

Lloyd Bergquist (B. 1929)
Lloyd Frederick Bergquist was born in Duluth, Minnesota, on May 29, 1929. He

Church of St. Mary, Melrose, 1898 (George Bergmann and A. E. Hussey). *Photograph by Bob Firth.*

received a bachelor's degree in architecture from the University of Minnesota in 1951, then served in the armed forces during the Korean War. He joined the firm of Bergstedt, Hirsch, Wahlberg and Wold in 1957 and remained there for the rest of his career, becoming a partner in 1974. He retired in 1995.

Notable Buildings

WITH MILTON BERGSTEDT AND JAMES HIRSCH
Degree of Honor Building, 325 Cedar Street, St. Paul (1961)
Inver Hills Community College, 8445 College Trail, Inver Grove Heights (1961)

WITH MILTON BERGSTEDT, CHARLES WAHLBERG AND FRITZ ROHKOHL
Arrowhead Resort, Lake Darling, Alexandria (1968–70)
Christ the King Lutheran Church, New Brighton (1969)
First Presbyterian Church, Stillwater (1969)
Sister Kenny Institute at Abbott Northwestern Hospital, 800 E. 28th Street, Minneapolis (1974)

Degree of Honor Building, St. Paul, 1961 (Bergstedt, Hirsch, Wahlberg & Wold). *Photograph 1963 by* St. Paul Dispatch and Pioneer Press. *Courtesy of Minnesota Historical Society.*

Milton Bergstedt (1907–1998)
Milton Victor Bergstedt was born in St. Paul on November 18, 1907, and attended public schools in the city. He graduated from the University of Minnesota with a degree in architecture in 1931 and attended the Harvard Graduate School of Design in 1932–33. He worked for the state architect of Illinois and in the firm of Talmadge & Watson of Chicago before returning to Minnesota. He was employed successively by Mather and Fleischbein, Edwin Lundie, Clarence H. Johnston, and Ellerbe & Company. In 1941, Bergstedt left Ellerbe and joined William Ingemann in St. Paul. When Ingemann entered the Army Air Force during World War II, Bergstedt ran the office.

After the war, the firm was reestablished as Ingemann and Bergstedt, and W. Brooks Cavin associated with them from 1948 to about 1951. Bergstedt left the firm in 1951 and set up his own practice with James Hirsch as junior partner, the firm being known as Bergstedt and Hirsch. Charles Wahlberg and Clark Wold entered the office in the mid-1950s and the name was changed to Bergstedt, Hirsch, Wahlberg & Wold in 1957. The partnership split up in 1962 when Hirsch left to set up his own office in Hudson, Wisconsin. Wold departed in 1968 to form The Wold Association, and Lloyd Bergquist and Fritz Rohkokl were added as principals and then partners. The firm thus became Bergstedt, Wahlberg, Bergquist and Rohkohl (BWBR) in 1974, under which name it continues to operate at the present time.

Bergstedt retired in 1974, although he remained active as chairman for ten more years. He died in St. Paul on June 18, 1998.

Notable Buildings
Mt. Zion Temple, 1300 Summit Avenue, St. Paul (1954–55) (with Eric Mendelsohn)
Degree of Honor Building, 325 Cedar Street, St. Paul (1961) (Bergstedt, Hirsch, Wahlberg & Wold)
Inver Hills Community College, 8445 College Trail, Inver Grove Heights (1961) (Bergstedt, Hirsch, Wahlberg & Wold)
Arrowhead Resort, Lake Darling, Alexandria (1968–70)
Christ the King Lutheran Church, New Brighton (1969)
First Presbyterian Church, Stillwater (1969)
Sister Kenny Institute at Abbott Northwestern Hospital, 800 E. 28th Street, Minneapolis (1974) (BWBR)

Louis Bersback (1891–1964)
Louis Boynton Bersback was born in Chicago on February 21, 1891. He studied at the Harvard University School of Architecture and graduated with his bachelor's degree in 1918. He served in the Photographic Division of the U.S. Army Air Corps during World War I and, after the war, worked in various offices in the East and Midwest before settling in Minneapolis sometime before 1922. In that year, he was placed in charge of the Civil Works Administration's (CWA) Mapping Project for the city of Minneapolis, overseeing sixty-five draftsmen. The following year, Bersback became an inspector for the Home Owners' Loan Corporation and, in 1935, a junior architect on a U.S. housing project. His career after that is unknown, but it appears he continued as an architect for some time.

Despatch Laundry, Minneapolis, 1929 (Louis Bersback). *Photograph ca. 1970. Courtesy of Minneapolis Public Library, James K. Hosmer Special Collection, MC088.*

Bersback died in Arizona in February 1964.

Notable Buildings
Windsor Apartments, 2001–2019 Third Avenue S., Minneapolis (1922)
J. K. Kolar residence, 174 Malcolm Avenue SE, Minneapolis (1927)
Despatch Laundry, 2611 1st Avenue S., Minneapolis (1929)
St. Stephen's Episcopal Church, 50th Street and Wooddale Avenue, Minneapolis (1938) (with Cram and Ferguson)

George Bertrand (1859–1931)
George Emile Bertrand was born in Superior, Wisconsin, on June 22, 1859. He attended the public schools of Superior and then studied architecture in Boston and spent several years in architects' offices learning the profession. He came to Minneapolis in 1886 and set up a private practice. Four years later Bertrand entered into a partnership with Walter Keith, and, after the partnership dissolved in 1894, resumed private practice. In 1896 he became a partner of Arthur Chamberlin (Bertrand and Chamberlin) and the firm remained active until 1931.

Bertrand died in Minneapolis on October 31, 1931.

Notable Buildings

BERTRAND & CHAMBERLIN
Asbury Hospital, 915 E. 15th Street, Minneapolis (1898)
Dean & Company warehouse, 406–410 Washington Avenue N., Minneapolis (1902)
Salisbury Mattress Company (now part of St. Anthony Main development), 212 SE Main Street, Minneapolis (1909)
Minneapolis Athletic Club (now Grand Hotel), 619 2nd Avenue S., Minneapolis (1912)
Chamber of Commerce Annex, 3rd Street S. and 4th Avenue S., Minneapolis (1919)

Shriner's Hospital, 2025 E. River Road, Minneapolis (1921)

Philip Bettenburg (1900–1968)
Philip Charles Bettenburg was born on September 23, 1900, in St. Paul. He graduated from the University of Minnesota's School of Architecture and began practicing in St. Paul in 1922. Eventually he was joined in partnership by George B. Townsend, Sidney L. Stolte, and Gordon M. Comb; by 1960, the firm had a staff of twenty-five. Bettenburg was also a career officer in the U.S. Army and rose to the rank of major general and commander of the Minnesota National Guard. His firm specialized in designing armories in many towns and cities across the state in the 1930s; later he branched out into a variety of commercial and institutional architectural work. The firm continued to be operated through the 1970s and 1980s by the last partner, William Estebo.

Bettenburg died on March 20, 1968, in St. Paul.

Notable Buildings

P. C. BETTENBURG & COMPANY
Armory, Brainerd (1936)
National Guard Armory, 500 S. 6th Street, Minneapolis (1935)

BETTENBURG TOWNSEND STOLTE & COMB
City Hall, Anoka (1954)

National Guard Armory, Minneapolis, 1935 (P. C. Bettenburg & Company). *Photograph 1935 by Norton & Peel. Courtesy of Minnesota Historical Society.*

Northwestern Hospital, Thief River Falls (ca. 1958)
Sheridan School, 525 N. White Bear Avenue, St. Paul (1960)
Edgewater Baptist Church, 5501 Chicago Avenue S., Minneapolis (1961)

Merrill Birch (1919–2003)
Merrill Arthur Birch was born in Minneapolis on April 17, 1919. He grew up in the city and attended public schools. After graduating from Edison High School in 1937, he entered the University of Minnesota and received a bachelor's degree in architecture in 1942. After military service in World War II, Birch joined the firm of McEnary & Krafft in 1946 and remained there for the rest of his career. The firm became known as McEnary, Krafft, Birch & Kilgore in 1963 after Robert Kilgore entered the practice and he and Birch were named partners.

Birch died in Delano, Minnesota, on October 6, 2003.

Notable Buildings
Aldersgate Methodist Church, 3801 Wooddale Avenue, St. Louis Park (1951)
Valleyview Hospital and Sanitarium, Jordan (1956)
Peace Presbyterian Church, 7624 Cedar Lake Road, St. Louis Park (1957)

Cyrus Bissell (1885–1976)
Cyrus Y. Bissell was a native of New Jersey, born in Hoboken on June 6, 1885. He graduated from Columbia University in 1908 with his bachelor's degree in architecture. Bissell worked as a draftsman and project manager in various New York City offices, including Delano and Aldrich, and Nelson and Van Wagonen. He then moved to Montreal and joined Brown and Vallance. Between 1908 and 1917 he was employed by Marcus T. Reynolds in Albany, New York.

During World War I, Bissell served as assistant chief estimator in the Construction Division of the War Department, the division that had charge of the construction of army camps, depots, and bases. Bissell moved to Minneapolis after the war and became an associate, and later a partner, with R. V. L. Haxby and Edward Stebbins in 1920.

The firm of Stebbins, Haxby and Bissell became one of the most successful in Minneapolis, specializing in the design of schools and commercial structures. The name changed as partners came and went (see "Bissell, Belair and Green"). Bissell retired in the 1960s and the firm existed until about 2000 as Green, Nelson & Weaver.

Bissell died on September 30, 1976.

Notable Buildings
STEBBINS, HAXBY AND BISSELL
Phi Sigma Kappa fraternity house, 317 18th Avenue SE, Minneapolis (1926)
Columbia Heights High School, Columbia Heights (1926)
J. H. Ravlin residence, 1615 E. River Road, Minneapolis (1927)
Cyrus Bissell residence, 4545 Fremont Avenue S., Minneapolis (1928)
Theta Chi fraternity house, 315 16th Avenue SE, Minneapolis (1928)
St. Louis Park High School, St. Louis Park (1937)

Christopher Boehme (1865–1916)
The son of a German-born immigrant who settled in St. Anthony in the 1850s, Christopher Adam Boehme was born on

Bissell, Belair and Green

It is a frequent occurrence in the architecture profession that firms change names as partners leave and new ones are added. Nowhere is this truer, perhaps, than in the case of Bissell, Belair and Green.

It all began in 1877 when Edward Stebbins moved to Minneapolis from New York and set up a practice, first with a former classmate from the Massachusetts Institute of Technology, George Mann—who was to go on to a distinguished career of his own in Missouri—and then alone for many years until forming a second partnership, this time with Robert Van Loan Haxby in 1914. Stebbins and Haxby flourished for six years and added Cyrus Bissell in 1920.

The firm, Stebbins, Haxby and Bissell, continued under this name until the passing of Stebbins in 1934. For about eight years it operated as Haxby and Bissell, then added John Belair as a partner (Haxby, Bissell & Belair). Haxby was tragically killed in an auto accident in 1947 and his name was subsequently dropped. Bissell and Belair were joined by Gene L. Green in 1960 and the firm was known as Bissell, Belair and Green until Bissell retired in the 1960s, after which the name changes seemed to occur thick and fast. Partners Arthur E. Nelson, John K. Weaver, Mark F. Winsor, L. Vern Watten, and Kenneth Quass were added at various times and the firm was known as Green, Nelson, Watten and Winsor and then Green, Nelson, Weaver and Winsor for several years and, finally, simply Green, Nelson and Weaver. The firm went out of business about 2000, after almost 125 years of continuous practice.

Cyrus Bissell residence, Minneapolis, 1928 (Stebbins, Haxby & Bissell). *Photograph 1929 by Norton & Peel. Courtesy of Minnesota Historical Society.*

January 16, 1865, in Minneapolis. Boehme was educated at the University of Minnesota, where he took the special course in architecture, which was all that was available before the establishment of the school of architecture. He was employed by Warren Dunnell for fourteen years, both during and after his training. In 1896, Boehme set up his own practice and worked alone until 1903 when he entered partnership with Victor Cordella. The partnership was dissolved in 1911 and Boehme returned to private practice.

Boehme died in Minneapolis on November 24, 1916.

Notable Buildings

WITH VICTOR CORDELLA
Swan Turnblad residence (now the American Swedish Institute), 2600 Park Avenue, Minneapolis (1903–07)
St. Joseph's Catholic Church, Browerville (1908–09)
Our Lady of Lourdes Catholic Church, Little Falls (1911)

Francis C. Boerner (1889–1936)
Francis Clarence Boerner was born in Duluth on July 24, 1889. He graduated from Central High School in 1907 and entered the University of Minnesota, from which he earned his bachelor's degree in civil engineering in 1911. He subsequently worked for architects in New York City before returning to Minnesota in 1916 to become a partner of Ernest Croft in Minneapolis. Croft and Boerner were fellow students at the University and both practiced in New York City, perhaps in some of the same offices. Boerner left to serve in the armed forces during World War I and, after the war, resumed his partnership with Croft. The firm dissolved in 1930 when Boerner moved back to his hometown. He maintained a practice there, except for brief employment with the Works Projects Administration in 1935–36, until his death in Duluth from pneumonia on December 12, 1936.

Notable Buildings

WITH ERNEST CROFT
Northwest Terminal Warehouse, 630–658 Stinson Boulevard NE, Minneapolis (1920)
Lafayette Building, 10th Street and Nicollet Avenue, Minneapolis (1922)
Mille Lacs County Courthouse, Milaca (1922)
Minneapolis Auditorium, Minneapolis (1925) (razed 1988)
Children's Gospel Mission, 1407 Washington Avenue S. (1932)

Septimus Bowler (1868–1940)
Septimus James Bowler was born in London, England, on February 11, 1868. Nothing is known of his education or work experience until he arrived in Minneapolis about 1884. He worked first as a carpenter and then, about 1888, established an architectural practice. He maintained a busy office until the early 1930s, designing a variety of buildings including apartment houses, commercial structures, and Jewish temples. In 1939 he was hospitalized in the Rochester (Minn.) State Hospital for an unknown illness.

In 1921, George Chapman, president of the Minneapolis Chapter of the American Institute of Architects, made this less than flattering assessment of Bowler's character and reputation in a letter he wrote to William Stanley Parker, secretary of the national organization: "In regard to Septimus James Bowler, Mr. Bowler has

Mikro Kodesh Synagogue (now Disciples Ministry Church), Minneapolis, 1927 (Septimus Bowler). *Photograph 1937 by Minneapolis Star Journal Tribune. Courtesy of Minnesota Historical Society.*

never been considered eligible for Chapter membership and to the best of my knowledge has never made application to the Chapter. I have not heard much of him for the past few years since Prohibition went into effect; previous to that time, I believe he was sober only occasionally. His work, architecturally, consisted of rough sketch plans made mostly for the cheaper class of speculative builders. He has never been considered a man of any standing and particularly one eligible for Institute membership." Bowler, however, did a flourishing business during the 1920s and into at least the early 1930s, despite his alleged alcoholism. While the date of his retirement from practice has not been found, he moved to Rochester, Minnesota some time in 1939.

Bowler died in Rochester on April 16, 1940.

Notable Buildings
Temple Israel Cemetery Chapel, 4153 3rd Avenue S., Minneapolis (1894)
First Church of Christ Scientist, 614–620 E. 15th Street, Minneapolis (1897)
Mikro Kodesh Synagogue (now Disciples Ministry Church), 1000 Oliver Avenue N., Minneapolis (1927)

William T. Bray (1868–1959)
William Thayer Bray was born in New York State on July 30, 1868. He received his architectural training through apprenticeships in his home state and moved to Duluth in 1891, where he began working as a draftsman. One of his earliest jobs, if not his first in the city, was in the firm of Traphagen and Fitzpatrick, where he was employed from 1892 to 1895 or 1896. In 1896, Bray formed a partnership with John J. Wangenstein (Wangenstein and Bray) which was dissolved in 1898. In 1901 he was a partner of Carl Wirth. He subsequently joined I. Vernon Hill in partnership (Hill & Bray, 1902–1904), practiced alone for a year, then joined Carl Nystrom for eight or nine years in a firm called Bray and Nystrom. After the dissolution of this firm, Bray returned to private practice until 1923, when he partnered with Claude Smith (Bray & Smith) until his retirement to California in 1925.

Bray died in Beverly Hills, California, on his birthday in 1959.

Notable Buildings
Robert Smith residence, 2330 E. 5th Street, Duluth (1903) (with I. Vernon Hill)

Henry A. Meyers residence, Duluth, 1910 (William T. Bray and Carl Nystrom). *Photograph courtesy of Northwest Architectural Archives, University of Minnesota.*

Edward L. Bradley residence, 2229 E. 1st Street, Duluth (1904) (with I. Vernon Hill)

Carl A. Luster residence, 1629 E. Superior Street, Duluth (1905)

Ward Ames Jr. residence, 2216 E. 2nd Street, Duluth (1908) (with Carl Nystrom)

Thomas J. Davis residence, 2104 E. 1st Street, Duluth (1909) (with Carl Nystrom)

Henry A. Meyers residence, 2505 E. 1st Street, Duluth (1910) (with Carl Nystrom)

Edwin Brown (1875–1930)

Edwin Hacker Brown was born in Worcester, Massachusetts, on July 27, 1875. He attended Harvard University and graduated in 1896 with a Bachelor of Arts degree. He entered Worcester Polytechnic Institute and received a Bachelor of Science degree. He came to Minneapolis and entered into a partnership with Edwin Hewitt in 1910. During World War I, Brown served in the United States and Europe with the Red Cross. After the war, Hewitt and Brown resumed their partnership. Brown established the Architects Small House Service Bureau, an organization that eventually became national in scope, and which provided architect-produced plans for inexpensive houses to help alleviate the postwar housing shortage.

Brown died of pneumonia in Minneapolis on April 21, 1930.

Notable Buildings

WITH EDWIN HEWITT

Cathedral Church of St. Mark, 519 Oak Grove Street, Minneapolis (1908–11)

Hennepin Avenue Methodist Church, 511 Groveland Avenue, Minneapolis (1916)

Architects and Engineers Building, 1200 2nd Avenue S., Minneapolis (1922)

James Brunet (B. 1906)

James Abelardo Brunet was born in Monroe, Wisconsin, on July 21, 1906. He graduated from the University of Minnesota's School of Architecture in 1930 and, after working for a year in various

Minneapolis architectural offices, joined Hans Wessel in partnership. Marvin Kline became a partner in 1934 and the partnership continued until the early 1960s. Brunet left the partnership about 1966 and moved to Santa Fe, New Mexico, where he joined Philippe Register and Terrance Ross as a partner. He retired in 1980 and resided in Santa Fe.

Notable Buildings
V. Mel Kaufmann residence, 20 Park Lane, Minneapolis (1935)

Emma Brunson (1887–1980)
Emma F. Gruetzke was born on February 17, 1887, probably in St. Paul. Her early life and education are unknown. She married Harry S. Brunson, a St. Paul boiler inspector, and began working for Augustus Gauger as a draftsman in 1905. She continued with Gauger until 1920, then she set up her own practice, which she maintained as a one-person office until her retirement in 1968. Her practice consisted mainly of residences. Brunson died in St. Paul on December 5, 1980.

Notable Buildings
Hugo Koch residence, Osceola Avenue between Albert and Hamline Avenues, St. Paul (1923)
Emma Brunson residence, Maryland Street between Arcade and Mendota Streets, St. Paul (1925)
Theodore Maier residence, 616 Gotzian, St. Paul (1926)
C. E. Smith residence, 673 Nebraska Avenue, St. Paul (1926)

Charles Buechner (1859–1924)
Charles William Buechner was born in Darmstadt, Germany, on April 27, 1859, the son of Carl Ernst and Josephine (Buchs) Buechner. Young Charles was educated in France and Germany, ending his education at Solothurn, Switzerland. It is not known when he immigrated to the United States, but he arrived in St. Paul in 1874 and began working as a surveyor for the St. Paul, Milwaukee and

Christ Lutheran Church, St. Paul, 1913 (Buechner & Orth). *Photograph ca. 1930. Courtesy of Minnesota Historical Society.*

Manitoba Railway. He was later employed in the Tracks, Bridges and Buildings Division of the Northern Pacific Railway and, in 1883, began an architectural apprenticeship in the office of Clarence Johnston. Buechner left Johnston in 1892 and started his own practice as a partner of John H. Jacobsen for the next ten years. At Jacobsen's death in 1902, Buechner joined Henry Orth in partnership for the rest of his career. The firm of Buechner and Orth specialized in courthouses, theaters, and public buildings.

Buechner died in St. Paul on August 13, 1924.

Notable Buildings
Dr. Edward Walther residence, 443 Dayton Avenue, St. Paul (1893) (Buechner & Jacobsen)
Lac Qui Parle County Courthouse, Madison (1899) (Buechner & Jacobsen)
Norwegian Evangelical Lutheran Church (now Christ Lutheran Church), University Avenue and Park Street, St. Paul (1913) (Buechner & Orth)

Carl Buetow (1893–1987)
Carl Herbert Buetow was born on December 28, 1893, in St. Paul. He attended public schools in the city and in February 1910, after graduating from high school, began working as a draftsman in the office of Reed and Stem in St. Paul, to study architecture. Buetow attended night school at the University of Minnesota and took courses in mathematics, architectural modeling, and engineering and drawing. After about three and a half years with Reed and Stem, Buetow moved to Clarence H. Johnston's office, where he remained for about two and a half years. He then joined Alban & Lockhart for two

Auditorium and fire station, Deerwood, 1935 (Carl Buetow). *Photograph ca. 1940. Courtesy of Minnesota Historical Society.*

years (1915–17), supervising the construction of a number of their buildings, until the start of World War I. During the war, he worked for the Great Northern Railroad as a draftsman and as an accountant for a time. As soon as the war ended, Buetow joined Lambert Bassindale's firm in St. Paul, where he remained only long enough to finish the Northern Pacific (now Samaritan) Hospital in the Midway district.

Following his employment with Bassindale, Buetow was employed as head of the architectural department in the Louis F. Dow Company, designers of small-town banks, then moved to the office of the city architect of St. Paul. After three and a half years there, he formed his own practice.

In the 1930s and through World War II he was hired by the federal government in its WPA and PWA programs to design a variety of public works structures, including hospitals and airfield facilities. He resumed his private practice after the war and retired in 1960.

Buetow died in St. Paul on July 22, 1987.

Notable Buildings
Northern Pacific Hospital (later Samaritan Hospital), St. Paul (1918–19) (razed ca. 1988) (with Bassindale)
Hospital, Glencoe (1935)
Auditorium and fire station, Deerwood (1935)
Memorial Hospital, International Falls (1948)
Hospital, Redwood Falls (1953)

Gerald Buetow (1917–1978)
Gerald Herbert Buetow was born on June 15, 1917 in St. Paul. He graduated from the University of Minnesota in 1940 with his bachelor's degree in architecture. He worked briefly as a draftsman in the firm of Jones & Cerny in 1938, and was employed in a similar position with the Oliver Iron Mining Company in Duluth from 1941 to 1942. He then joined his father, Max, in St. Paul and worked first as a draftsman before becoming a partner in 1945. He remained in the firm for the remainder of his career, continuing to practice after his father's death in 1957.

Buetow died in St. Paul on February 9, 1978.

Notable Buildings
Gerald Buetow residence, 1433 Forest Lane, Arden Hills (1948)
Marigold Foods plant, Rochester (1965)
Community Hospital, New York Mills (1966)

Max Buetow (1892–1957)
Max Otto Buetow, younger brother of Carl Buetow, was born in St. Paul, Minnesota on February 19, 1892. He attended the University of Minnesota (1912–14) and the St. Paul School of Art (dates unknown). He worked as chief draftsman in the office of Buechner & Orth of St. Paul until 1917, and then he worked for Philip Bettenburg for three years. In 1920, he established a partnership with C. Kampfer, which lasted ten years, after which Buetow set up his own office, specializing in the design of churches, schools, and hospitals. He was joined by his son Gerald in 1945, who carried on the practice after Buetow's death in St. Paul on February 23, 1957.

Notable Buildings
Gymnasium (now Graebner Memorial Chapel), Concordia College, St. Paul (1911)

Breck School, St. Paul (1927) (razed ca. 1990)
Police department building, Little Falls (1935)
Lutheran Memorial Center, Concordia College, St. Paul (1951–52)
Walther Hall (dormitory), Concordia College, St. Paul (1956–58) (razed 2007)

Leroy Buffington (1847–1931)

Leroy Sunderland Buffington was born on September 22, 1847, in Cincinnati, Ohio. He studied architecture and engineering at the University of Cincinnati, graduating in 1869. Two years after his graduation, Buffington moved to St. Paul where he became a partner of Abraham Radcliffe and was employed on the remodeling of the State Capitol. He relocated to Minneapolis in 1874 and remained there the rest of his life.

Buffington was one of the most successful architects in Minnesota. He specialized in designing hotels (forty-two of them during his career), plus public and commercial buildings, churches, and residences. In 1881 Buffington claimed to have thought up the idea of building skyscrapers by using load bearing iron frames, the same method used today. He applied for a patent for his invention in November 1887; it was granted in May 1888. Frustrated that none of the subsequent builders of high-rise buildings using his patented method paid him royalties, he formed the Buffington Iron Building Company to sue the infringers. He lost all the lawsuits he brought to court. The only builder to ever pay him a royalty was Rufus Rand of Minneapolis in 1929. Buffington also battled for several years to obtain acceptance of his patents for a type of acetylene gas application, a struggle finally won in 1900 after a serious challenge from John Schumacher of Chicago.

He maintained a private practice in Minneapolis until his death on February 15, 1931. An obituary noted that a week before his death, he had "made the rounds of his friends to dissipate a rumor he was dead. A resident of Stillwater of similar name had died and eastern papers had thought it was the Minneapolis architect and had so carried the story."

Notable Buildings
Pillsbury A Mill, Main Street and 3rd Avenue SE, Minneapolis (1880–82)
Boston Block, Minneapolis (1881–84) (razed 1942)
Shipman, Greve House, 445 Summit Avenue, St. Paul (1882)

Pillsbury A Mill, Minneapolis, 1880–82 (Leroy Buffington). Photograph ca. 1885 by Henry R. Farr. Courtesy of Minnesota Historical Society.

Ware Auditorium (later Grand Theater), Northfield 1898–99 (Harry Carter). *Photograph courtesy of Northfield Historical Society.*

Minneapolis Tribune Building, Minneapolis (1883–84) (razed 1889)

West Hotel, Minneapolis (1884) (razed 1940)

Burton Hall, University of Minnesota, Minneapolis (1892)

Harry Carter (1843–1910)

Harry G. Carter was born in England on March 20, 1843. It is not known when he came to the United States, but it probably was in his childhood and certainly before the Civil War, when he served in the Union Army. There is also no information available about what kind of training he had to prepare him for a career in architecture. By 1885, Carter had an office in St. Paul and moved to Minneapolis eight years later. He specialized in theatrical architecture, designing theaters and opera houses throughout the Upper Midwest. A notice in *The Improvement Bulletin* in 1894 announced that "Harry G. Carter . . . is the only architect in the Northwest making a specialty of theatrical architecture. He is the architect of the handsome new People's theatre, Minneapolis, the Minneapolis Bijou and many others."

Carter spent the rest of his life in Minneapolis and died there on February 27, 1910.

Notable Buildings

Metropolitan Theatre, Minneapolis (1894) (razed 1937)

Veteran's Service Building, St. Paul, 1953–54, 1973 (Brooks Cavin Jr.). *Photograph courtesy of Northwest Architectural Archives, University of Minnesota.*

Bijou Theatre, 20 N. Washington Avenue, Minneapolis (1897) (razed 1961)
Ware Auditorium (later Grand Theater), Northfield (1898–99)
Princess Theatre, Minneapolis (1920) (razed ca. 1975)

Brooks Cavin Jr. (1914–2002)
William Brooks Cavin Jr. was born in Philadelphia, Pennsylvania, on November 3, 1914. He received a Bachelor of Arts degree from Harvard University in 1937, a bachelor's degree in architecture from Harvard in 1940, and a master's degree in architecture from the same institution in 1941. He then worked as a designer-draftsman with four firms in Washington, D.C.: Kastern & Hibben (1941–43); Faulkner & Kingsbury (1943–44); Saarinen & Swanson (1944–45); and Louis Justement (1945–46). Cavin was a conscientious objector during World War II, but served in a civilian capacity with the above firms and in the War Department analyzing enemy aircraft.

He moved to St. Paul in 1946 and set up his own company after winning an international design competition for the Veteran's Service Building in St. Paul. He had a private practice until 1960 when he entered into a partnership with Clayton Page and they opened an office in Minneapolis in addition to their St. Paul office. The Cavin and Page partnership ended in 1969 with Page's death. Cavin and John Rova, who had joined the firm three years earlier, continued in business, with Rova as an associate until 1980 when he became a full partner.

Cavin taught in the University of Minnesota's School of Architecture from 1947 to 1967, served as director of the St. Paul Gallery and School of Art from 1951 to 1957, was a charter member of the Minneapolis Heritage Preservation Commission (1971–1978), and a member of the State Review Board for the National Register of Historic Places. As a leading supporter of historic preservation in the Twin Cities, he worked on the restoration of the Minnesota State Capitol, the old Federal Courts Building (now Landmark Center in St. Paul), Fort Snelling, and the old Post Office in New Ulm.

Cavin died in Shelburne, Vermont, on December 19, 2002.

Notable Buildings
See also Clayton Page
Veteran's Service Building, 20 W. 12th Street, St. Paul (1953–1954, 1973)
Central Apartments, 554 Central Avenue W., St. Paul (1964)
Fort Snelling Historic Site restoration, St. Paul (1965–80)
Loring Towers, Grant Street and 1st Avenue S., Minneapolis (1969–70)
Brown County Historical Museum, New Ulm (1983–84)

Robert Cerny (1908–1985)
Robert George Cerny was born in La Crosse, Wisconsin, on June 11, 1908. As a high school student, he was an apprentice in the office of Parkinson and Dockendorff, a leading firm in the city. Cerny graduated in 1926 and entered the University of Minnesota in 1928, where he received a bachelor's degree in architecture in 1932. During his summer vacations, he worked as a student draftsman in the offices of William Ingemann, Jacobson and Jacobson, and A. Moorman, all in St. Paul. Cerny went to Harvard University and earned a master's degree in architecture in 1933. He was employed as an architect with the Tennessee Valley Authority (TVA) for a year, then traveled in Europe under a Nelson-Robinson Traveling Fellowship. He returned to the United States and the TVA in 1935, and in 1937 he moved to Minneapolis and formed the partnership of Jones and Cerny, which lasted until 1942. Then Cerny joined Long & Thorshov, and the firm was renamed Thorshov & Cerny in 1951. In 1960 the partnership was dissolved and Cerny formed his own practice, Cerny & Associates, which became one of the most successful in Minnesota. He taught architecture at the Univesity of Minnesota from 1937 until his retirement in 1976, and he closed his firm in 1978.

Cerny died in St. Paul on January 31, 1985.

Notable Buildings
St. Olaf Catholic Church, 805 S. 2nd Avenue, Minneapolis (1953–54) (Thorshov & Cerny)
Weyerhaeuser Memorial Chapel, Macalester College, St. Paul (1967–68) (Cerny & Associates)
Radisson South Hotel, Bloomington (1968–70) (Cerny & Associates)
Brooklyn Center Civic Center, Brooklyn Center (1968–71) (Cerny & Associates)
Health Sciences Unit A (now Moos Tower), University of Minnesota, Minneapolis (Cerny & Associates with Architects Collaborative and Hammel Green & Abrahamson) (1973)

Weyerhaeuser Memorial Chapel, St. Paul, 1967–68 (Robert Cerny). *Photograph by Bob Firth*.

Arthur Chamberlin (1865–1933)
Arthur Bishop Chamberlin was born in Solon, Ohio, on March 12, 1865. When he was two years old, his family moved to Milwaukee where he grew up. In 1882, his father, a railroad ticket agent, was transferred to Minneapolis, and two years later Chamberlin began his architectural career by hiring on as a draftsman in the prestigious firm of Long & Kees. He remained there, except for a brief time in 1887, until 1890. During part of that time he studied perspective drawing with Harvey Ellis, who was the top architectural delineator in the Midwest.

Chamberlin moved his family to Seattle and over the next six years worked successively for Saunders & Houghton, John Parkinson, and William Boone, then entered into a partnership with Carl Siebrand. He returned to Minneapolis in 1896, worked as a draftsman in Orff

Minneapolis Athletic Club (now Grand Hotel), Minneapolis, 1912 (Bertrand & Chamberlin). *Photograph 1915 by Charles J. Hibbard. Courtesy of Minnesota Historical Society.*

and Joralemon's office, and then formed a highly successful partnership with George Bertrand (Bertrand & Chamberlin) in 1897 that lasted until 1931.

Chamberlin died in Minneapolis on September 18, 1933.

Notable Buildings

BERTRAND & CHAMBERLIN
Asbury Hospital, 915 E. 15th Street, Minneapolis (1898)
Dean & Company warehouse, 406–410 Washington Avenue N., Minneapolis (1902)
Salisbury Mattress Company (now part of St. Anthony Main development), 212 SE Main Street, Minneapolis (1909)
Minneapolis Athletic Club (now Grand Hotel), 619 2nd Avenue S., Minneapolis (1912)
Chamber of Commerce Annex, 3rd Street S. and 4th Avenue S., Minneapolis (1919)
Shriner's Hospital, 2025 E. River Road, Minneapolis (1921)

Rollin Chapin (1888–1952)
Rollin Chapin was born in Minneapolis on July 12, 1888, and grew up in the city. He graduated from the School of Architecture at the University of Pennsylvania in 1912 and returned to his hometown to enter the firm of Tyrie & Chapman. He worked as a draftsman in the firm for three years before joining Hewitt & Brown. When the United States entered World War I, Chapin enlisted and was assigned first to the Construction Division of the U.S. Army, where he designed army camps, and then served in the Surgeon General's office designing new facilities for Walter Reed Hospital in Washington.

Chapin came back to Minneapolis after the war and worked briefly as a draftsman in Frederick Mann's office (1919–20) before establishing his own practice in 1920. He became best known as a designer of small homes, for which he won at least one national design award, and was active in the Chapin Publishing Company which published *The Improvement Bulletin* (later the *Construction Bulletin*). In the mid-1930s, he became junior architect on the Sumner Field Housing Project in north Minneapolis.

Chapin moved to Seattle in 1949 and set up a firm there. He also served as president of Pacific Builder & Engineer Inc., publishers of a magazine for the architecture and building industry. The magazine later became a sister publication of *Construction Bulletin*, which was published in Minneapolis for many years. He died in Seattle on April 4, 1952.

Notable Buildings
Thomas Joseph residence, 1583 Northrop Avenue, Falcon Heights (1936)
W. M. Lauer residence, 2255 Folwell Avenue, Falcon Heights (1940)
W. E. Peik residence, 2225 Hoyt Avenue, Falcon Heights (1941)

Cecil Chapman (1876–1918)
Cecil Bayless Chapman was born in 1876 in Dubuque, Iowa. He moved to Minneapolis as a child with his family and grew up there. It is not known how he got his professional training. He first appears in 1898 as a draftsman with William Channing Whitney. Chapman started his own practice before 1907; in 1912 he joined Gottlieb Magney in a partnership that ended in 1917.

Chapman died in Minneapolis on August 27, 1918, after a lingering illness.

Notable Buildings
E. J. Scriver residence, 2631 E. Lake of the Isles Parkway, Minneapolis (1908)
Grace Evangelical Lutheran Church (now Grace University Lutheran Church), 324 Harvard Street SE, Minneapolis (1915) (with Gottlieb Magney)
Sumner Branch Library (now Sumner Community Library), 611 Van White Memorial Boulevard, Minneapolis (1915) (with Gottlieb Magney)

George Chapman (CA. 1877–1950)
George Augustus Chapman—no relation, as far as is known, to Cecil Chapman—was born in New York State around 1877. His education and training are unknown. He first appears as a partner of William Tyrie in Ogdensburg, New York, in 1897. Chapman moved to Minneapolis and was in partnership there with Charles Bell in 1908, when he invited Tyrie to come to the city and enter their firm. After Bell left

Sumner Branch Library, Minneapolis, 1915 (Cecil Chapman and Gottlieb Magney). *Photograph 1954. Courtesy of Minneapolis Public Library, James K. Hosmer Special Collection, M1348.*

Fawkes Building, Minneapolis, 1910 (George Chapman). *Photograph ca. 1920 by Charles P. Gibson. Courtesy of Minnesota Historical Society.*

in 1913, the practice continued as Tyrie & Chapman. Tyrie left the partnership in 1929 to join Long and Thorshov and Chapman continued in private practice. He also served as president of the Minneapolis Chapter of the American Institute of Architects and was a consulting architect in the 1930s.

He died in Minneapolis on October 20, 1950.

Notable Buildings
Fawkes Building, 1625 Hennepin Avenue, Minneapolis (1910)

Elizabeth Clarke residence, 2525 Pillsbury Avenue S., Minneapolis (1912)

Wilbur Clark Jr. (B. 1921)
Wilbur B. Clark Jr., was born on July 23, 1921, in Minneapolis. He attended Washburn High School, graduating in 1939. He entered the University of Minnesota and received a bachelor's degree in architecture in December 1946. In January 1947 Clark joined Pfeifer and Shultz, engineers, in Minneapolis as a draftsman and remained there for a year.

Afterward, he was employed by Grosz and Anderson in Grand Forks, North Dakota, from February to August 1948, when he returned to Minneapolis to enter the firm of Armstrong and Schlichting. In 1960, Clark formed a partnership with Richard Peterson and Newton Griffith, which became one of the most successful in the Twin Cities. After Griffith's death in 1968, the firm became Peterson, Clark and Associates. Peterson left the partnership in 1983 and Clark continued to operate it until about 1989, after which he practiced privately for several years.

Notable Buildings
Housing for the Elderly, 1707 3rd Avenue S., Minneapolis (ca. 1962) (Peterson, Clark & Griffith)
Housing for the Elderly, 1515 Park Avenue, Minneapolis (1965) (Peterson, Clark & Griffith)
Ray Mithun residence, Northome (n.d.)

Frederick Clarke (1853–1942?)
Frederick A. Clarke is one of the most interesting and eclectic personalities among Minnesota architects. He was born in Connecticut in 1853 and attended the local public schools, where, because he was exceptionally talented in Latin, he was sent to high school before his twelfth birthday. After leaving school, Clarke went to work in a piano factory while studying music and art in his spare time. When he was twenty-two, he moved to California and traveled there for a year before settling in San Francisco to continue his piano-making trade. He soon became the chief designer and manager of the company while serving as organist of the great Tabernacle organ.

During his residence in San Francisco, Clarke entered the San Francisco Medical College, but in the second year he burned himself out from overwork and left for a year's rest and to seek a brand-new career. He chose architecture and moved to Minneapolis in 1885 to take up his practice. He worked first as a draftsman for Harry Wild Jones, then in 1888 set up an office of his own. Clarke was in partnership in 1892 with Frank E. Rotchka; it dissolved two years later and he resumed solo practice. He specialized in designing apartment houses and private residences—several of his apart-

San Mateo Flats (now Fitzgerald Condominiums), St. Paul, 1894 (Frederick Clarke). *Photograph ca. 1964 by Eugene Debs Becker. Courtesy of Minnesota Historical Society.*

ment buildings are included in the South Ninth Street Historic District in Minneapolis. A news article in *The Improvement Bulletin*, May 14, 1898, reported that while he was a highly capable designer, his "greater experience was in the line of economy and practical work, saving thousands of dollars to his clients and in no instance tolerating anything freakish in the aim to do something original, holding his clients' interests as paramount at all times."

It appears that Clarke could not altogether forsake the practice of medicine, either, for the same article noted that since leaving San Francisco he had been quietly studying and providing free medical advice to his friends "who [held] him in grateful remembrance for efficient medical relief." In the lean years after the panic of 1893, Clarke took advantage of the downturn of business in his office to obtain a degree in osteopathy and a Doctor of Medicine degree. At the same time, just so he did not remain idle for long, he served as president of the Minneapolis Wire & Iron Works. In 1898, Clarke moved back east to practice medicine. Edwin Overmire succeeded to his architectural practice and took over the office at 1043 Lumber Exchange.

From this point on, Clarke's life fades into obscurity. It appears that he may have set up a medical practice in Portland, Maine, which he maintained well into the 1930s, and that he died there in 1942. Thus, it is uncertain whether the Dr. Frederick A. Clarke of Portland, Maine, is the same individual as Mr. Frederick A. Clarke, architect, of Minneapolis and points West, but it appears likely that he was.

Notable Buildings
Mayhew Apartments, 614–626 S. 9th Street, Minneapolis (1886)
Adams Apartments, 500 10th Street S., Minneapolis (1888)
Salisbury and Satterlee Co. Warehouse, 221 Main Street SE, Minneapolis (1892)
S. J. Cooke Company warehouses (now Gaar Scott Historic Lofts and Minnesota Opera Center, respectively), 614 and 620 1st Street N., Minneapolis (1892)
San Mateo Flats (now Fitzgerald Condominiums), 475–481 Laurel Avenue, St. Paul (1894)
Residence, 2400 Girard Avenue S., Minneapolis (1897)
Residence, 2303 Colfax Avenue S., Minneapolis (1897)

Arthur Clausen (CA. 1875–1952)
Arthur C. Clausen was born about 1875 in Illinois. His education and training are unknown. He first appears in Minneapolis employed as a draftsman for Long & Long in 1899. He remained there for about ten years, and then set up his own practice. Some time around the mid- to late 1910s, Clausen moved to California where he worked as a mechanical engineer in a steel company in South San Francisco and San Mateo, and practiced architecture at the same time. During this period, he assisted in designing "Pan Town," a company-owned community of fifty-eight residences for workers in the Pan automobile factory in St. Cloud, Minnesota (1920–21). Most of his architectural career in California remains unknown.

Clausen died in Portland, Oregon, on May 7, 1952.

Mudbaden Sulphur Springs Sanitarium, Jordan, 1915 (Arthur Clausen). *Photograph ca. 1920. Courtesy of Minnesota Historical Society.*

Notable Buildings
Mudcura Sanitarium, Chanhassen (1908–09) (razed 1997)
George Kline residence (now the public library), Chaska (1909)
Residence, 4609 Lyndale Avenue S., Minneapolis (1911)
Mudbaden Sulphur Springs Sanitarium, Jordan (1915)
Pan Town, St. Cloud (1920–21)

Horace Cleveland (1814–1900)
Horace William Shaler Cleveland was born in Lancaster, Massachusetts, on December 16, 1814. He attended a school operated by his mother, whose curriculum stressed the observation and study of nature and landscape. Cleveland moved to Cuba with his family in the late 1820s where his father was in the diplomatic service and where he learned mulching techniques on the coffee plantations.

In the 1830s, having returned to the United States, he was employed as a surveyor in Illinois and other western states. He moved back to Massachusetts in the late 1830s and stayed for a time with his brother, Henry, in Jamaica Plain. Cleveland purchased a farm, called "Oatlands," in Burlington, New Jersey, in the early 1840s and practiced scientific farming.

Back in Massachusetts in 1854, he opened a landscape practice with Robert Morris Copeland. The firm designed the Sleepy Hollow Cemetery in Concord, working for Ralph Waldo Emerson and other members of the committee that headed the cemetery association. Copeland and Cleveland also served as advisors to the city of Boston on a park system and street layout for the Back Bay area.

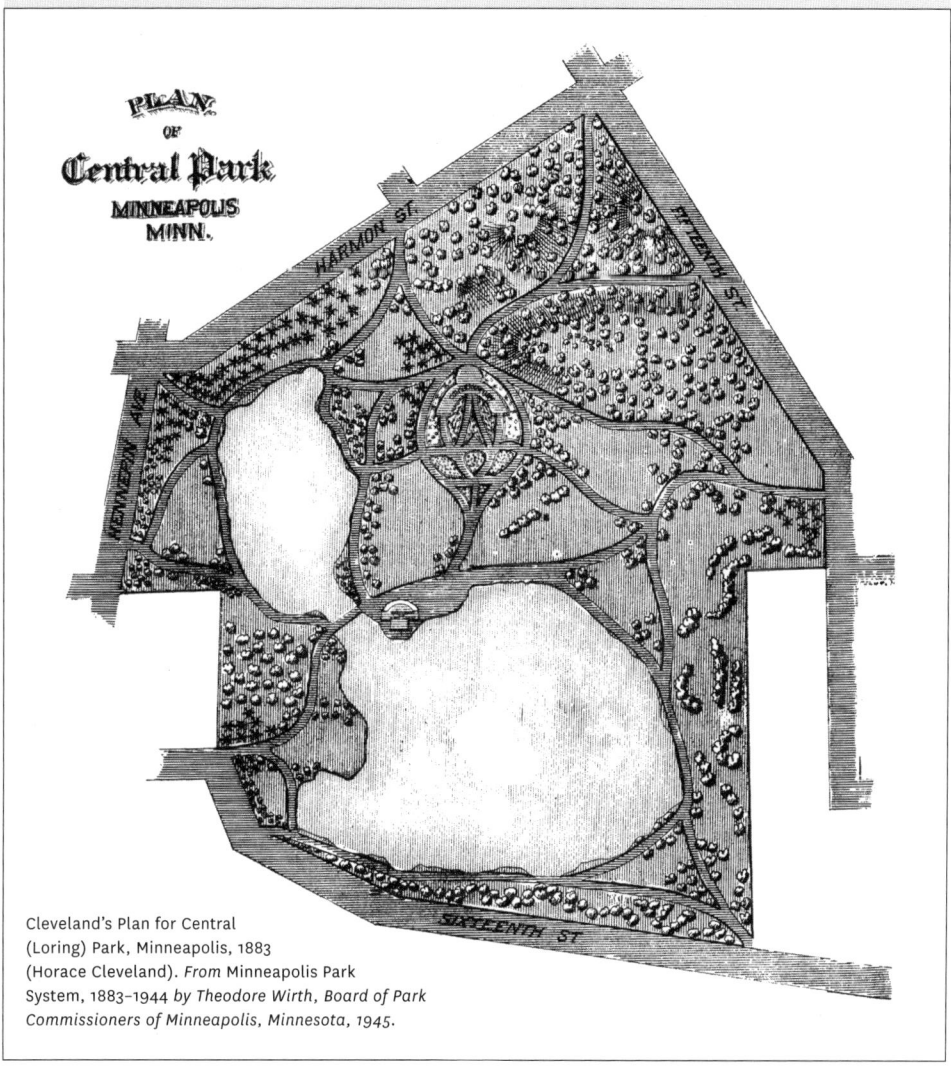

Cleveland's Plan for Central (Loring) Park, Minneapolis, 1883 (Horace Cleveland). *From* Minneapolis Park System, 1883–1944 *by Theodore Wirth, Board of Park Commissioners of Minneapolis, Minnesota, 1945.*

Cleveland moved to Chicago in 1866 and secured work with railroads as well as forming an association with William French, a civil engineer and founding director of the Art Institute of Chicago. The two men collaborated on the design of cemeteries and residential subdivisions. Cleveland also worked on Drexell Boulevard, South Parks, and Graceland Cemetery in the 1870s. His office burned in the Chicago fire of 1871, destroying his extensive library. He published *Landscape Architecture as Applied to the Wants of the West* in 1873, which defined and developed the new field of landscape architecture.

In 1883, Cleveland began working on a plan for the Minneapolis park system, moving to the city in the mid-1880s and remained there much of the rest of his life.

He died on December 5, 1900 in Hinsdale, Illinois.

Notable Buildings

PARK PLANS

Oakland Cemetery, 927 Jackson Street, St. Paul (1874) (with William French)

Loring Park, 1382 Willow Street, Minneapolis (1883)

Elliot Park, 1000 E. 14th Street, Minneapolis (n.d.)

Fairview Park, 609 29th Avenue N., Minneapolis (n.d.)

Logan Park, 690 13th Avenue NE, Minneapolis (n.d.)

Elizabeth Close (B. 1912)

Born in Vienna, Austria, on June 4, 1912, Elizabeth Scheu was the daughter of a lawyer and alderman. She grew up in a landmark house designed by Adolf Loos, an early practitioner within the Modern Movement in Europe. The unusual residence was devoid of decoration, and attracted artists, writers, musicians, and journalists as guests. Among them were Ezra Pound, John Gunther, and Richard Neutra, who met his wife Dione during one such visit.

Influenced by outstanding architecture every day, young Elizabeth was naturally drawn to it as a profession and entered the Technische Hochschule to take a degree in architecture. She left Vienna in 1935 because of prejudice against women at the school and because of the rise of Nazi influence in Austria. She entered the Massachusetts Institute of Technology (MIT) for graduate study and then moved to Philadelphia to work under Oskar Stonorov designing a public housing project. She was brought to Minneapolis by Winston Close, a fellow MIT classmate, to help design the Sumner Field housing project, and became a designer for two years in Magney and Tusler, one of the firms working on the designs.

In 1938, Elizabeth married Winston Close and together they opened an architectural practice, which they maintained for the remainder of their careers, except for a period during World War II. Today the firm continues as The Close Associates, under the presidency of Gar Hargens.

Notable Buildings

WITH WINSTON CLOSE

Benjamin and Gertrude Lippincott residence, 252 Bedford Street SE, Minneapolis (1938, 1940)

Rood studio, 1650 Dupont Avenue S., Minneapolis (1948)

Winston and Elizabeth Close residence, 1588 Fulham Street, Falcon Heights (1953)

Philip Raup residence, 1572 Fulham Street, Falcon Heights (1954)

J. J. Jenkins residence, 2190 Folwell Avenue, Falcon Heights (1957)

Freshwater Biological Institute, Navarre (1974)

Winston Close (1906–1997)

Winston Arthur Close was born in Appleton, Minnesota, on April 27, 1906. He attended public schools there and took a degree in architecture from the University of Minnesota in 1927. After graduation, he worked as a draftsman successively in the firms of Toltz, King & Day, St. Paul; Long & Thorshov, Minneapolis; Ellerbe & Company, St. Paul; Erickson & Company, Minneapolis; and Magney & Tusler, Minneapolis. At the latter firm, he was chief draftsman from 1935 to 1937. Close earned a master's degree in architecture at the Massachu-

Benjamin and Gertrude Lippincott residence, Minneapolis, 1938, 1940 (Elizabeth and Winston Close). *Photograph courtesy of Northwest Architectural Archives, University of Minnesota.*

setts Institute of Technology in 1935 and, in 1938, married Elizabeth Scheu and formed an architectural partnership with her in Minneapolis. Close served in the navy from 1943 to 1946 and was advisory architect to the University of Minnesota from 1950 to 1971, helping to develop master plans for the University's West Bank campus (1956–1961) and the Duluth campus (1949). He and Elizabeth were elected fellows of the American Institute of Architects in 1969, the first time a married couple had been given this honor.

Elizabeth and Winston Close specialized in residential design and produced more than 150 houses. Fourteen of them were designed for University of Minnesota faculty and administrators in the University Grove area in Falcon Heights near the St. Paul campus. The firm also produced classroom structures for the University.

Close died in Falcon Heights, Minnesota, on June 15, 1997.

Notable Buildings

WITH ELIZABETH CLOSE
Benjamin and Gertrude Lippincott residence, 252 Bedford Street SE, Minneapolis (1938, 1940)
Rood studio, 1650 Dupont Avenue S., Minneapolis (1948)
Winston and Elizabeth Close residence, 1588 Fulham Street, Falcon Heights (1953)

Advance Thresher Company, Minneapolis, 1900 (Kees and Colburn). *Photograph 1966 by Norton & Peel. Courtesy of Minnesota Historical Society.*

the latter having left a very successful practice with Franklin Long. Colburn remained with Kees until his death in Minneapolis on January 13, 1927. Kees died two months later, almost to the day.

Notable Buildings

KEES & COLBURN
Advance Thresher Company, 700 S. 3rd Street S., Minneapolis (1900)
Emerson Newton Plow Company, 708 S. 3rd Street, Minneapolis (1904)
Orpheum Theater, Minneapolis (1904) (razed 1940)
Jacob Leuthold residence, Kasson (1905)
Flour Exchange addition, 310 4th Avenue S. Minneapolis (1907)
Lowry Medical Building, 28 W. 5th Street, St. Paul (1910)
Northern Implement Company, 616–622 S. 3rd S., Minneapolis (1910–11)
Colburn family residence, 2829–2837 E. Lake of the Isles Parkway, Minneapolis (1922)

Philip Raup residence, 1572 Fulham Street, Falcon Heights (1954)
J. J. Jenkins residence, 2190 Folwell Avenue, Falcon Heights (1957)
Freshwater Biological Institute, Navarre (1974)

Serenus Colburn (1871–1927)
Serenus Milo Colburn was born on October 12, 1871, in Ansonia, Connecticut. He received a public education and, at the age of fifteen, moved to Minneapolis where he was employed as a draftsman in the office of James C. Plant. He remained in Plant's office for five years and then moved to a succession of offices, including William C. Whitney's, where he was head draftsman (1891–1898). Colburn then joined Frederick Kees in what became a hugely productive partnership,

Gordon Comb (1912–1996)
Gordon MacCallum Comb was born in Minneapolis on July 9, 1912. He was educated in public schools and graduated from the University of Minnesota with a bachelor's degree in architecture in 1935. He was in private practice for a period of time in the late 1930s, and then joined Rilco Laminated Products in St. Paul as an engineer. About 1949, Comb became a partner of Philip Bettenburg, George Townsend, and Sidney Stolte in St. Paul

and remained with them for the rest of his career. He specialized in the design of churches and hospitals. Late in his career, he worked on the renovation of Westminster Presbyterian Church in Minneapolis.

Comb died in Minneapolis on December 28, 1996.

Notable Buildings

BETTENBURG TOWNSEND STOLTE & COMB
City Hall, Anoka (1954)
Northwestern Hospital, Thief River Falls (ca. 1958)
Sheridan School, 525 N. White Bear Avenue, St. Paul (1960)
Edgewater Baptist Church, 5501 Chicago Avenue S., Minneapolis (1961)

E. Richard Cone (1905–1980)
Earle Richard Cone was born in Northfield, Minnesota, on December 28, 1905. He graduated from the University of Minnesota with his bachelor's degree in architecture and took a master's degree in architecture at Harvard University. It is not known whom he worked for after graduating or the dates of his degrees. Cone entered partnership with Fred Slifer in St. Paul in 1936 and remained in the firm until the latter's death in 1948. Cone then joined Gerhard Peterson in forming Northfield Architects, Inc., which they moved to St. Paul in 1950. The firm remained active until 1972, when Cone retired and the partnership dissolved.

He died in St. Paul on October 4, 1980.

Notable Buildings

WITH FREDERICK SLIFER
St. Mary's Church, Winona (1938–39)

WITH GERHARD PETERSON
St. Anne's Roman Catholic Church, 2627 Queen Avenue N., Minneapolis (1948–49)
Trinity First Lutheran Church, 1900–1904 13th Avenue S., Minneapolis (1951)
Peace Evangelical Lutheran Church, Faribault (1957)
St. John's Lutheran Church, 2451 Fairview Lane, Mound (1963)
Our Savior's Lutheran Church, 9185 Lexington Avenue N., Circle Pines (1970–77)

Victor Cordella (1872–1937)
Victor Cordella was a native of Krakow, Poland, where he was born on January 1, 1872. The son of a sculptor, he studied at the Royal Academy of Art in Krakow and at the technological institute in Lvov in Ukraine. He moved to the United States in 1893 and apprenticed or worked under a number of architects in Minneapolis and St. Paul, including Cass Gilbert, William H. Dennis, Warren Dunnell, and Charles Aldrich. In 1903 he became a partner of Christopher Boehme. Their partnership lasted for eight years, during which time they produced a number of notable buildings. After the partnership dissolved in 1911, Cordell established a private practice for the remainder of his career, except for a very brief association with Edwin E. Olson in the mid-1920s.

Cordella died on April 12, 1937, in Minneapolis.

Notable Buildings

WITH CHRISTOPHER BOEHME
Swan Turnblad residence (now the American Swedish Institute), 2600 Park Avenue, Minneapolis (1903–07)

Swan Turnblad residence, Minneapolis, 1903–07 (Victor Cordella and Christopher Boehme). *Photograph ca. 1907. Courtesy of Minnesota Historical Society.*

St. Joseph's Catholic Church, Browerville (1908–09)
Our Lady of Lourdes Catholic Church, Little Falls (1911)

Frederick Corser (1849–1924)
Frederick Gardner Corser was born in Rochester, New York, on June 12, 1849. He was educated in the Rochester public schools and at the Rochester Free Academy. He studied architecture at the Massachusetts Institute of Technology, all before coming to Minneapolis about 1877. After arriving, Corser went into business with Charles Haglin where he stayed until 1881 when Haglin left to form a construction company with Charles Morse. Corser maintained a private practice from then on. He was the architect of the Minneapolis Fire Department for two years, and, besides designing fire stations, he designed a number of churches, schools, and residences throughout the Upper Midwest. Corser was editor of *Western Architect* magazine for three years (1902–05) and a charter member of the local association of architects. He and his family resided for forty years at 615 James Avenue North but by the time of his

Wesbrook Hall, Minneapolis, 1895-96 (Frederick Corser). *Photograph 1904 by Sweet. Courtesy of Minnesota Historical Society.*

death they had moved to 3925 2nd Avenue South.

Corser died in Minneapolis on September 3, 1924.

Notable Buildings
Griswold residence, 11 Maple Place, Minneapolis (1886)
St. Stephen Roman Catholic Church, Clinton Avenue and E. 22nd Street, Minneapolis (1888-89)
Griswold residence, 107-109 Island Avenue, Minneapolis (1891)
North Branch Library, 1834 Emerson Avenue N., Minneapolis (1894, 1914)
Little Sisters of the Poor (now Stonehouse Square Apartments), 215 Broadway Street NE, Minneapolis (1895)
Wesbrook Hall, University of Minnesota, Minneapolis (1895-96)

Eugene Corwin (1889-1973)

Eugene D. Corwin was born in Peoria, Illinois, on October 29, 1889. He moved to St. Paul ten years later and was educated in the public schools. In 1907 he entered the studio of A. A. Gewalt where he studied anatomy and modeling for two years, then was employed by Reed and Stem, and Herbert Sullwold. He moved to Los Angeles in 1914 and worked in the office of Myron Hunt for a year before moving again, this time to Chicago, where he joined the firm of Rapp and Rapp. Corwin also studied in the atelier of the Chicago Architectural Club and at the Institute of Fine Arts. He entered the military in 1917 and came back to St. Paul after World War I, working for Clarence Johnston. In 1923, he formed an association with Serenus Colburn in Minneapolis, which ended four years later with the latter's death. He then worked successively with Larson and McLaren, and Buechner and Orth. For much of his later life, Corwin was in private practice in St. Paul, where he died on June 9, 1973.

Notable Buildings
No buildings attributable to Corwin have been found.

John Coxhead (1863–1943)
John Hopper Coxhead was born in Fort Lee, New Jersey, in 1863. He attended public schools in New York City and graduated from high school in Englewood, New Jersey, in 1879. He studied architecture at Cooper Union School of Design in New York for two years, then attended Columbia College for a year before leaving to join the offices of Edward Dewson and then Van Brunt & Howe in Boston. In 1883 Coxhead relocated to Sioux Falls, South Dakota, where he worked in the office of Wallace Dow, the state's leading architect. His employment there was brief, and he moved around to various locations afterward, including New York and Chicago, and became a junior partner of F. S. Allen in Streator, Illinois, in 1886 for less than a year, designing several structures in the town.

Coxhead moved to St. Paul in 1887 and opened an office in March 1888, which swiftly became very successful at first. Three years later, however, business began to wane and Coxhead developed an association with William Worth Carlin of Buffalo, New York, early in 1892, while continuing to maintain an office in St. Paul until either later that year or early in 1893, when he left for Buffalo. The fledgling partnership soon took in another partner, C. Powell Karr, also a New Jersey native. Karr departed by the end of 1893, Carlin died in March 1894, and Coxhead practiced on his own until 1918 when he began working for the War Department designing facilities for the Army Air

Charles Carman Double House, St. Paul, 1888 (John Coxhead). *Photograph by Paul Clifford Larson.*

Corps. In 1923 he moved with his family to McCook Field in Dayton, Ohio, and continued to design airfields nationwide. He lost his job in 1925 but was reinstated about two years later, this time with the Veterans Administration in Washington, D.C.

Coxhead retired in the 1930s and died in Brewster, New York, on May 21, 1943.

Notable Buildings
Frederick Swift residence, 962 St. Clair Avenue, St. Paul (1888)
First Baptist Church, Stillwater (1888)
D. H. Tandy flats, 668–674 E. 4th Street, St. Paul (1888)
Charles Carman Double House, 534 Laurel Avenue, St. Paul (1888)
Daniel Lawler residence, 546 Marshall Avenue, St. Paul (1889)

Harold Crawford (1888–1981)
Harold Hamilton Crawford was born on April 6, 1888, in Beaver Creek, Minnesota. He lived in Eyota as a child for a number of years before moving to Rochester in 1907. He graduated from high school there the following year and studied architecture at the University of Illinois, from which he took his bachelor's degree in 1913. From 1913 to 1914, Crawford worked as a draftsman in the office of James B. Dibelka in Chicago, and was employed in the same capacity in Frank Chouteau Brown's firm in Boston in 1915. He entered Harvard University and earned a master's degree in architecture in 1916. After leaving Harvard, he returned to Rochester and set up his own practice where he remained, except for two years in the U.S.

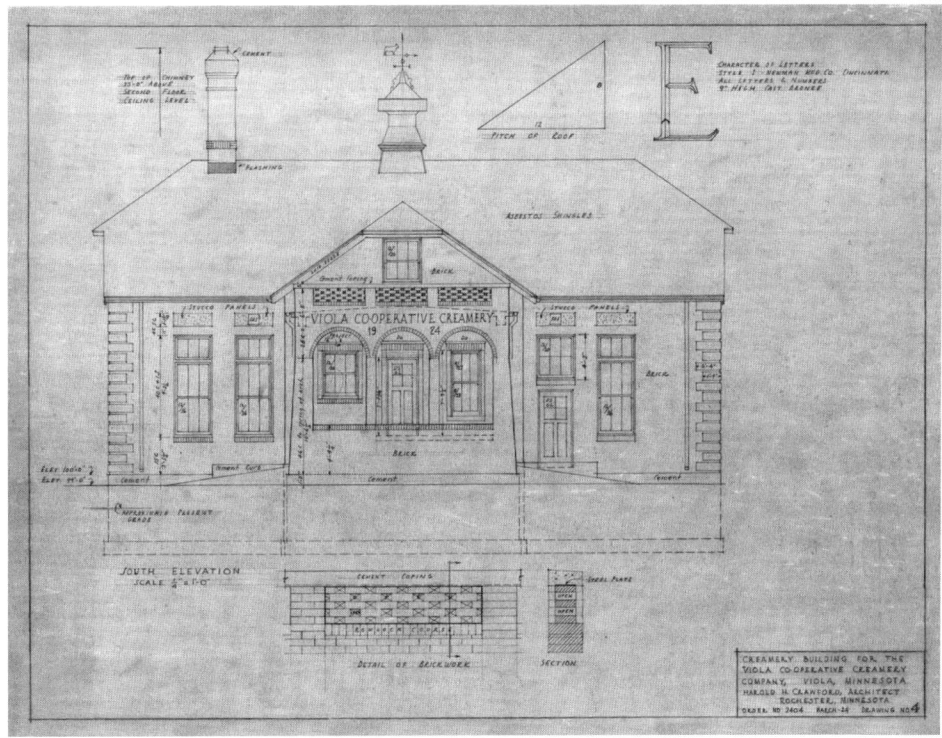

Viola Cooperative Creamery, Viola, 1924 (Harold Crawford). *Photograph courtesy of Olmsted County Historical Society.*

Minneapolis Auditorium, Minneapolis, 1925 (Ernest Croft and Francis Boerner). *Photograph ca. 1927 by Lee Brothers. Courtesy of Minnesota Historical Society.*

Army during World War I, for the rest of his life. He retired around 1965.

Crawford died in Rochester on May 8, 1981.

Notable Buildings
Viola Cooperative Creamery, Viola (1924)
Harold Crawford residence, 514 8th Avenue SW, Rochester (1926)
Rochester Bread Company, 300 11th Avenue NW, Rochester (1928)
Rochester Public Library, Rochester (with Peter Bross) (1936–37)
Parish Hall, Calvary Episcopal Church, Rochester (1950)

Ernest Croft (1889–1959)
Ernest Bernard Croft was born in Herman, Minnesota, on November 19, 1889. He received a degree in civil engineering from the University of Minnesota in

1911, and, after working for about three years in New York City for various firms, returned to Minneapolis and set up a partnership with Francis C. Boerner (1916–1930). After the partnership dissolved, Croft remained in private practice for the rest of his career.

He died in Minneapolis on May 23, 1959.

Notable Buildings

WITH FRANCIS BOERNER
Northwest Terminal Warehouse, 630–658 Stinson Boulevard NE, Minneapolis (1920)

Lafayette Building, 10th Street and Nicollet Avenue, Minneapolis (1922)
Mille Lacs County Courthouse, Milaca (1922)
Minneapolis Auditorium, Minneapolis (1925) (razed 1988)
Children's Gospel Mission, 1407 Washington Avenue S. (1932)

Perry Crosier (1890–1953)
Perry E. Crosier was born on November 17, 1890, in Minneapolis. He began his career in 1909 as a draftsman for Harry W. Jones in Minneapolis. From 1910 to 1913 he worked for Bertrand and Chamberlin, architects; Harrington-Skiles, a

Belmont Apartments, Minneapolis, 1919 (Perry Crosier). *Photograph 1920 by Charles J. Hibbard. Courtesy of Minnesota Historical Society.*

real estate company; and J. L. Hedden, building contractors, all in Minneapolis. Between 1914 and 1916 Crosier had his own company of architects and contractors, the Crosier Construction Company. When this firm broke up, he continued to practice architecture independently for the rest of his life, except briefly in 1921 when he worked for Liebenberg & Kaplan. Crosier continued to collaborate with them for many years thereafter, especially in the design of movie theaters. He also designed dozens of apartment houses in Minneapolis in the course of his career, along with a variety of other structures. Crosier's son Paul joined his father in practice in 1946 and the firm became Perry E. Crosier & Son.

Crosier died in Minneapolis on July 25, 1953, and his firm was continued for two more years by his son.

Notable Buildings
Belmont Apartments, 1000 W. Franklin Avenue, Minneapolis (1919)
Westgate Theatre, 3903 Sunnyside Avenue, Edina (1934) (with Liebenberg & Kaplan)
Avalon Theatre (now, In the Heart of the Beast puppet and mask theater), 1500 E. Lake Street, Minneapolis (1937)
Boulevard Twins Theatre (now Hollywood Video), 5315 Lyndale Avenue S., Minneapolis (1939)
Fair Oaks Apartments, 3rd Avenue S. and E. 24th Street, Minnneapolis (1939)
Hopkins Theatre, 429 Excelsior Boulevard W., Hopkins (1941)
Village Theatre, Faribault (1944–46)

Charles Daniels (CA. 1830–CA. 1900)
Charles N. Daniels was born in New York State around 1830. His precise place of birth is unknown and nothing is known of his childhood or education. He appears to have been a self-taught carpenter or, more likely, apprenticed under master carpenters to learn the trade. He worked as a cabinetmaker in Minneapolis at an unknown date before moving to Faribault, where he practiced as an architect and contractor. Daniels moved on to Fargo, North Dakota, in 1879 and practiced architecture there until 1884 when he relocated again, to Washington State, and, deciding that architecture was not for him, became an insurance agent. He was a member of the Masonic Order during his career and through that connection designed temples in Fergus Falls, Minnesota, and Casselton and Fargo, North Dakota.

It is not known where or when Daniels died, but it probably was in Tacoma, Washington, before 1900.

Notable Buildings
Masonic Temple (now Dakota Business College), Fargo, North Dakota (1884)

Beaver Day (1884–1931)
Beaver Wade Day was born in Lisbon, North Dakota, on March 28, 1884. He graduated from the University of Pennsylvania in 1908 with his bachelor's degree in architecture. While attending school, he worked with Cope and Stewardson as a draftsman for a year and a half, and with Newman and Harris for two years, both in Philadelphia. He moved to Indianapolis and was employed in the office of Brubaker and Stern for an additional two years before moving to St. Paul and joining Allen Stem about 1912. In 1918 Day became a partner of Max Toltz and Wesley King in what grew into one of the most successful architecture and engineering

firms in Minnesota (Toltz, King & Day). He remained in the company until his untimely death on February 28, 1931, of spinal meningitis.

Notable Buildings

WITH MAX TOLTZ AND WESLEY KING
Hamm Building, 408 St. Peter Street, St. Paul (1920)
Stearns County Courthouse, St. Cloud (1921–22)
Carl Cummins residence, 2237 Princeton Avenue, St. Paul (1924)
Spink County Courthouse, Redfield, South Dakota (1925–27)
Ward County Courthouse, Minot, North Dakota (1928–30)
Aitkin County Courthouse, Aitkin (1929)

Victor De Brauwere (1883–1919)
Much of Victor Felix V. De Brauwere's life is cloaked in mystery. He was born in Islington, England, in 1883 of Dutch and

Stearns County Courthouse, St. Cloud, 1921–22 (Beaver Day, Max Toltz, and Wesley King). *Photograph courtesy of Northwest Architectural Archives, University of Minnesota.*

French ancestry. It is not known where he was educated or what architectural training he may have had, nor is it known when he came to the United States, but he practiced in Minneapolis from 1911 to 1918, for one year of that time with a partner, possibly named Harry L. Hopper, who was practicing as a civil engineer in Minneapolis around 1912. De Brauwere moved to California about 1918 and died there of pneumonia in August 1919.

Notable Buildings
Residence, 2103 2nd Avenue S., Minneapolis (1912)
Printer's Exchange Building (now L. A. Rockler Fur Company), 16–18 N. 4th Street, Minneapolis (1915)

William Dennis (1845–1917)
William H. Dennis was born in Delaware County, New York, on March 29, 1845. At the age of fifteen, he moved with his family to New York City, where he studied architecture, although it is not known if this was formal training or apprenticeships. He also studied for two years in Paris, but again it is not known what type of education he received. He returned to the United States and either was employed by another firm or had his own practice in Buffalo, New York, for a time. Dennis moved to Minneapolis about 1878 and worked first for William Grimshaw as a draftsman (1879–80) before setting up his own office. He was joined by his brother Oliver in 1884, and after the latter

Augustana Lutheran Church, Minneapolis, 1881–83 (William Dennis). *Photograph ca. 1885. Courtesy of Minnesota Historical Society.*

left for California in 1888, Dennis was employed as vice president and executive secretary of the American Universal Lighting Company in Minneapolis and then moved to Buffalo, New York, to work as an architect. He closed his office in Minneapolis in 1910 and relocated to Pasadena, California, where he practiced for a few years.

Dennis died in Pasadena on November 12, 1917.

Notable Buildings
Chute Building, Minneapolis (1881–82) (razed 1979)
Augustana Lutheran Church, 704 11th Avenue S., Minneapolis (1881–83)
Citizen's Bank, Minneapolis (1884) (razed 1941)
Times Annex (Century Piano Company), Minneapolis (1889–90) (razed 1992)
S. E. Olson Department Store (later Powers), Minneapolis (1893) (razed 1993)

Menno Detwiler (1868–1907)
Menno S. Detwiler was born on February 14, 1868, in Blair, Ontario. He studied at the Chicago Art Institute and Mechanical School and was first employed in the office of an unknown Chicago architect, and possibly did some design work on the Chicago World's Fair of 1893. He opened his own office in Columbus, Ohio, about 1895 and then moved to La Crosse, Wisconsin, and subsequently to Austin, Minnesota, where he became a partner of Frank W. Kinney. The men moved their office to Minneapolis in September 1902 and remained in business for two more years. From 1904 to 1907 Detwiler was a partner of Charles E. Bell.

He died suddenly in Rochester, Minnesota, on December 19, 1907.

Notable Buildings
Beltrami County Courthouse, Bemidji (1902) (with Frank Kinney)
Martin County Courthouse, Fairmont (1906) (with Charles Bell)
South Dakota State Capitol, Pierre, South Dakota (1907) (with Charles Bell)

Arthur Dickey (1928–2001)
Arthur Harold Dickey was born on December 7, 1928, in Sioux Falls, South Dakota, and graduated from high school there in 1947. He entered the University of Nebraska in Lincoln and received his bachelor's degree in architecture in 1952. In 1951, he joined the firm of Davis and Wilson in Lincoln as a draftsman and, after graduation, moved to Minneapolis and was employed as a draftsman in the office of Shifflet, Backstrom & Carter. He started his own firm, Arthur Dickey Architects, in Edina in 1962. The firm won many architectural awards and was credited with designing more than three hundred residences and several fire stations in the Twin Cities.

Dickey died in Minneapolis on January 19, 2001.

Notable Buildings
Immaculate Conception Church, 4059 Quincy Street NE, Columbia Heights (1956)
Wayzata County Club, Wayzata (1956)
Worzalla Publishing Plant, Stevens Point, Wisconsin (1956–57)
Residence, 6824 Valley View Road, Edina (1967)

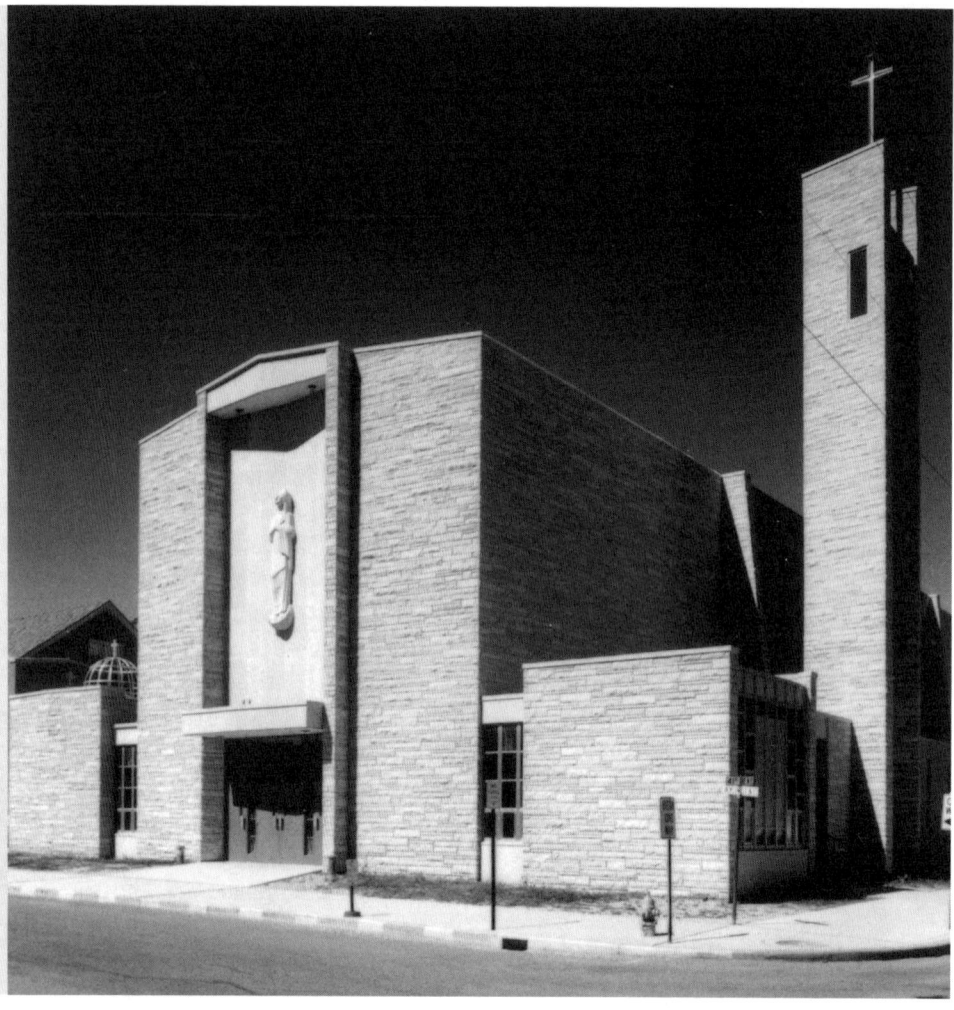

Immaculate Conception Church, Columbia Heights, 1956 (Arthur Dickey). *Photograph 1959 by Cunningham Incorporated. Courtesy of Minnesota Historical Society.*

Grover Dimond (1888–1977)
Grover Willard Dimond was born on September 3, 1888, in Minnesota. He received his Bachelor of Science degree in civil engineering from the University of Minnesota in 1912. He worked as a draftsman in Minneapolis for an unknown firm and served in World War I. In 1925 Dimond found employment as an estimator with St. Paul Foundry Company and remained in that position until 1942. He became a consulting engineer for a few years and then, in 1946, formed an architectural firm with Habbley W. Clarke in St. Paul. The two partners dissolved the firm in 1948 and Dimond started Grover Dimond Associates, in which he remained until his retirement as chairman of the board in 1965. His son, Grover Dimond Jr., succeeded as head of the company.

Dimond died in St. Paul on September 12, 1977.

Notable Buildings
O. M. Taylor residence, Deephaven (1941)
Gillette State Hospital Children's Center Building, Phalen Park, St. Paul (1954)
O'Halloran and Murphy Mortuary, Snelling and Watson Avenue, St. Paul (1954)
Oakdale Community Church, 1066 Carrie Street, West St. Paul (1955)

Grover Dimond Jr. (1915–1993)
Grover Willard Dimond Jr., was born in Minneapolis on May 21, 1915. He grew up in St. Paul and graduated from Central High School and the University of Minnesota's School of Architecture (1949). Early on, he demonstrated an aptitude for design, winning first place in an airplane design contest sponsored by a St. Paul newspaper. During World War II, Dimond worked at the Curtiss Wright aircraft factory in St. Louis. He returned to St. Paul after the war and began drafting residential plans for a national magazine. In the 1950s he joined Grover Dimond Associates, an architectural and engineering firm founded by his father in 1946. He became a partner of Louis Lundgren and Donald Haarstick in Interpro, and also joined Lundgren in Convention Center Architects & Engineers, an interoffice consortium formed to develop the St. Paul Civic Center. Dimond served on a committee to formulate the Capitol Centre plan for downtown St. Paul in the late 1960s and early 1970s. The firm closed in 1973.

Dimond died in St. Paul on November 12, 1993.

Notable Buildings
Kellogg Square, 111 Kellogg Boulevard, St. Paul (1968–72) (Interpro)
Capitol Centre Skyway Building, 5th and Cedar Streets, St. Paul (1969) (Interpro)
Northwestern National Bank, 55 E. 5th Street, St. Paul (1969–74) (Interpro)
Lakewood Community College, White Bear Lake (1971)

Edward Donohue (1869–1915)
Edward J. Donohue was born in St. Paul in 1869. He attended the public schools in the city and received his architectural training as an apprentice in the offices of several St. Paul architects. He entered partnership with Edward P. Bassford in 1890 and remained in the firm for five years. After leaving Bassford, Donohue opened a private practice that he maintained for the rest of his life. He was best known as a designer of public buildings and Catholic churches and schools.

Church of St. Bridget, De Graff, 1901 (Edward Donohue). *Photograph by Bob Firth.*

Donohue died in St. Paul on November 29, 1915, after an illness of several years.

Notable Buildings
Convent and School for Sisters of St. Joseph, Graceville (1900)
Church of St. Bridget, De Graff (1901)
Colonel Edward Farr residence, Pierre, South Dakota (1904)
J. P. Crowley residence, 761 Linwood Avenue, St. Paul (1908)
Harriet Egan residence, 757 Linwood Avenue, St. Paul (1908)
Thomas McKary residence, 925 Dayton Avenue, St. Paul (1915)

Adam Dorr (1854–1928)
Adam Lansing Dorr was born in New York State on December 21, 1854, the son of German immigrants. It is not known exactly where he was born, or what kind of early education he received. He was trained in architects' offices in Canada and Buffalo, New York. After his marriage, he and his wife moved to Minneapolis in 1882, where he was employed with the firm of Plant and Whitney as a draftsman. A year later Dorr joined George and Fremont Orff, and then formed his own practice starting in 1886. He was briefly a partner with William P. Appleyard in 1888–89 and, in 1910, his son, William, joined him to form Dorr and Dorr. The firm specialized in designing fine residences and commercial buildings, including hotels and apartment houses. Dorr was reported to have been deaf through much of his adult life and communicated with people by writing in a small notebook. He retired in 1915 and moved to California in 1925.

Dorr died in Pasadena, California, on October 14, 1928.

Notable Buildings
Bull residence, 1628 Elliott Avenue S., Minneapolis (1887)
C. F. Keyes residence, 2225 E. Lake of the Isles Parkway, Minneapolis (1904)

Continental Hotel (now Continental Apartments), Minneapolis, 1910 (Adam Dorr). *Photograph 1950 by Norton & Peel. Courtesy of Minnesota Historical Society.*

E. Keller residence, 2507 Humboldt Avenue S., Minneapolis (1904)

A. L. Dorr residence, 2402 Irving Avenue S., Minneapolis (1907)

E. J. Moles residence, 2301 Humboldt Avenue S., Minneapolis (1907)

S. M. Klarquist residence, 2406 Irving Avenue S., Minneapolis (1908)

Continental Hotel (now Continental Apartments), 66–68 S. 12th Street, Minneapolis (1910)

William Dorr (1883–1967)

William Grey Dorr was born in Minneapolis on January 25, 1883, son of Adam and Clara Dorr. He graduated from the School of Engineering at the University of Minnesota and studied architecture at the University of California and the Armour Institute of Technology (now the Illinois Institute of Technology), Chicago. He was a member of Alpha Tau Omega fraternity at the University of Minnesota and designed their fraternity house in 1923. Dorr joined his father's office in 1910 and became a partner in 1912. He continued his father's practice after the latter's retirement three years later and continued to operate the firm until his own retirement about 1950. Like his father, Dorr specialized in residential architecture.

He died on November 13, 1967, in White Bear Lake, Minnesota.

Notable Buildings

J. M. Bennett residence, 1600 W. 22nd Street, Minneapolis (1911)

C. E. Daniels residence, 4626 Dupont Avenue S., Minneapolis (1913)

C. A. Fuller residence, Interlachen, Lake Minnetonka (1913)

M. H. Potter residence, 5456 Shoreview Avenue, Minneapolis (1948)

Harry Downs (1868–1929)

Harry Taylor Downs was born on March 16, 1868, in St. Peter, Minnesota, and attended the public schools there. He moved with his family to Minneapolis in 1883 where he finished high school. He became an apprentice draftsman in the office of George and Fremont Orff and, in 1889, joined the firm of Long and Kees as a draftsman. In 1894, Downs set up his own practice. Nine years later he became a partner of Harold Eads; the partnership lasted until September 1928, when Downs retired to Tacoma, Washington, for health reasons. While in Minneapolis, he served as an officer and director of the Architects Small House Service Bureau and as secretary and treasurer of the Minnesota State Board of Registration for architects and engineers.

Downs died in Tacoma, Washington, on January 5, 1929.

Notable Buildings

WITH HAROLD EADS

Charles L. Hoffman residence, Lake Minnetonka (1906)

Joyce Memorial Methodist Church, 1219 W. 31st Street, Minneapolis (1907)

Williams Hardware Company warehouse, 215 N. 1st Street, Minneapolis (1909)

Lake Harriet (Linden Hills) Commercial Club (now Wild Rumpus bookstore), 2718–2720 W. 43rd Street, Minneapolis (1910)

Charles Woodward residence, 2529 Irving Avenue S., Minneapolis (1913)

Plymouth Lodge (now Upper Midwest American Indian Center), 1035 W. Broadway, Minneapolis (1922)

Central Lutheran Church, Minneapolis, 1926–28 (Arthur Dunham and Engebret Sund). *Photograph 1928 by Hibbard Studio. Courtesy of Minnesota Historical Society.*

Arthur Dunham (1887–1972)
Arthur Barrett Dunham was born in Chicago on September 9, 1887. The family later moved to La Salle, Illinois, and young Dunham studied engineering at the University of Illinois, graduating in 1911. He worked in several architects' offices in Illinois during and after attending the university and moved to Minneapolis a few years after his graduation. He opened a private practice and subsequently merged with Engebret Sund in what was to become a very successful firm. In the early 1930s, Dunham left the partnership and moved to Omaha, Nebraska, to work with the Home Owners Loan Corporation, a Depression-era relief agency. He joined the Atomic Energy Commission in 1944 and moved to Washington, D.C. Dunham served in the field of property evaluation in both agencies.

He retired in 1968 and died in Springfield, Virginia, on November 2, 1972.

Notable Buildings

WITH ENGEBRET SUND
Mineral Springs Sanatorium, Cannon Falls (1915–29) (razed 1991)

Minnesota Training School for Boys, Red Wing, 1889 (Warren Dunnell). *Photograph ca. 1895. Courtesy of Minnesota Historical Society.*

Glen Lake Sanatorium Nurses Home, Chaska (1922)
Glen Lake Children's Camp, Eden Prairie (1925)
Wooddale School, Edina (1926)
Central Lutheran Church, 1300 4th Avenue S., Minneapolis (1926–28)

Warren Dunnell (1851–1931)
Warren Barnes Dunnell was born in Norway, Maine, on August 23, 1851, the son of Mark and Sarah Dunnell. In 1863 the family moved to Winona, Minnesota, and two years later to Owatonna. Dunnell attended the University of Minnesota in 1869 and later transferred to the Massachusetts Institute of Technology. He began his career in architecture with the supervising architect of the treasury in Washington, D.C., and then went to Paris to study at the École des Beaux-Arts. Upon his return, he rejoined the federal government and supervised the construction of buildings in Memphis, Tennessee (1878), and Kansas City, Missouri. He had a brief stint in St. Paul in 1876 during which he and partner Samuel J. Brown designed a Methodist Episcopal church in Owatonna.

Dunnell left government service in 1880 and returned to St. Paul where he entered the office of Abraham Radcliffe. A year later, he opened his own practice in Minneapolis, one that became devoted to churches, public buildings, and institutions, including hospitals and schools.

Dunnell died in Minneapolis on December 28, 1931.

Notable Buildings
Minnesota Training School for Boys, Red Wing (1889)
First Baptist Church, Owatonna (1892–93)
Douglas School, Minneapolis (1894) (razed 1980)
Fergus Falls State Hospital, Fergus Falls (1895)

Foster Dunwiddie (B. 1925)
Foster Wilfred Dunwiddie was born in Fox Lake, Wisconsin, on January 29, 1925. He graduated from high school in Port Washington, Wisconsin, in 1942 and studied engineering at the University of Cincinnati (1943) while serving in the U.S. Army. After World War II, he entered the University of Wisconsin where he earned a bachelor's degree in civil engineering in 1948. Dunwiddie then studied at the University of Minnesota's School of Architecture and was awarded a bachelor's degree in architecture in 1951. He joined the firm of Thorshov and Cerny in 1950 as a job captain and draftsman. He progressively became a project manager (1952), associate (1955), and vice president (1959). In 1963 he formed a partnership with William Miller and Kenneth Whitehead, both of whom Dunwiddie had worked with in the Thorshov and Cerny office. Whitehead left in 1966 to accept a position with United Airlines, and the firm continues to this day as Miller Dunwiddie. Dunwiddie also taught in the School of Architecture at the University of Minnesota from 1979 to 1983, after earning a master's degree in architecture there in 1979. He retired from practice in 1990.

Notable Buildings

MILLER, WHITEHEAD AND DUNWIDDIE
Bethlehem Congregational Church, International Falls (1963–64)
Metropolitan Stadium east grandstand, Bloomington (1964–65) (razed 1985)
Olivet Congregational Church, 1850 Iglehart Avenue, St. Paul (1964)

MILLER DUNWIDDIE
Metropolitan Airports Commission office building, Wold Chamberlain Field, Bloomington (1966)
Minnesota Valley Memorial Hospital, Le Seuer (1966–67)
C. A. Weyerhaeuser Memorial Museum, Little Falls (1973)
Commandant's house restoration, Fort Snelling, St. Paul (1975 and 1982)
Minneapolis City Hall restoration, 4th Street and 3rd Avenue S., Minneapolis (1982–86)
James J. Hill residence restoration, 240 Summit Avenue, St. Paul (1983)

Arndt Duvall Jr. (1904–1990)
Arndt John Duvall Jr. was born in Stillwater, Minnesota, on December 13, 1904. He received a degree in civil engineering from the University of Minnesota in 1925. He joined the firm of Toltz, King & Day in St. Paul and became a partner in 1956. It was at that time that the firm changed its name to Toltz, King, Duvall & Anderson (TKDA). Duvall became president after

Wesley King's death in 1959, and remained in the office until 1979. He continued as chairman of the board until his retirement in 1981.

It is difficult to ascertain what projects Duvall had a hand in designing or engineering in a firm as large as TKDA. Also, because he was an administrative officer for many years, he may have had little or no involvement with the design process during that period.

Duvall died in St. Paul on September 14, 1990.

Notable Buildings
No buildings attributable to Duvall have been found.

Harold Eads (1872–1936)
Harold H. Eads was a native of Champaign, Illinois, where he was born on August 18, 1872. He and his family moved to Minneapolis early in his life and he attended the public schools. Eads graduated from the University of Minnesota in 1892 and practiced architecture in Minneapolis for the remainder of his career. From 1903 to 1928 he was a partner of Harry T. Downs, and continued a private practice after Downs moved to Tacoma, Washington.

Eads died in Minneapolis on May 21, 1936.

Notable Buildings

WITH HARRY DOWNS
Charles L. Hoffman residence, Lake Minnetonka (1906)
Joyce Memorial Methodist Church, 1219 W. 31st Street, Minneapolis (1907)
Williams Hardware Company warehouse, 215 N. 1st Street, Minneapolis (1909)

Lake Harriet (Linden Hills) Commercial Club (now Wild Rumpus bookstore), 2718–2720 W. 43rd Street, Minneapolis (1910)
Charles Woodward residence, 2529 Irving Avenue S., Minneapolis (1913)
Plymouth Lodge (now Upper Midwest American Indian Center), 1035 W. Broadway, Minneapolis (1922)

Edwin Eckert (1926–1990)
Edwin Eckert was born in Winona, Minnesota, on April 16, 1926. He graduated from Winona Senior High School in June 1942, attended Iowa State College from 1943 to 1944, and served in the U.S. Army Air Force from 1944 to 1946. After World War II, he returned to Iowa State College and received his bachelor's degree in architectural engineering in 1949. Eckert was employed in the firm of Boyum, Schubert and Sorenson in La Crosse, Wisconsin, from 1949 to 1954, when he became an associate architect in their Winona office. During this time, he worked with James K. Carlson and the two men formed a partnership in 1956. After the partnership dissolved in 1969, Eckert became a senior partner in HSR Associates, Inc., architects and engineers in La Crosse, until his retirement in 1989.

Eckert died in La Crosse on May 16, 1990.

Notable Buildings
Fillmore County Courthouse, Preston (1958)
Dunn County Courthouse, Menomonie, Wisconsin (ca. 1963)
Winona Senior High School, Winona (1967)
Radisson Hotel, La Crosse, Wisconsin (ca. 1989)

Franklin Ellerbe (1870–1921)
Franklin Herbert Ellerbe was born in Mississippi in 1870. He came to Minnesota as a child, living first in Mankato and then St. Paul. He became an architect and builder, learning his craft as a St. Paul building inspector before setting up his own firm in 1909. At first, Ellerbe used space offered to him by James McLeod, a successful St. Paul architect. Ellerbe's first commissions were for the Old Fireside Inn in St. Anthony Park (1909) and a warehouse for the fledgling Minnesota Mining and Manufacturing Company (1910). In 1911 Ellerbe was joined by Olin Round and the partners secured the commission for the Zumbro Hotel in Rochester. A few years later, after Round had left the partnership in 1913, Ellerbe obtained the commission for the first building for the Mayo Clinic and, two years later, won the commission for the Crile Clinic (later the Cleveland Clinic) in Cleveland, Ohio. After Round left, Ellerbe maintained a private practice for the rest of his life.

He died in Rochester, Minnesota, following emergency surgery on July 21, 1921.

Notable Buildings
Old Fireside Inn (now Milton Square), 2260 Como Avenue, St. Paul (1909)
Zumbro Hotel, Rochester (1911–12) (with Olin Round)
Greve Oppenheim residence, 509 Summit Avenue, St. Paul (1913) (with Olin Round)
Mayo Clinic, Rochester (1914) (razed 1986)

Thomas Ellerbe (1892–1987)
Thomas Farr Ellerbe was born in St. Paul on December 21, 1892, the son of architect Franklin Ellerbe. Nothing is known of his education or training. He served in the National Guard on the Mexican border and then in Europe during World War I. In 1919, he joined his father's architectural firm and assumed direction of it after his father's death two years later. Ellerbe continued to serve as president of the firm, known variously as Ellerbe Architects and Ellerbe & Company, until his retirement in 1966. He continued as chairman of the board until 1969. In 1988, the company merged with Welton Becket of Los Angeles to become Ellerbe Becket and in October 2009 the firm was purchased by AECOM Technologies, Inc., of Los Angeles.

Ellerbe died in St. Paul on November 5, 1987.

Notable Buildings

ATTRIBUTED TO THE FIRM
Plummer Building, Mayo Clinic, Rochester (1923–28)
Garfield Schwartz residence, Rochester (1925)
Chateau Dodge Theatre (now Barnes and Noble bookstore), Rochester (1928)
O'Shaughnessy Field, College of St. Thomas, St. Paul (1928)
E. Starr Judd residence, Rochester (1929)
Northern States Power Company, 360 Wabasha Street, St. Paul (1930)
St. Paul City Hall and Ramsey County Courthouse, 15 W. Kellogg Boulevard, St. Paul (1932) (with Holabird & Root, Chicago)
Mayo Clinic Diagnostic Building, Rochester (1953, 1969)
Fairview-Southdale Hospital and Clinic, Edina (1964)

Plummer Building, Mayo Clinic, Rochester, 1923–28 (Ellerbe Architects). *Photograph courtesy of Northwest Architectural Archives, University of Minnesota.*

Willeik Ellingsen (1892–1959)
Willeik Emil Ellingsen was born in Norway on May 16, 1892. The family immigrated to the United States while he was a small child and settled in Duluth about 1907. Ellingsen attended the University of Minnesota and received a bachelor's degree in architecture about 1913. He spent most of his career practicing in Duluth, where he was noted for designing schools, churches, and public buildings. In the 1940s, he was a partner of Ephraim Giliuson, but it probably was only for a few years. Late in his life, he gave up private practice and associated with the firm of Stanius, Morgenstern and Ellingsen.

Ellingsen died in Duluth on February 11, 1959.

Notable Buildings
Downtown Motel, Duluth (1958)

Harvey Ellis (1852–1904)
Harvey Ellis, artist, architect, and craftsman, was born in Rochester, New York, on October 17, 1852. Early on, he demonstrated an interest in, and talent for, the arts. After his education, he worked briefly as a surveyor, and then was sent to West Point by his father in July 1871. His stay there was even briefer than his tenure as a surveyor: he was dishonorably discharged for tardiness, personal untidiness, and getting married. His marriage was annulled and he traveled to Europe to study art and architecture.

Returning to New York in 1873, Ellis set out to study art under Edwin White at the National Academy of Design (1875–76), but instead became an architectural draftsman with Arthur G. Gilman. He moved to Albany and is rumored to have worked for the highly distinguished architect, H. H. Richardson. Ellis returned to Rochester in 1879 and entered practice with his brother, Charles (H. & C. S. Ellis). The firm was quite successful, but friction between them ended the partnership in 1885.

Ellis moved to Utica, New York, and then to St. Paul, arriving sometime in 1885 or 1886. He worked first as a draftsman for J. Walter Stevens, then Charles Mould, and finally with Leroy Buffington in Minneapolis. Ellis left Minneapolis in 1890 and joined Eckel & Mann in St. Joseph, Missouri, remaining with the firm when it moved to St. Louis. After the Eckel & Mann partnership dissolved in 1892, Ellis continued working for George Mann and doing freelance drafting for several St. Louis firms. He returned to Rochester, New York, about 1894 and rejoined his brother's firm, continuing in it until 1903. In that year, Gustav Stickley invited Ellis

Pillsbury Hall, University of Minnesota, Minneapolis, 1888 (Harvey Ellis and Leroy Buffington). *Photograph courtesy of Northwest Architectural Archives, University of Minnesota.*

to join the staff of *The Craftsman* magazine, for which Ellis executed a number of articles and illustrations between July 1903 and his death early the next year.

Ellis died in Rochester, New York, on January 2, 1904.

Notable Buildings
Pillsbury Hall, University of Minnesota, Minneapolis (1888) (with Leroy Buffington)
Mabel Tainter Memorial Library, Menomonie, Wisconsin (1888) (with Leroy Buffington)

George Elmslie (1871–1952)
George Grant Elmslie was born in Huntley, Scotland, on February 20, 1871. He immigrated to the United States with his family in 1884, settling in Chicago. He probably received the bulk of his training in architecture through employment as an architect, finding work as a draftsman with Joseph Silsbee in 1887. It was in Silsbee's office that he met Frank Lloyd Wright and George Maher. Two years later he was hired by Louis Sullivan, at Wright's urging, and rose to become chief draftsman. Elmslie remained with Sullivan for twenty years, leaving late in 1909 to join William Purcell and George Feick in partnership in Minneapolis. He moved back to Chicago in 1913, after the death of his wife, Bonnie, and maintained the firm's office there until 1924, when the partnership with Purcell officially ceased. Elmslie opened a private practice which existed through the mid-1930s, when he closed it for lack of business. Thereafter, he lived in retirement with a sister until his death on April 23, 1952.

Notable Buildings
National Farmer's Bank, Owatonna (1907) (with Louis Sullivan)
Charles Crane estate, Woods Hole, Massachusetts (1912) (with William Purcell)
Edna Purcell residence, 2328 Lake Place, Minneapolis (1912–13) (with William Purcell)
Capitol Building and Loan, Topeka, Kansas (1922–1923) (razed 1968)
Clayton Summy residence, Hinsdale, Illinois (1925)
Forbes Hall, Yankton College, Yankton, South Dakota (1929–30)
Oliver P. Morton School, Hammond, Indiana (1936) (with William Hutton)

Arvid Elness (1939–1996)
Arvid Edward Elness was born in 1939 and grew up in Windom, Minnesota. He graduated from the University of Minnesota with a bachelor's degree in architecture in 1962. After working for several firms, the last being Miller, Hanson, Westerbeck and Bell, he formed Arvid Elness Architects in 1975. He had been engaged in the restoration and renovation of Butler Square in Minneapolis and, after forming his own firm, he continued to specialize in restoration work. Elness was also considered an innovator in the design of public housing, group and senior housing, and low-income housing.

In about 1994, he merged his office with BRW to form BRW-Elness. Mark Swenson and David Graham came into the firm from BRW and after Elness's sudden death in 1996 they continued on in their own practice, Elness Swenson Graham Architects.

Elness died in Tampa, Florida, on December 9, 1996.

BRW Incorporated

BRW Incorporated represents the initials of the last names of three founding members: David J. Bennett, Donald W. Ringrose, and Richard P. Wolsfeld. This large firm was responsible for the design of a number of major buildings in Minnesota and elsewhere.

By 1985 it was called Bennett, Ringrose, Wolsfeld, Jarvis, Gardner, Inc., with the addition of Peter E. Jarvis and Lawrence J. Gardner. Mark G. Swenson was also in the firm by then and became a partner after Arvid Elness assumed leadership.

Elness merged his company, Arvid Elness Architects, with BRW in 1994 and the firm was renamed BRW-Elness. In 1995, BRW-Elness and BRW Group, Inc., became two separate companies. In 1996, BRW-Elness was renamed Elness Swenson Graham Architects. That same year, BRW Group Inc. was acquired by Dames & Moore of Los Angeles (since purchased, in turn, by URS).

Notable Buildings
Butler Square renovation, 1st Avenue N. and 6th Street, Minneapolis (1974–76) (with Miller Hanson Westerbeck & Bell)
Advance Thresher Building (now Thresher Square) renovation, 700–708 3rd Street S., Minneapolis (1984–86) (Arvid Elness Architects)

Charles Elwood (1883–1960)
Charles Saxby Elwood was born on February 28, 1883, in Ovid, Michigan. His family descended from William Bradford, second governor of the Plymouth Colony in Massachusetts. He was educated in the public schools of Superior, Wisconsin, at Superior State Normal School, and the Art Institute of Chicago. He also took classes through the International Correspondence Schools. Elwood was employed by the Milwaukee Railroad in Itasca, Wisconsin (1901–02), and the U.S. Post Office (1903–06). He then worked for the Aluminum Cooking Utensil Company for a year before becoming a draftsman successively for Arthur Heun, Charles E. White Jr., Dean & Dean, William Drummond, George Maher, and John S. Van Bergen, all in Chicago. He

James Shiely residence, St. Paul, 1925 (Charles Elwood). *Photograph by Paul Clifford Larson.*

moved to Clinton, Iowa, about 1908 and was employed at the Gordon Van Tine Company, designers and manufacturers of woodwork and cabinetry, and then left to join the U.S. Housing Project at Rock Island, Illinois, under Cervain and Horn (1916–1919).

Elwood moved to Minneapolis in 1919 and worked for two years as draftsman at the Thompson Yards, Inc., and then American Farm Buildings in St. Paul. He entered private practice in 1921 in St. Paul and became a partner of Kenneth Worthen in 1926. After the demise of that partnership, he worked in a variety of offices and jobs for years and returned to private practice late in his career.

Elwood died in St. Paul on June 18, 1960.

Notable Buildings
James Nolan residence, 151 Woodlawn Avenue, St. Paul (1923)
Leo Hugo residence, 1286 N. Dale Street, St. Paul (1924)
James Shiely residence, 1460 Ashland Avenue, St. Paul (1925)
George Cahill residence ("The Castle"), 1999 Sargent Avenue, St. Paul (1930)
Charles Elwood residence ("Beyond Avalon"), 648 Lexington Avenue S., St. Paul (1949)

Richard Faricy (B.1928)
Richard Thomas Faricy was born on June 1, 1928, in St. Paul. He attended public and parochial schools in the city, graduating from St. Thomas Academy in 1946. He spent the next two years at the College of St. Thomas in a course of pre-engineering, then attended the University of Minnesota before entering the army in 1952. Following his military service, Faricy returned to the University of Minnesota in 1957 and graduated with his bachelor's degree in architecture in 1960. While he was studying at the University, he worked in the office of Grover Dimond in St. Paul and, upon graduation, was employed by Cerny and Associates in Minneapolis, where he remained for ten years. In 1970, Faricy and Wayne Winsor, former president of Ellerbe Architects, formed a highly successful partnership which they maintained until the firm merged with Symmes, Main, McGee and Associates (SMMA). Faricy continued with SMMA as a consultant and later joined the Collaborative Design Group as a consultant.

Notable Buildings

WINSOR FARICY
Landmark Center (adaptive reuse) (former Old Federal Courts Building), 75 W. 5th Street, St. Paul (1976)
International Market Square (adaptive reuse) (formerly Munsingwear factory), Glenwood and Lyndale Avenues, Minneapolis (1985–86)

Carleton Farnham (1898–1978)
Carleton Willard Farnham was born in Minneapolis on February 6, 1898. He graduated from North High School in the city in 1916 and took extension classes in architecture through the University of Minnesota without attaining a degree. He received his training mainly through employment in several firms, most of them as a draftsman, starting with Northwest Lumberman's Association, Minneapolis (1918–20). He went on to work for Thompson Yards, Minneapolis; O. K. Westphal, architect, Minneapolis; H. J. Scherer, architect, Minneapolis; Fallow, Huey & Macomber, architects, Minneapolis; U.S. Forest Service, St. Paul; Charles

W. Cole & Son, South Bend, Indiana; Fegles Construction Company, Minneapolis; and General Mills, Minneapolis. He established his own firm by 1924 and designed a large number of private dwellings and apartment houses in the 1920s and 1930s. During World War II, Farnham supervised the construction of war plants (1942–44). He returned to Minnesota in 1945 and resumed private practice.

Farnham died in Minneapolis on April 6, 1978.

Notable Buildings
Alfred Johnson residence, 343 W. Elmwood Place, Minneapolis (1926)
H. M. Peterson residence, 5256 Washburn Avenue S., Minneapolis (1926)
Franklin Groves residence, 4885 E. Lake Harriet Parkway, Minneapolis (1928)
Henry Gray residence, 1100 E. Minnehaha Parkway, Minneapolis (1929)
Anderson store building, 2110 Lyndale Avenue S., Minneapolis (1929)
Marie Antoinette apartments, 26–30 W. 22nd Street, Minneapolis (1939)

George Feick Jr. (1881–1945)
Johann George Feick Jr., was born in Sandusky, Ohio, on January 27, 1881. He graduated from the school of architecture at Cornell University in 1903 and entered his father's construction business in Sandusky. From March to December 1906 he traveled through Europe with Cornell classmate William Purcell. When they returned to the United States, they set up an architectural practice in Minneapolis in January 1907. During the years of the partnership, Feick was the specifications writer and was responsible for other business duties, but did little design work. No buildings can be directly attributed to him. He divided his time between the architecture firm and his father's business and eventually, in 1913, left to make another tour of Europe, and afterwards rejoined his father's company full-time in Sandusky. He remained there the rest of his life.

Feick died in Sandusky, Ohio, on November 29, 1945.

Notable Buildings
Stewart Memorial Presbyterian Church (now Redeemer Missionary Baptist Church), 116 E. 32nd Street, Minneapolis (1909) (with William Purcell)

Charles Ferrin (1853–1929)
Charles Foss Ferrin's exact place and date of birth are unknown, but it is known that he was born in New Hampshire in 1853. After that, details of his life are lacking until his appearance in Minneapolis in 1874 as a carpenter. His career as an architect began the following year when he joined Allen E. Hussey in partnership. The partnership lasted only a year, after which Ferrin went into business for himself. In 1887 he became a partner of Edgar Joralemon and, after two years, the firm broke up and Ferrin worked at a variety of jobs, including clerk of the works during the construction of the Minneapolis City Hall and Courthouse in the mid- and late 1890s. Between 1900 and 1910 he was the architect and superintendent for Twin City Rapid Transit Company. Afterward, he resumed his trade of carpentry and was superintendent of an apartment building late in his life.

Ferrin died in Minneapolis on March 12, 1929.

Notable Buildings
Crowell Block, 614 W. Lake Street, Minneapolis (1888) (with Joralemon)
St. Paul Street Railway Co. Midway Carhouse (now Midway Commons), 2324 University Avenue W., St. Paul (1891)
Twin City Rapid Transit Company car shops, Snelling Avenue and I-94, St. Paul (1907) (razed ca. 2003)

Harry Firminger (1888–1962)
Harry Firminger was born on June 24, 1888, in St. Louis, Missouri. He attended public schools in St. Louis and Kirkwood, Missouri, and, after graduating from high school in 1905, began taking correspondence courses and night classes in architecture in St. Louis while working in the office of Hal Lynch. About 1908 he moved to St. Paul, where he continued the study of art, architecture, and structural engineering at the St. Paul School of Art and the University of Minnesota. Firminger was employed in James McLeod's office as a junior draftsman in 1908 while attending school and then joined Edward Donohue as a senior draftsman and designer (1909–11). He next moved to the office of Charles Hausler in the same position and, in 1915, rose to be senior draftsman in the city architect's office. From 1916 to 1918, he was senior draftsman and designer under Olin H. Round.

For three years, beginning in 1919, Firminger had a private practice, then joined, first, O'Meara & Hills as senior draftsman (1923–27), and then his old boss Charles Hausler (1928–1934). From 1935 to 1941 he was a partner of Harold T. Purtell, and between 1929 and 1939 he and his partners produced several fine examples of Art Deco and Streamline Moderne buildings. Firminger became a civilian employee of the U.S. Navy during World War II, designing facilities in Idaho and California. He returned to private practice in St. Paul after the war and died there on October 10, 1962.

Notable Buildings
Minnesota Building, 4th and Cedar Streets, St. Paul (1929) (with Hausler)
Church of Our Lady of Mt. Carmel, Opole (1929) (with Hausler)
Abe Engelson residence, 1775 Hillcrest Avenue, St. Paul (1939) (with Purtell)
Farmers' Union Grain Terminal Association building (now TIES Education Center), 1667 N. Snelling Avenue, Falcon Heights (1946) (with Raymond Gauger)
Dennis Scanlon residence, 404 N. River Boulevard, St. Paul (n.d.)

Albert Fisher (1913–2000)
Albert Fisher was born in Minneapolis on November 10, 1913. He graduated from the University of Minnesota's School of Architecture with a degree in architectural engineering in 1934. From 1935 to 1944 he worked for the Insulite Chemical Company of Aurora, Illinois, a manufacturer of wood pulp insulation material for walls and ceilings whose main factory was located in Fort Frances, Ontario. Then he worked at George Washington University in Washington, D.C., from 1944 to 1946, before returning to Minneapolis and joining the firm of Hills, Gilbertson and Hayes, where he was chief draftsman until becoming a partner in 1956, following the death of Hayes.

Fisher retired on December 27, 1978, and died in Minneapolis on November 27, 2000.

Notable Buildings

WITH VICTOR GILBERTSON
St. Charles Borromeo Catholic Church rectory, Stinson and St. Anthony Boulevards NE, Minneapolis (1961–62)
St. Constantine's Ukrainian Catholic Church, University Avenue and 5th Street NE, Minneapolis (1970–72)

Nairne Fisher (1899–1980)
Nairne W. Fisher was born in Illinois on November 23, 1899, but the exact location is unknown. He attended a technical school in Minneapolis where he received training in drafting. He also briefly studied at the École des Beaux-Arts in Paris, but the dates of his term there are unknown. Fisher also worked as a draftsman in lumberyards in Minnesota and South Dakota. He entered the U.S. Army during World War I, serving in intelligence. In about 1922, he established a practice in St. Cloud, then became a partner of Leo W. Schaefer (1923–24). He is reported to have flourished to such an extent that he opened offices in Chicago, St. Paul, Milwaukee, and Washington, D.C. In 1929, Fisher obtained a commission to design the Mundelein College building in Chicago in association with Joseph W. McCarthy. Mundelein was a women's college that later became part of Loyola University in Chicago. Today the beautiful Art Deco building, one of several he executed in this style, is on the National Register of Historic Places. He moved his practice to Minneapolis in 1939 and then relocated to Chicago in 1945, where he had an office up to at least 1957.

Fisher made a career of specializing in the design of public buildings. He retired about 1972.

Fisher died in Deltona, Florida, on July 30, 1980.

Notable Buildings
Polk County Courthouse, Crookston (1930)
Pope County Courthouse, Glenwood (1930)
Rice County Courthouse, Faribault (1932–34)
Central High School, Devils Lake, North Dakota (1936)

Francis Fitzpatrick (1863–1931)
Francis Willford Fitzpatrick was born on April 9, 1863, in Montreal, Quebec. Little is known of his early life, education, or career. He was living with his family and working in Duluth by 1884. In that year, he moved to Minneapolis and was employed as a draftsman by Leroy Buffington. Three years later Fitzpatrick entered the office of George and Fremont Orff where he remained until about 1890, when he briefly became manager of the Minnesota Decorating Company. He moved back to Duluth in 1890 and entered a partnership with Oliver Traphagen, which lasted until 1896 when he relocated to Washington, D.C., and worked as foreman in the Office of the Supervising Architect of the Treasury (1897–1903). During that time, Fitzpatrick supervised the construction of the Chicago Post Office and possibly the U.S. Government Building in Chicago as well. He was also a freelance draftsman during this time.

In 1903 he set up a private practice, which he maintained until about 1918 when he became head of the architectural

Board of Trade Building, Duluth, 1894-95 (Francis Fitzpatrick and Oliver Traphagen). *Photograph ca. 1895. Courtesy of Minnesota Historical Society.*

department of the Bankers Realty Investment Company in Omaha, Nebraska. But this job must have lasted only a short while, for by 1920 he was residing in Evanston, Illinois, where he was described by a contemporary as a "hearty, red-faced, stoutish man who seemed older than the fifty-six years" he was by then. Whether he had a private practice or was retired during the 1920s is unknown.

Fitzpatrick died in Evanston, Illinois, on July 11, 1931.

Notable Buildings

WITH OLIVER TRAPHAGEN
Chester Terrace Apartments, Duluth (1890)
Fitger's Brewing Company (now a hotel), Duluth (1890)
First Presbyterian Church, Duluth (1891)
Munger Terrace Apartments, Duluth (1891-92)
Torrey Building, Duluth (1892)
Board of Trade Building, Duluth (1894-95)

Mark Fitzpatrick (1866-1956)

Mark Fitzpatrick was born on June 27, 1866, in St. Paul. He studied architecture at Fordham University, from which he graduated with honors about 1887. He returned to St. Paul, and first appears as supervising architect of the James J. Hill mansion on Summit Avenue (1889-91), designed by Peabody & Stearns of Boston. This means that Fitzpatrick either already had a reputation or had good connections on the East Coast in order to be given this task by the preeminent firm from Boston. He was a partner of Charles Joy for a time before setting up his own practice in St. Paul by the turn of the century. He lived and worked in St. Paul the rest of his life, except for a year in Minneapolis (1902-03). He was also associated with the magazine *Western Architect* from near its inception throughout its entire publishing history (1903-1940).

Fitzpatrick died on September 27, 1956, in St. Paul.

Notable Buildings

George Taylor residence, Summit and Oakland Avenues, St. Paul (1904)
Carling's Uptown Restaurant, St. Paul (1908) (razed 2000)
Guiterman Brothers Men's Apparel (now Frogtown Family Lofts), 653 Galtier Street, St. Paul (1910, 1917)
Tuttle residence, 2148 Iglehart Avenue, St. Paul (1912-13)

Alan Fleischbein (1886-1964)

Little is known of Alan Charles Fleischbein's early life and career. He was born in Belleville, Illinois, on August 9, 1886, but his education and training is unknown. About 1917 he joined Ralph Mather in practice in St. Paul and they maintained the firm for a number of years.

He died in St. Paul on September 5, 1964.

Notable Buildings
Roy Molen residence, 3076 Hamline Avenue N., Roseville (1925) (with Ralph Mather)
Municipal building, Forest Lake (1939)

LeRoy Gaarder (1891–1984)
LeRoy Leinial Gaarder was born in Highland, Wisconsin, on June 10, 1891. He attended public schools in Highland and Dodgeville and entered St. Olaf College for one year (1912–13). He enrolled in night school at the University of Minnesota from 1913 to 1917, studying architecture while working in the offices of Cecil Chapman (1913), Mather and Boerner (1914), Howard Parsons (1915), and Purcell and Elmslie (1916–17). He was also a student of the viola under the tutelage of the concertmaster of the Minneapolis Symphony Orchestra. Gaarder moved back to Dodgeville and opened a private practice for one year, then served in the U.S. Army from 1918 to 1919. In 1920, he established a practice in Albert Lea, maintaining it in a studio attached to his house until well into the 1970s. Except for stints in 1934–35 as a consulting architect to the U.S. Treasury on federal buildings and a year (1943–44) as a project planner for the regional office of the Public Buildings Administration in Seattle, Washington, he spent the rest of his career in Albert Lea.

Gaarder died in Albert Lea on January 27, 1984.

Notable Buildings
Queen of Angels Catholic Church, Austin (1937–38, 1954–56)
Christ Church (Episcopal), Austin (1951)
Zion Lutheran Church, Albert Lea (1958–61)

Carl Gage (1881–1950)
Carl Alexander Gage was born on November 26, 1881, in Newport, New Hampshire. The family moved to Minneapolis the following year and Gage was educated in the public schools and spent a year at the Minneapolis School of Fine Arts. He seems to have been first employed as a designer in the Flour City Ornamental Iron Company in Minneapolis, where he stayed for three and a half

Zion Lutheran Church, Albert Lea, 1958–1961 (LeRoy Gaarder). *Photograph by Bob Firth.*

Lutheran Ladies' Seminary, Red Wing, 1892–94, 1907–08 (Augustus Gauger). *Photograph courtesy of Goodhue County Historical Society, Red Wing.*

years. He then moved into architecture, working first for Thomas Holyoke in St. Paul, then Ernest Kennedy in Minneapolis, after which he associated with Edwin Hewitt. He remained in Hewitt's office for three years, then joined the firm of Bertrand and Chamberlin (1910). In 1914, Gage associated with Tyrie and Chapman and, three years later established his own practice. He was briefly in partnership with Joseph V. Vanderbilt in 1925; otherwise, he practiced alone. He was a joint organizer and first secretary of the Architects Small House Service Bureau and served in the U.S. Army in World War I.

Gage died in Laguna Beach, California, on January 8, 1950.

Notable Buildings
Edgar Smith residence, 3520 W. Calhoun Boulevard, Minneapolis (1921)
Frank Chatfield residence, 5013 Belmont Avenue S., Minneapolis (1926)
Henry Clark residence, 5017 Belmont Avenue S., Minneapolis (1926)
Hoyt residence, 3430 W. Calhoun Boulevard, Minneapolis (1928)
W. E. Goodfellow residence (now Bakken Museum), 3537 Zenith Avenue S., Minneapolis (1928)
Lloyd Lynch residence, 3316 W. 34th Street, Minneapolis (1932)

Augustus Gauger (1852–1929)
Augustus F. Gauger was born in Germany on February 16, 1852. He immigrated to the United States in 1862 with his parents and grandfather and became a naturalized citizen. The family settled first on a farm in the vicinity of Oshkosh, Wisconsin. Young Gauger became a carpenter and worked in Oshkosh until moving to Chicago at an unknown age. He attended schools in Oshkosh as well as Chicago and probably learned architecture through his

carpentry experience. In 1875, he moved to St. Paul and became a draftsman in the office of Edward Bassford. Three years later he set up his own practice which he maintained the rest of his life. For one year (1894–95), he was a city building inspector in St. Paul, and he was a member of a committee that revised the city's building code in 1896 and again in 1910–11. Gauger also served as architect to the State Board of Education from 1881 to 1887, and was named a fellow of the American Institute of Architects in 1889. He married Albertine Nitschke in 1878 and the couple had seven children, all sons. One of them, Raymond, carried on his father's practice into the 1970s.

Gauger died in St. Paul on February 17, 1929.

Notable Buildings
Augustus Gauger residence, 1183 Como Lake Drive W., St. Paul (ca. 1883)
Zion German Lutheran Church, 780 N. Cortland Place, St. Paul (1888)
Lutheran Ladies' Seminary, Red Wing (1892–94, 1907–08)
William Schornstein Saloon and Grocery, 223 Bates Avenue, St. Paul (1884)
Samuel Dearing House, 241 W. George Street, St. Paul (1886)
Marshall County Courthouse, Warren (1899)
Post Office, Sleepy Eye (1904)

Raymond Gauger (1895–1977)
Raymond Richard Gauger was born in St. Paul on January 3, 1895. He graduated from St. Paul Central High School and the Massachusetts Institute of Technology. While in college, he worked summers as a draftsman for Emmanual Masqueray. He also attended George Washington University. Gauger joined his father, Augustus Gauger, in practice and continued the business after his father's death in 1929. His company was called Gauger-Parrish in later years and continued to operate for some time under that name. It specialized in courthouse and jail architecture.

Gauger retired in 1975 and died in St. Paul on May 6, 1977.

Notable Buildings
Gustavus Adolphus Lutheran Church, 27th Avenue and Lincoln Street NE, Minneapolis (1937)
Pilgrim Lutheran Church, Prior and St. Clair Avenues, St. Paul (1940)
Grace Lutheran Church, 1730 Old Hudson Road, St. Paul (1961–62)

Frederick German (1863–1937)
Frederick George German was born in Bath, Ontario, on November 9, 1863. He was educated at the University of Toronto and Brentford College Institute, and obtained his first employment as an architect in Detroit. He later moved to New York and worked in the office of prestigious architects McKim, Mead & White. German moved to Duluth in 1889 and designed a number of homes in Lakeside and Lester Park for the Lakeside Land Company. He went to Kansas City, Missouri, in 1899 to join his father-in-law and a Mr. Strohe in forming the firm of Strohe, Brown and German. Something evidently didn't work out, for German returned to Duluth in 1900 and remained there the rest of his life. He was a partner of John DeWard for a short time following his return to Duluth and then joined A. Werner Lignell in partnership. In 1923 he became a partner of Leif Jenssen, but the partnership was brief, for Jenssen died

Pilgrim Congregational Church, Duluth, 1917 (Frederick German). *Photograph ca. 1920 by Charles P. Gibson. Courtesy of Minnesota Historical Society.*

that same year. German then practiced alone for the remainder of his career.

He died in Duluth on October 13, 1937.

Notable Buildings
A. C. Weiss residence, Duluth (1904) (with Lignell)
Glen Avon Presbyterian Church, Duluth (1905) (with Lignell)
Donald B. MacDonald residence, Duluth (1908) (with Lignell)
Marshall Wells Wholesale Hardware building, Duluth (1910)
Pilgrim Congregational Church, Duluth (1917)

Cass Gilbert (1859–1934)
By all odds, Cass Gilbert was one of Minnesota's most important architects and certainly its best known. He was born in Zanesville, Ohio, on November 24, 1859. His family moved to St. Paul in 1867 where Gilbert attended Macalester College. In 1878–79 he transferred to the Massachusetts Institute of Technology and then went to Europe for another year of study in England and on the Continent. Following his travels he returned to the United States and went to work for the distinguished New York firm of McKim, Mead & White, becoming a protégé of

Endicott Building, St. Paul, 1889–90 (Cass Gilbert and James Knox Taylor). *Photograph ca. 1964 by Eugene Debs Becker. Courtesy of Minnesota Historical Society.*

Minnesota State Capitol, St. Paul, 1895–1905 (Cass Gilbert). *Photograph ca. 1913 by Charles W. Jerome. Courtesy of Minnesota Historical Society.*

William Mead. After two years, Gilbert moved to St. Paul and in December 1882 opened an office as a representative of McKim, Mead & White. In 1884 he formed a partnership with a boyhood friend, James Knox Taylor and the firm of Gilbert & Taylor became one of the most prosperous in the city. The partnership dissolved in 1892. In 1895 Gilbert won the competition to design a new Minnesota State Capitol. During the decade-long project, his national reputation grew to such an extent that he moved to New York City and opened an office there. He lived in New York for the rest of his life.

Gilbert died while visiting Brockenhurst, England, on May 17, 1934.

Notable Buildings

Gotzian Shoe Co. (now Parkside Apartments), 242–250 E. 5th Street, St. Paul (1883)

Elizabeth Gilbert House, 471 Ashland Avenue, St. Paul (1884)

Charles and Emily Noyes House, 89 Virginia Street, St. Paul (1887) (with James Knox Taylor)

William Lightner-George Young Double House, 322–324 Summit Avenue, St. Paul (1888) (with James Knox Taylor)

Endicott Building, 4th Street between Robert and Jackson Streets, St. Paul (1889–90) (with James Knox Taylor)

Cass Gilbert residence, 1 Heather Place, St. Paul (1890)

St. Clement's Episcopal Church, 901 Portland Avenue, St. Paul (1894)

Minnesota State Capitol, St. Paul (1895–1905)

Episcopal Church of St. Paul the Divine, Moorhead (1898–99)

Northern Pacific Railroad depot, Little Falls (1899)

New York Custom House, New York, New York (1899–1907)

Woolworth Building, New York, New York (1910–12)

Federal Reserve Bank, 5th Street and Marquette Avenue, Minneapolis (1922–24)

U.S. Supreme Court building, Washington, D.C. (1928–1934)

Victor Gilbertson (1911–2005)

Victor Curtis Gilbertson was born in Velva, North Dakota, on December 11, 1911. He attended high school in Towner, North Dakota, and Luther College in Decorah, Iowa. In 1935 he earned a degree in architecture from the University of Minnesota, and the following year entered the Massachusetts Institute of Technology. That

St. Constantine's Ukrainian Catholic Church, Minneapolis, 1970–72 (Victor Gilbertson). *Photograph by Bob Firth.*

same summer he worked as a draftsman for the North Dakota Highway Department in Minot, and then joined O'Meara and Hills in St. Paul as a draftsman, where he was employed from 1936 to 1939. Gilbertson formed an architectural practice with James Hills and Mark Hayes in 1940 (Hills, Gilbertson and Hayes) in Minneapolis. During World War II, he worked with Shanley, Van Teylingen and Henningson in Great Falls, Montana (1941), and Mason and Hanger, New York City (1942), on government defense projects. Gilbertson returned to Minneapolis after the war and resumed his partnership, adding Albert Fisher after Hayes's death in 1956 (Hills, Gilbertson and Fisher).

Gilbertson retired in 1984 and died on March 13, 2005, in Minnetonka, Minnesota.

Notable Buildings
St. Francis of Assisi Church, Rochester (1940–51)
Oak Grove Presbyterian Church, Bloomington (1946–47)
Christ Lutheran Church, 3244 34th Avenue S., Minneapolis (1949–50) (with Saarinen & Saarinen)
Lutheran Church of the Good Shepherd, 4801 France Avenue S. (1949–50)
First Congregational Church, Austin (1954–56)
Baudette Hospital, Baudette (1956)
St. Charles Borromeo Catholic Church rectory, Stinson and St. Anthony Boulevards NE, Minneapolis (1961–62)
St. Constantine's Ukrainian Catholic Church, University Avenue and 5th Street NE, Minneapolis (1970–72)

Ephraim Giliuson (1888–1947)
Ephraim Carl Giliuson was born on January 8, 1888, in Stillwater, Minnesota. His parents were Swedish immigrants who settled in the area in 1881. When he was three years old, his family moved to Duluth and he was educated in the public schools there. He graduated from Duluth Business University in 1903 and entered John J. Wangenstein's firm as an apprentice. In 1907, Giliuson went to Chicago and trained for two years at the Art Institute of Chicago. He returned to Wangenstein's practice in 1909 and they formed a partnership four years later. It is not known how long it lasted. Between 1913 and 1922, Giliuson and Anthony Puck were partners for an unknown number of years. At the time of his death, he was in partnership with Willeik Ellingsen.

Giliuson died in Duluth on June 6, 1947.

Notable Buildings
Granada Theater, Duluth (1935) (razed 1987)

Florence Glindmier (1896–1974)
Florence Dorothy Glindmier was born on August 8, 1896, in St. Paul. She graduated from high school in 1915, the College of St. Catherine in 1922, and from the St. Paul School of Art the following year. She worked with George Lockhart, architect, in St. Paul in 1924–25, and was associate editor of the *National Building Journal* at the same time. She became head of the art department at St. Margaret's Academy in Minneapolis in 1927. She also attended the University of Minnesota pursuing postgraduate work (1933–36). Glindmier worked at various times for the Jefferson Lumber Company and the Carr-Cullen

Company in Minneapolis, drafting stock plans. She also was a color consultant on state projects beginning in 1946, and was designer of the Minnesota Territory commemorative postage stamp in 1948. In 1964 she joined the State Architect's Office, where she worked for an undetermined number of years.

Glindmier died in St. Paul on August 24, 1974.

Notable Buildings
No buildings attributable to Glindmier have been found.

Joel Glotter (B. 1925)
Joel Harvey Glotter was born in Minneapolis on April 17, 1925. He graduated from West High School in 1943 and received his bachelor's degree in architecture from the University of Minnesota in 1951. He began working as a draftsman in the firm of Dimond, Haarstick and Lundgren in St. Paul, and in 1952 was employed by Magney, Tusler and Setter in Minneapolis. Glotter became a partner with Liebenberg and Kaplan in 1960, and continued the firm after Liebenberg's retirement in 1980, eventually joining Saul Smiley and Garold R. Nyberg in partnership.

Notable Buildings
Hennepin County Medical Center, 7th Street S. and Park Avenue, Minneapolis (1972–76) (Liebenberg, Kaplan and Glotter)
Minnetonka Fire Station, Minnetonka (1974) (Liebenberg, Smiley and Glotter)

Carl Graffunder (B. 1919)
Carl Graffunder was born in Rock Island, Illinois, on March 23, 1919. He attended public schools in Hibbing, Minnesota, and graduated from high school there in 1936. He studied at Hibbing Junior College for a year before transferring to the University of Minnesota, where he received his bachelor's degree in architecture in 1942. Graffunder served in the U.S. Navy in World War II, working in naval architecture in a shipyard at Bremerton, Washington. After the war, he attended the New York Structural Institute for a year (1946) and then entered Harvard University where he received a master's degree in architecture in 1948.

While at the University of Minnesota, Graffunder worked during the summer of 1939 as a draftsman in the office of J. C. Taylor in Hibbing, spent the summer of 1940 with Antonin Raymond in New Hope, Pennsylvania, and the summer of 1941 with Eino Jyring in Hibbing. In 1946 and 1947 he was chief draftsman in Antonin Raymond's office and returned to Minneapolis in 1949 to set up his own practice. In 1950 he began teaching in the School of Architecture at the University in addition to maintaining his office, Carl Graffunder and Associates. For a time, he partnered with Norman Nagle until the latter's death in 1965.

Notable Buildings
Stevens Square Nursing Home, Stevens Avenue S. and 32nd Street, Minneapolis (ca. 1960)
St. Anthony Housing, University and Third Avenues NE, Minneapolis (1961)
Clayton A. Gay Hall, University of Minnesota–Morris, Morris (1965–66)
Science building, University of Minnesota–Morris, Morris (1966)

Curtis Green (B. 1925)
Curtis Harlan Green was born in Minneapolis on March 29, 1925. He attended Edison High School and the University of Minnesota, graduating from the latter in 1946 with a bachelor's degree in architecture. He worked for about a year in the firm of Magney, Tusler and Setter, and then attended the Massachusetts Institute of Technology (MIT) where he studied under Alvar Aalto. Green earned a master's degree in architecture in 1948 from MIT and then joined the Milwaukee firm of Grassold-Johnson to design an addition to the public library. He returned to Minneapolis and entered Thorshov and Cerny's office in 1949. Two years later, he moved to Dimond, Haarstick and Lundgren in St. Paul, and then, in 1953, became a partner with Richard Hammel, where he remained for the rest of his career.

Green retired from practice in December 1993.

Notable Buildings

WITH RICHARD HAMMEL
Lutheran Church of the Reformation, 2544 S. Highway 100, St. Louis Park (1958, 1969)
Colonial Church of Edina (now Wooddale Church), 5532 Wooddale Avenue, Edina (1965) (Interior)
O'Shaughnessy Auditorium, College of St. Catherine, St. Paul (1968–70)
St. John's Episcopal Church, St. Cloud (1971)
Northeast Branch, Minneapolis Public Library, 2400 Central Avenue NE, Minneapolis (1971–72)

Gene Green (B. 1926)
Gene Loren Green was born in Madelia, Minnesota, on September 23, 1926. He graduated from South High School in Minneapolis in 1944 and then spent a year at Missouri Valley College in Marshall, Missouri. He transferred to the University of Minnesota and received a bachelor's degree in architecture in 1950. Green joined Haxby, Bissell and Belair in Minneapolis in 1947 as a draftsman, and subsequently became job captain, field superintendent, and designer in the same firm. He went on to become a member of Cerny & Associates in Minneapolis, and then a principal in Bissell, Belair and Green in 1959. Green retired from practice in 1991.

Notable Buildings
Hans Christian Andersen Elementary School, 10th Avenue S. and E. 27th Street, Minneapolis (1975)

Newton Griffith (1924–1968)
Newton Ellis Griffith was born in Omaha, Nebraska, on January 30, 1924. He moved to Minneapolis as a child and graduated from Roosevelt High School in 1941. He received his bachelor's degree in architecture from the University of Minnesota in 1946 and earned a master's degree in architecture at Harvard University in 1949. He returned to Minneapolis that same year and joined the firm of Thorshov & Cerny, becoming an associate member in 1953. Griffith was awarded a Johns Hopkins fellowship in 1952 and a merit award from *Institutional* magazine in 1959. In 1960 he, together with Wilbur Clark Jr. and Richard Peterson, founded a firm that became one of the most successful in Minnesota (Peterson, Clark, Griffith).

Griffith died in Edina, Minnesota, on June 2, 1968.

IBM building, Minneapolis, 1962 (Newton Griffith, Richard Peterson, and Wilbur Clark). *Photograph 1964 by Norton & Peel. Courtesy of Minnesota Historical Society.*

Notable Buildings

WITH RICHARD PETERSON AND WILBUR CLARK
Griffith residence, 7028 Wexford Road, Edina (1960)
IBM building, 245 Marquette Avenue, Minneapolis (1962) (razed 1986)
Fuji-ya Restaurant, 420 1st Street S., Minneapolis (1967)

William Grimshaw (1853–1922)
William H. Grimshaw was born on December 6, 1853, in Philadelphia, Pennsylvania. He came to Minneapolis with his father in 1857 and attended public schools there. Beginning about 1875, Grimshaw worked as an architect and contractor in Minneapolis, but it is not known how or where he obtained his training. He was elected to the state legislature in 1885 and served for a number of years while continuing to maintain his practice. He managed the senatorial campaigns of Cushman Davis, Knute Nelson, and Moses Clapp, and served as a member of the Minneapolis water board for six years. He left the field of architecture in 1899 when he was appointed as United States Marshal by President William McKinley

and served in that position for seventeen years.

    Grimshaw died in Minneapolis on May 24, 1922.

Notable Buildings
St. Anthony Lodge IOOF (now The Bulldog Tavern), 401 E. Hennepin Avenue, Minneapolis (1891–92)
Bellevue Hotel (now Ozark Flats), 1227 Hennepin Avenue, Minneapolis (1892)

David Griswold (B. 1918)
David Jackson Griswold was born in Minneapolis on July 8, 1918. He attended West High School and graduated from Washburn High School in 1936. He received a bachelor's degree in architecture from the University of Minnesota in 1941, and served in the U.S. Navy Postgraduate School from 1942 to 1945 designing landing craft and submarines while supervising the drafting rooms. After the war, Griswold returned to Minneapolis and entered the firm of Magney, Tusler and Setter, where he remained until 1948. He joined Long and Thorshov as chief draftsman that same year, and two years later became chief engineer at the Fred O. Watson Company, general contractors. In 1952 he established his own practice (David J. Griswold and Associates) and in 1956 joined with Loren Abbett in a short-lived partnership. After the latter's untimely death that year, Griswold practiced alone until partnering with John Rauma in 1963.

    Griswold retired from practice in 1994.

Notable Buildings
Good Shepherd Lutheran Church School, Spring Lake Park (1958)
William H. Ziegler Company, Bloomington (1959)
Pako Corporation, Golden Valley (1959)
Middlebrook Hall, University of Minnesota, Minneapolis (1969) (with John Rauma)
Cedar Hi Apartments, 630 Cedar Avenue, Minneapolis (1970) (with John Rauma)

Mildred Grunau (1909–1992)
"Millie" Grunau, as she was best known, was born in South St. Paul on November 23, 1909. She attended public schools there and received her further education at Macalester College and the University of Minnesota, finishing two years of architectural training at the latter in 1932. Grunau later said that she graduated from both schools on the same day. She taught high school mathematics for a time before becoming an employee with a contracting firm as a draftsman about 1937. The Federal Housing Administration requested use of her house plans as models to spur the construction of affordable housing across the United States. She worked for Brown-Blodgett in St. Paul for many years, producing literally hundreds of stock house plans for sale to builders and individual homeowners. It was estimated that by 1961, some 3,000 residences had been built from her plans.

    Grunau died in Miami, Florida, on September 7, 1992.

Notable Buildings
T. W. Kohlhoff residence, Litchfield (n.d.)
Robert Yount residence, 19th Street and Wentworth Avenue, South St. Paul (n.d.)

Donald Haarstick (1915–1980)
Donald Sydney Haarstick was born in Rochester, Minnesota, on June 2, 1915. He earned a bachelor's degree in architecture from the University of Minnesota in 1937, but his early work experience is not known. He formed a highly successful partnership, Interpro, with Louis Lundgren and Grover Dimond Jr. in 1949. After Dimond left to set up his own firm, Haarstick remained in business with Lundgren until the partnership was dissolved in 1972. Haarstick moved to Bloomington, Minnesota, and maintained a private practice until his retirement in 1975.

He died in St. Paul on January 19, 1980.

Notable Buildings

WITH LOUIS LUNDGREN
Burnsville High School, 600 Highway 13, Burnsville, (1958)
Aldrich Arena, 1850 White Bear Avenue N., Maplewood (1962)
Harding Senior High School, 1540 E. 6th Street, St. Paul (1965)
John Adams Junior High School, Rochester (1969)
Kellogg Square, 111 E. Kellogg Boulevard, St. Paul (1969–73)

Charles Haglin (1849–1921)
Charles F. Haglin was born on April 7, 1849, in Hastings, New York. He was educated in the public schools of that city and became a draftsman in the office of a Syracuse architect in his late teens. He moved to Chicago after a year and, in 1873, relocated to Minneapolis and entered practice with Franklin B. Long. The partnership ended in 1876 and Haglin formed another partnership with Frederick Corser.

In 1881 he left Corser and set up a construction company with Charles Morse, and together they built a number of large structures in Minneapolis,

Peavey Haglin Experimental Concrete Grain Elevator, St. Louis Park, 1899 (Charles Haglin). *Photograph ca. 1908. Courtesy of Minnesota Historical Society.*

including the Globe Building (1882) and the William Washburn residence ("Fairoaks," 1883). The company also erected the Minneapolis City Hall and Courthouse (1895–1905). While the city hall was underway, the partnership was dissolved and Haglin operated the firm alone until 1909 when B. H. Stahr joined as partner. The new company, Haglin-Stahr, lasted for a number of years and erected such notable Minneapolis buildings as the Radisson Hotel (1909), Orpheum Theater, Plaza Hotel, and numerous residences.

Later in life, Haglin admitted his three sons into the partnership and the firm operated as C. F. Haglin & Sons. In 1920 the company contracted to rebuild the town of Hibbing, Minnesota, after the entire townsite was moved to make way for an expansion of an iron ore pit mine. Haglin is well known for constructing the first reinforced concrete grain elevator in the United States, in St. Louis Park for Frank H. Peavey (1899). The structure still exists near the junction of Highway 100 and Highway 7.

Haglin died in Long Beach, California, on February 23, 1921.

Notable Buildings
Milwaukee Road Freight House (now Dunn Bros. Coffee), 201 Third Avenue S., Minneapolis (1879)
William Washburn residence ("Fairoaks"), 24th Street and 3rd Avenue S., Minneapolis (1883) (contractor) (razed 1924)
Minneapolis City Hall and Courthouse, 4th Street and 3rd Avenue S., Minneapolis (1895–1905) (contractor)
Peavey Haglin Experimental Concrete Grain Elevator, Highway 7 and Highway 100, St. Louis Park (1899)
Radisson Hotel, 7th Street between Nicollet and Hennepin Avenues, Minneapolis (1907) (contractor) (razed 1982)

Ernest Haley (1867–1954)
Ernest C. Haley, son of architect Joseph Haley, was born in Malone, New York, on September 25, 1867. The family moved to Minnesota the same year and settled in Minneapolis in 1873. Haley was educated in the public schools of Minneapolis and studied architecture with his father. He became a partner in the firm, along with his brother Arthur, about 1897. After his father's death in 1904, Haley continued the practice for many years.

He retired from practice about 1948 and died in Minneapolis on July 2, 1954.

Notable Buildings
Fife residence, 1808 Knox Avenue S., Minneapolis (1903)
Silas King residence, 2927 Clinton Avenue S., Minneapolis (1903)
Flour City Odd Fellows Building, 2701–2707 E. Lake Street, Minneapolis (1910)
Swedish Emanuel Methodist Church, 1900 11th Avenue S., Minneapolis (1919)
Roy Witt residence, 2820 Benton Boulevard, Minneapolis (1920)

Joseph Haley (1835–1904)
Joseph Haley was born in Bangor, New York, on May 15, 1835. Nothing is known of his education or professional training, but it appears from the few existing clues, that he obtained his architectural training through apprenticeship, a common occurrence in the nineteenth century. He had a practice in Malone, New York, for several years prior to 1867. Haley moved to

Minnesota late in 1867 and worked intermittently in Minneapolis and Dayton, Minnesota, before settling down in Minneapolis in 1873 for the rest of his life. His sons Arthur and Ernest studied architecture in their father's office; Arthur was a partner in 1887–88 before moving on. Ernest entered his father's firm in 1897 and assumed the practice after the elder Haley died on August 9, 1904, in Minneapolis.

Notable Buildings
Moline, Milburn, and Stoddard Co. (now Traffic Zone Center for Visual Arts), 250 3rd Avenue N., Minneapolis (1886)
National Biscuit Company warehouse, 248–258 3rd Avenue N., Minneapolis (1901)

Lucien Hall (1855–1933)
Lucien P. Hall was born in New York State in March 1855. Nothing is known of his education or professional training. He lived in New York until about 1882, and appears in Duluth in 1890 as a partner of Emmet Palmer. William Hunt joined the firm in 1893. The partnership was very successful during the next decade, erecting many buildings in the city and elsewhere in northern Minnesota. Hall left the firm in 1904, retiring to his summer home on Bay Lake near Brainerd to raise flowers and fruit.

Hall died on his farm near Brainerd on July 28, 1933.

Moline, Milburn and Stoddard Co. (now Traffic Zone Center for Visual Arts), Minneapolis, 1886 (Joseph Haley). *Photograph 1969. Courtesy of Minneapolis Public Library, James K. Hosmer Special Collection, M0349.*

Central High School, Duluth, 1891–92 (Lucien Hall and Emmet Palmer). *Photograph 1899. Courtesy of Minnesota Historical Society.*

Notable Buildings
Central High School, Duluth (1891–92)
   (with Emmet Palmer)
Joseph Sellwood residence, Duluth (1902)
   (with Emmet Palmer and William Hunt)

Richard Hammel (1923–1986)
Richard F. Hammel was born in Owatonna, Minnesota, on May 30, 1923, into a family of contractors. His grandfather helped build the National Farmers Bank, designed by Louis Sullivan. He graduated with a bachelor's degree in architecture from the University of Minnesota in 1944 and, after serving two years in the U.S. Navy, attended Harvard Graduate School of Design where he studied under Walter Gropius. He received a master's degree in architecture in 1947. Hammel joined the firm of Richard E. Windisch in Honolulu from 1947 to 1950 and returned to Minneapolis to teach part-time in the School of Architecture at the university. He also worked as assistant consulting architect to the university. In 1951, Hammel became the consulting architect to the St. Paul Public Schools and two years later, he and Curtis Green formed a partnership, joined by Bruce Abrahamson in 1954. The firm of

Hammel, Green & Abrahamson (HGA) remains one of the largest and most important architectural firms in Minnesota.

Hammel remained active in the firm until his death on November 18, 1986, in Wayzata, Minnesota.

Notable Buildings

WITH CURTIS GREEN AND BRUCE ABRAHAMSON
Lutheran Church of the Reformation, 2544 S. Highway 100, St. Louis Park (1958, 1969)
Colonial Church of Edina (now Wooddale Church), 5532 Wooddale Avenue, Edina (1965) (Interior)
O'Shaughnessy Auditorium, College of St. Catherine, St. Paul (1968–70)
St. John's Episcopal Church, St. Cloud (1971)
Northeast Branch, Minneapolis Public Library, 2400 Central Avenue NE, Minneapolis (1971–72)

Olof Hanson (1862–1933)
Olof Hanson was born in Fjelkinge, Sweden, on September 10, 1862. He and his family immigrated to the United States in 1875. Hanson became permanently deaf at the age of ten. He attended the Minnesota School for the Deaf in Faribault, and Gallaudet College in Washington, D.C., from which he received a bachelor's degree in 1886. He began working as a draftsman in the firms of E. Townsend Mix and Isaac Hodgson in Minneapolis in 1886.

After receiving a master's degree from Gallaudet College in 1889, Hanson studied at the École des Beaux-Arts in Paris and traveled in Europe. When he returned to the United States, he was employed at Wilson Brothers & Company in Philadelphia, and then set up a practice in Faribault in 1894. He entered partnership with Frank Thayer in Mankato in 1901 and, after the firm won the competition for the courthouse and jail in Juneau, Alaska,

Lutheran Church of the Reformation, St. Louis Park, 1958, 1969 (Richard Hammel, Curtis Green, and Bruce Abrahamson). *Photograph by Bob Firth.*

Thompson Memorial Hall, St. Paul, 1916 (Olof Hanson). *Photograph 1929. Courtesy of Minnesota Historical Society.*

Thayer and Hanson moved to Seattle, Washington.

The partnership was dissolved in 1904 and Hanson continued to practice in Seattle, part of the time in the office of Schack, Young & Myers (1906–12). In 1924, he became a deacon in church ministries and in 1929 was ordained a priest and conducted services for the deaf in Seattle, Tacoma, Spokane, and Portland.

Hanson died in Seattle on August 8, 1933.

Notable Buildings
Dawes House, Gallaudet College, Washington, D.C. (1895)
Jonathan Noyes residence, Faribault (1896)
Jay Cooke Howard residence, Duluth (1899)
Thompson Memorial Hall, 1824 Marshall Avenue, St. Paul (1916)

Collis Hardenbergh (1912–1978)
Collis Morgan Hardenbergh was born in Kansas City, Missouri, on May 21, 1912. He attended Country Day School in Kansas City for seven years, graduating in 1929. He then entered Harvard University from which he received a Bachelor of Arts degree in 1933. In 1937 he earned a bachelor's degree in architecture from the University of Minnesota.

Hardenbergh worked as a junior draftsman in the office of McKenzie Hague in Minneapolis during the summer of 1936, and in the same capacity at McEnary & Krafft from October 1936 to the following February. From January to April 1938 he was employed as a junior draftsman in Hewitt Setter & Hamlin in Minneapolis and then joined Magney & Tusler for a month in 1938 before becoming employed by Haxby & Bissell for a year (May 1938–May 1939) as senior draftsman. He returned to Magney, Tusler & Setter in June 1939 and remained there until he entered service with the federal government during World War II as an engineer for several aircraft companies in Arkansas and New York.

After the war, Hardenbergh briefly worked for Madigan-Hyland in New York City and then returned to Minneapolis to set up his own firm in 1946. Later that same year he joined Karl Humphrey Jr. in partnership, which lasted for the remainder of his career.

Hardenbergh died in Beverly, Massachusetts, on April 23, 1978.

Notable Buildings

WITH KARL HUMPHREY JR.
Robert Longfellow residence, Alexandria (1953)
Charles Case residence, Red Oaks, Maplewood (1953)
Ruth Bovey Stevens residence, Ferndale (1956)
E. B. Wilson residence, Sunfish Lake (1973)

Gar Hargens (B.1943)
William Garman Hargens was born on April 16, 1943, in Pottstown, Pennsylvania. He attended Wesleyan University, earning his bachelor of arts degree in 1965, and he received a masters degree in architecture from the University of Minnesota in 1974. Hargens began working at Close Associates in 1968 and continued in the firm for the rest of his career. In 1980, he became principal architect and part owner of the practice, and eight years later purchased sole ownership of the firm. From 1976 to 1986, Hargens taught in the College of Architecture and Landscape Architecture at the University of Minnesota, and has served as chair of the St. Paul Heritage Preservation Commission and member of the board of the MacPhail Center for the Performing Arts in Minneapolis.

Notable Buildings
Dartmouth Place Town Homes, 901 Dartmouth Place SE, Minneapolis (1996–97)
Seward Co-op and Deli, 2111 E. Franklin Avenue, Minneapolis (1998)
Eigenfeld residence, 219 Mount Hope Drive, St. Paul (2001)
Louis and Maud Hill residence restoration, 260 Summit Avenue, St. Paul (2004)

Ernest Hartford (1881–1928)
Ernest Myrick Hartford was born in Minneapolis on July 2, 1881. He appears not to have had any formal education in architecture, but instead obtained it all through training in architects' offices. Nothing is known of his early career, although he was employed as a draftsman in Minneapolis by 1905. He joined Silas Jacobson in partnership in St. Paul about 1910. The partnership was dissolved when Jacobson bought Hartford's interest in August 1914. Hartford and Charles Hausler formed a very brief practice that same year, which continued while Hausler was serving as city architect of St. Paul, to which he was appointed in January 1914. After the Hausler-Hartford partnership was discontinued, Hartford continued to practice architecture for an unspecified time before relocating to Chicago where

he was employed as a structural engineer for the Burlington Railroad. He registered for the draft during World War I but no evidence has been found that he served in the armed forces.

He died in Lake County, Florida, in 1928.

Notable Buildings
J. B. Sanborn building, 26 E. 7th Street, St. Paul (1913–14) (with Jacobson)
Sacred Heart Hospital (Mount Marty Hospital of the Benedictine Sisters), Yankton, South Dakota (1914) (with Jacobson)
Malcolm McMillan residence, 1058 St. Clair Avenue, St. Paul (1915)

Roy Haslund (1888–1970)
Roy H. Haslund was born in Ashley, Minnesota, on November 6, 1888. He graduated from the College of Architecture at the University of Illinois in 1915. After serving in World War I, he came to St. Paul and worked in the firm of Toltz, King & Day before becoming a partner of Allen Stem for a brief period, prior to the latter's retirement in 1920. Haslund maintained the practice as a continuation of Stem's office as well as his own until about 1955. He then joined Ellerbe Architects where he remained until his retirement in 1964.

Haslund died on April 27, 1970, in Stillwater, Minnesota.

Notable Buildings
WITH ALLEN STEM
St. Paul Athletic Club, 340 Cedar Street, St. Paul (1917)
Allen Stem residence, Dellwood (ca. 1920)
St. Paul Casket Co., 1222 University Avenue N., St. Paul (1922)

Charles Hausler (1889–1971)
Charles Alfred Hausler was born in St. Paul on January 27, 1889. He attended Adams Elementary School and Mechanic Arts High School. As a youth, he was an avid baseball player and fan as well as an amateur boxer.

Early on, he determined to be a cartoonist and studied at the St. Paul School of Fine Arts. Eventually, he decided to be an architect instead and worked as an apprentice in Clarence Johnston's office for two years starting at age sixteen. He then went to work for Harry Jones in Minneapolis before journeying to Chicago to serve as an apprentice to Solon Beman and Louis Sullivan.

Hausler returned to St. Paul in 1908 and set up a practice with Peter Linhoff. After three years, he became a partner of William Alban; the firm broke up when Hausler was appointed city architect in January 1914, although he was briefly a partner of Ernest Hartford starting in October 1914. He remained city architect until 1922 and during his tenure a number of schools, branch libraries, fire stations, and other municipal facilities were designed in his office, some of them in partnership with Percy Bentley, with whom he practiced until about 1917. In 1921 he was asked by the city of St. Paul to draw up a building code, which was adopted that same year.

He was elected to the state legislature in 1922 and resigned from his position as city architect, but continued to practice architecture. He served for sixteen years in the legislature and left the state senate in 1939 to resume his career in architecture full-time.

He died in St. Paul on July 12, 1971.

Charles Hausler residence, St. Paul, 1917 (Charles Hausler). *Photograph 1974 by Kenneth M. Wright Studios. Courtesy of Minnesota Historical Society.*

Notable Buildings
Como Park Comfort Station, Lake Como, St. Paul (1915) (with Percy Bentley)
Charles Hausler residence, 1735 W. 7th Street (moved to 526 Grace), St. Paul (1917)
St. Anthony Park Branch Library, 2245 Como Avenue, St. Paul (1917)
St. James A.M.E. Church, 624 Central Avenue, St. Paul (1926)
Minnesota Building, 4th and Cedar Streets, St. Paul (1928)
St. Lawrence Catholic Church, Faribault (1934)

Robert Haxby (1882–1947)
Robert Van Loan Haxby was born in Garden City, Long Island, New York, on April 19, 1882. He graduated from Columbia University with a bachelor's degree in architecture in 1908, and then worked as a draftsman in New York City and St. Paul, where he joined Clarence Johnston's firm as senior draftsman in 1909. Two years later he moved to Minneapolis and was employed by Edward Stebbins, helping to design public schools. Haxby and Stebbins became partners in 1914 and he remained in the firm for the rest of his life. From 1915 to 1920 he was the architect for the Minneapolis Board of Education. In 1920 he and Stebbins were joined by Cyrus Bissell (Stebbins, Haxby & Bissell).

Haxby died from injuries suffered in an automobile accident near Casper, Wyoming, on June 24, 1947.

Notable Buildings

STEBBINS & HAXBY
Grand Meadow Grade and High School, Grand Meadow (1916)

STEBBINS, HAXBY & BISSELL
Hendricks Grade and High School, Hendricks (1921)
Zeta Psi fraternity house, 1829 University Avenue SE, Minneapolis (1925–26)
Theta Chi fraternity house, 315 16th Avenue SE, Minneapolis (1928)
Holy Rosary School and Convent, 2424 18th Avenue S., Minneapolis (1931)
Alpha Gamma Rho fraternity house, 2060 Carter Avenue, St. Paul (1936)

Mark Hayes (1909–1956)

Mark N. Hayes was born on April 24, 1909, in Williston, North Dakota. He and his parents moved to Minneapolis where he attended De La Salle High School and the University of Minnesota, from which he received a degree in architecture in 1931. He worked as a draftsman for the Minneapolis–St. Paul Sanitary District in St. Paul from 1933 to 1937, and then joined Patrick O'Meara in partnership in 1937. In 1940 he entered partnership with James Hills and Victor Gilbertson, and served in the Navy in World War II.

Hayes died in Minneapolis on June 24, 1956.

Notable Buildings

WITH VICTOR GILBERTSON

St. Francis of Assisi Church, Rochester (1940–51)

Oak Grove Presbyterian Church, Bloomington (1946–47)

Christ Lutheran Church, 3244 34th Avenue S., Minneapolis (1949–50) (with Saarinen & Saarinen)

Lutheran Church of the Good Shepherd, 4801 France Avenue S. (1949–50)

First Congregational Church, Austin (1954–56)

Wesley United Methodist Church, Minneapolis, 1889–90 (Warren Hayes). *Photograph 1949 by Norton & Peel. Courtesy of Minnesota Historical Society.*

Warren Hayes (1847–1899)
Warren Howard Hayes was born in Prattsburgh, New York, on August 22, 1847, into a family reputed to be related to President Rutherford B. Hayes of Ohio. He grew up on a farm and attended Watkins Academy and Genessee Wesleyan Seminary in Lima, New York. In 1868, he entered Cornell University and studied civil engineering, natural sciences, and modern languages. He graduated with his bachelor's degree in 1871 and opened an architectural practice in Elmira, New York, that same year. Hayes moved to Minneapolis in 1881 and began a highly successful firm specializing in churches. He also designed a number of commercial buildings, schools, and residences. Hayes employed the "Akron Plan" in several of his churches, which placed the auditorium at a forty-five degree angle to the main axis with seating in a semicircle around the platform and pulpit.

Hayes died in Minneapolis on August 27, 1899.

Notable Buildings
First Congregational Church, 500 8th Avenue SE, Minneapolis (1886)
Central Presbyterian Church, 500 Cedar Street, St. Paul (1889)
Wesley United Methodist Church, 1st Avenue S. and Grant Street, Minneapolis (1889–90)
Frey residence, 1206 5th Street SE, Minneapolis (1892)

William Hazel (1854–1929)
William Augustus Hazel was born in Wilmington, North Carolina, on September 12, 1854. At the age of three, his parents moved to Oberlin, Ohio, and then subsequently to Cambridge, Massachusetts. He attended public schools in Cambridge and, at the age of sixteen, became a servant in the household of Charles Russell Lowell. He remained there a month before moving on to work as a janitor in an architect's office in Boston. It was there that he decided to enter the profession and became an apprentice in the office, along with his janitorial duties. He gradually moved into a full-time drafting position, a rarity for African Americans in the early 1870s.

Hazel moved to New York in 1877 and sought work as a draftsman. He was finally employed by Charles Gambrill, former partner of H. H. Richardson. He remained there for one year, then moved back to Boston and studied the design of stained glass. In 1886 Hazel accepted the position of designer in the stained glass department of Forman Ford & Company of Minneapolis, and subsequently became the Minneapolis representative of Tiffany Glass Company. A year later he was appointed designer and manager of the St. Paul branch of Brown & Haywood, stained glass manufacturers of Minneapolis. At the same time, he moonlighted as an architect.

After one of his sons died, his wife moved the family back to Cambridge. Hazel remained in Minneapolis until 1904, when he joined them. He taught at Tuskegee Institute in 1909 and at Howard University from 1921 to 1924, where he established its School of Architecture. He moved to Philadelphia in 1924 and, three years later, in failing health, went to live with his wife, daughter, and son-in-law at Cardinal Gibbons Institute, a secondary and trade school for black students, in Ridge, Maryland. He died there on February 13, 1929.

Notable Buildings
St. Peter's African Methodist Episcopal Church, Minneapolis (1888) (razed 1973) (with Francis J. Roberson)
Stained glass windows, St. Paul's African Methodist Episcopal Church, Springfield, Illinois (1899)
Dining Hall and Home Economics Building, Howard University, Baltimore, Maryland (1921)

T. P. Healy (1844–1906)

Theron Potter Healy was born in Nova Scotia in 1844. He was a successful shipping company owner in Halifax, but the loss of two ships in 1882 caused him great financial loss and he left Nova Scotia for Bismarck, North Dakota. He remained there only briefly before moving to Minneapolis about 1883.

Healy went into the contracting business around 1886 and became known as a developer and builder, although he did design many of the houses he constructed, especially Queen Anne houses in south Minneapolis, up to 1897. A block of his homes between 3105 and 3145 2nd Avenue South, including his own residence at 3115 and two others, was placed on the National Register of Historic Places in 1993. After 1897 Healy worked chiefly as a contractor, building structures designed by Harry Wild Jones, Franklin Long and Frederick Kees, William Whitney, and others.

Healy died in Minneapolis on February 1, 1906.

Notable Buildings
Residences: 3105–3145 2nd Avenue S., Minneapolis (1886–98) (3120 2nd Avenue S. razed 1960)
Residences: 3116–3124 3rd Avenue S., Minneapolis (1886–98)
W. F. Wagner residence, 1712 Dupont Avenue S., Minneapolis (1897)
P. E. Skahen residence, 1805 Irving Avenue S., Minneapolis (1901)
William Dunwoody residence, Minneapolis (1905–06) (razed 1967) (William Whitney, architect)

Raymond Hermanson (1916–2003)

Raymond T. Hermanson was born in Lemmon, South Dakota, on August 17, 1916. He was raised in Staples and St. Cloud, graduating from high school in 1934, then studied engineering and architecture at St. John's College in Collegeville, graduating in 1938. He worked with Nairne Fisher in Minneapolis in about 1940 and then was employed with the U.S. Navy designing docks and other structures at naval bases throughout the world. In 1943 Hermanson was commissioned in the Naval Air Corps and studied meteorology at New York University. He was sent to a weather station in San Francisco, followed by a stint at the Scripps School of Oceanography for further study.

He returned to St. Cloud after the war and found employment in the office of Louis Pinault. In 1949 he formed a partnership with Fred V. Traynor and they were joined by Gilbert F. Hahn in the late 1960s. Traynor, Hermanson and Hahn merged with the St. Cloud firm of Pauly and Olsen in 1983, becoming part of Short Elliott Hendrickson (SEH) in the early 1990s.

Hermanson retired from practice about 1983 and died in St. Cloud on August 28, 2003.

Notable Buildings
- St. Anastasia's Elementary School, Hutchinson (1957) (Traynor & Hermanson)
- Halenbeck Hall, St. Cloud State University, St. Cloud (1965) (Traynor & Hermanson)
- Warner Palestra, St. John's University, Collegeville (1973–75) (Traynor, Hermanson & Hahn)

Edwin Hewitt (1874–1939)

Edwin Hawley Hewitt was born in Red Wing, Minnesota, on March 26, 1874, the son of a distinguished surgeon. Hewitt attended public schools and went on to Hobart College in New York for a year before returning to complete his undergraduate work at the University of Minnesota. While at the university, he attended the Minneapolis School of Fine Arts at night and worked in the office of Cass Gilbert during vacations.

After graduation, Hewitt studied for a year at the Massachusetts Institute of Technology, and then entered the office of Shepley, Rutan and Coolidge in Boston. He worked there for three and a half years, afterwards going to Paris to study for four years at the École des Beaux-Arts.

In 1904 he returned to Minneapolis and set up his own practice. In 1910 he established a partnership with Edwin Brown that was active until the latter's death in 1930. Hewitt resumed private practice but

Cathedral Church of St. Mark, Minneapolis, 1908–11 (Hewitt & Brown). *Photograph ca. 1912 by Charles P. Gibson. Courtesy of Minnesota Historical Society.*

business languished during the Depression and, in 1934, Hewitt closed the office and became chief architectural supervisor of the Federal Housing Administration for the Minneapolis area. He revived his firm briefly in 1937 with partners Donald Setter and Ralph Hamlin.

Hewitt died on August 11, 1939, in Minneapolis.

Notable Buildings
Edwin Hewitt residence, 126 E. Franklin Avenue, Minneapolis (1906)

HEWITT & BROWN
Cathedral Church of St. Mark, 519 Oak Grove Street, Minneapolis (1908–11)
Hennepin Avenue Methodist Church, 511 Groveland Avenue, Minneapolis (1916)
Architects and Engineers Building, 1200 2nd Avenue S., Minneapolis (1922)

I. Vernon Hill (1872–1904)
Isaac Vernon Hill was born in Stanton-under-Bardon, England, on May 9, 1872. He came to the United States in 1888 with his family and settled in Duluth. It is not known how Hill obtained his architectural training, but he first appears as a bookkeeper and draftsman in the Lakeside Land Company in Duluth in 1891, and by 1896 was a partner of Wallace Wellbanks in an architecture firm that lasted only about a year. Hill then practiced alone until he entered partnership with Gerhard Tenbusch in 1899. By 1902, he and Tenbusch had parted company and Hill was a partner of William T. Bray. This partnership ended with Hill's premature death from cancer and pneumonia in Los Angeles, California, on February 25, 1904.

Notable Buildings
Mrs. Augusta Letteau residence, 712 E. 1st Street, Duluth (1896)
S. G. Knox residence, 15th Avenue E. and 1st Street, Duluth (1896)

I. Vernon Hill residence, Duluth, 1902 (Hill & Bray). *Photograph ca. 1965. Courtesy of Minnesota Historical Society.*

HILL & TENBUSCH

Cook residence, 501 Skyline Parkway W., Duluth (1900)

Frederick A. Patrick residence, 2306 E. Superior Street, Duluth (1901)

HILL & BRAY

I. Vernon Hill residence, 2220 E. Superior Street, Duluth (1902)

Crosby residence, 2029 E. Superior Street, Duluth (1902)

Robert Smith residence, 2330 E. 5th Street, Duluth (1903)

Sacred Heart Cathedral School, 206 W. 4th Street, Duluth, (1904)

James Hills (1888–1979)

James Bertram Hills was born in Binghamton, New York, on April 8, 1888. He attended Cornell University, from which he received a degree in architectural engineering. He began practicing in St. Paul in 1917 and was a partner of Patrick O'Meara. After O'Meara's death, Hills organized a partnership in 1940 with Victor Gilbertson and Mark Hayes. The firm was one of the most successful in Minneapolis for many years. After the death of Hayes in 1956, Albert Fisher became a full partner.

Hills retired shortly before his death in Minneapolis on January 28, 1979.

Notable Buildings

WITH VICTOR GILBERTSON AND MARK HAYES

St. Francis of Assisi Church, Rochester (1940–51)

Oak Grove Presbyterian Church, Bloomington (1946–47)

Christ Lutheran Church, 3244 34th Avenue S., Minneapolis (1949–50) (with Saarinen & Saarinen)

Lutheran Church of the Good Shepherd, 4801 France Avenue S. (1949–50)

First Congregational Church, Austin (1954–56)

Baudette Hospital, Baudette (1956)

WITH VICTOR GILBERTSON AND ALBERT FISHER

St. Charles Borromeo Catholic Church rectory, Stinson and St. Anthony Boulevards NE, Minneapolis (1961–62)

St. Constantine's Ukrainian Catholic Church, University Avenue and 5th Street NE, Minneapolis (1970–72)

James Hirsch (B. 1922)

James Hirsch was born in Medford, Wisconsin, in 1922. He attended Notre Dame University and Texas A&M University before earning a bachelor's degree in architecture at the University of Minnesota in 1948. He joined Milton Bergstedt in 1951 and remained in the firm until 1962. Hirsch then opened a private practice in Hudson, Wisconsin, in 1962, which he sold to BWBR (Minneapolis) in 1978, and subsequently retired to the state of Washington in 1980.

Notable Buildings

WITH MILTON BERGSTEDT

Mt. Zion Temple, 1300 Summit Avenue, St. Paul (1954–55) (with Eric Mendelsohn)

Degree of Honor Building, 325 Cedar Street, St. Paul (1961)

Inver Hills Community College, 8445 College Trail, Inver Grove Heights (1961)

BWBR Architects

BWBR traces its origins to the establishment of William Ingemann's firm in 1922. He was joined by Milton Bergstedt in 1941, who soon after became a partner in the practice. In September 1951, they dissolved the partnership, citing differences in how to manage the firm, and Bergstedt and James Hirsch, who had joined Ingemann and Bergstedt in 1948, organized the firm that would eventually become BWBR. Charles "Chuck" Wahlberg had been hired in April 1950 and, after a one-year sojourn with Brooks Cavin after he left Ingemann and Bergstedt, rejoined them in early 1951. When that partnership broke up later in the year, Wahlberg stayed with Ingemann for a short time and then moved to the office of Magney, Tusler and Setter in Minneapolis. In 1954, he returned to Bergstedt's practice. Thus, the "B" and "W" of the future office was in place.

The following year, the "R" arrived: Fritz Rohkohl was elevated to full-time, after having worked part-time in the office since 1953. In 1957, the second "B", Lloyd Bergquist, was hired, but the firm operated as Bergstedt, Hirsch, Wahlberg and Wold (Clark Wold became a principal in 1957) until Hirsch left to set up his own office in Hudson, Wisconsin, in 1962. The company was known as Bergstedt, Wahlberg & Wold until Wold's departure in 1968 and it remained Bergstedt, Wahlberg and Bergquist up until 1974 when Rohkohl was at last added to the firm's name. The acronym BWBR followed shortly thereafter.

Minneapolis Industrial Exposition Building, Minneapolis, 1886 (Isaac Hodgson). *Photograph ca. 1938. Courtesy of Minnesota Historical Society.*

Isaac Hodgson (1828–1909)
Isaac Hodgson was born in Belfast, Ireland, in 1828. Nothing is known of his education or training or when he came to the United States. He was living in Greensburg, Indiana, by 1850, employed as a carpenter. He moved to Indianapolis about 1862 and established a very successful architectural practice. In 1882 he came to Minneapolis and spent the remainder of his life there. Hodgson obtained many large commissions in Minneapolis during the 1880s and 1890s, and his firm had offices in St. Paul, Omaha, Kansas City, and elsewhere. He was joined in business by his son Edgar about 1882, and it is possible that another son, Isaac Jr., was in the firm as well, maintaining offices successively in Denver and Portland, Oregon, in the 1880s and 1890s.

Hodgson died in Minneapolis on April 17, 1909.

Notable Buildings
Bartholomew County Courthouse, Columbus, Indiana (1874)
Minnesota Loan and Trust Company, Minneapolis (1883) (razed ca. 1920)
Chamber of Commerce building, Minneapolis (1883) (razed 1926)
Minneapolis Industrial Exposition Building, Minneapolis (1886) (razed in two stages, 1940, 1946)
Bank of Minneapolis, Minneapolis (1886) (razed 1958)

Thomas Hodne (B. 1927)
Thomas Harold Hodne Jr., was born in Minneapolis on May 5, 1927. He received his bachelor's degree in architecture from the University of Minnesota in 1955 and his master's degree in architecture from the Massachusetts Institute of Technology (MIT) in 1956. In 1954, Hodne taught at the School of Architecture at the University of Minnesota, the first instructor hired by Ralph Rapson after the latter assumed the directorship of the school. Hodne also taught at the Boston Architectural Center while pursuing his master's degree. After leaving MIT, he practiced with architectural and planning firms in Cleveland; Cambridge, Massachusetts; Minneapolis; and St. Paul. He rejoined the School of Architecture at the University of Minnesota as a professor in 1964 and remained there for the next twenty years. He also served as an urban designer with the Minneapolis City Planning Commission in the late 1950s.

In 1962, Hodne formed Hodne Associates, Inc., and the following year won a competition sponsored by Ruberoid to design a housing project for East Harlem in New York City. Hodne formed The Hodne/Stageberg Partners with James Stageberg in July 1968 to assist in designing the huge, $65 million complex. Construction did not start for several years, and by the time it was finished in 1975, it had been named 1199 Plaza after its sponsor, Local 1199 Drug and Hospital Union. The project ultimately won nine design awards between 1975 and 2001.

In 1982 The Hodne/Stageberg Partners dissolved and the next year Hodne moved to Winnipeg, where he assumed the directorship of the School of Architecture at the University of Manitoba. He remained as head of the school until 1988, after which he was appointed professor in the Department of Architecture, a post he held until 1997. In the meantime, he had a private practice in Minneapolis, Thomas Hodne Architects, which later became

Thomas Hodne Junior, FAIA Architect. He is now retired from practice.

Notable Buildings
1199 Plaza, New York, New York (1968–75) (with James Stageberg)
Native American Center for the Minneapolis Region (now Minneapolis American Indian Center), 1530 E. Franklin Avenue, Minneapolis (1974) (with James Stageberg)
West Campus, University of Iowa, Iowa City, Iowa (1984–85)

Abraham Holstead (1879–1955)
Abraham Holstead was born in England on August 15, 1879. He graduated from Bradford College with a degree in architecture and became head designer for Sir Alfred Gelder in Hull, and a member of the Royal Institute of British Architects. He came to the United States in 1906 and worked as chief designer in the Shepley, Rutan & Coolidge office in Chicago, where he designed a number of major buildings throughout the United States. It is not known when Holstead moved to Duluth, but he entered partnership with William Sullivan there in 1912, a practice that continued to 1928. He remained in Duluth after the partnership dissolved. During World War II, he worked as a designer in the Riverside shipyards in Duluth.

Holstead retired about 1946 and moved to California. He died in Manhattan Beach on April 2, 1955.

Notable Buildings
See also William Sullivan
Corn Exchange Bank, Chicago, Illinois (1907)
Harper Library, University of Chicago, Chicago, Illinois (1910–12)
Frank and Ida Kemp residence, Duluth (1914)
Buhl Public Library, Buhl (1917–18)

Thomas Holyoke (1866–1925)
Thomas Gannett Holyoke was born into a prominent family in South Natick, Massachusetts, on April 1, 1866. He attended schools in Medford, Massachusetts,

Buhl Public Library, Buhl, 1917–18 (Abraham Holstead). *Photograph ca. 1918. Courtesy of Minnesota Historical Society.*

George Gardner residence, St. Paul, 1905 (Thomas Holyoke). *Photograph 1948 by* St. Paul Dispatch & Pioneer Press. *Courtesy of Minnesota Historical Society.*

including Medford High School. His father died while he was in high school and, after graduation, he moved to St. Paul to live with his sister, Mrs. William Davis. She and her husband had hired Cass Gilbert to design their house, and Gilbert asked them if they knew anyone who would be interested in an apprenticeship. They suggested young Holyoke, and he began working for Gilbert in 1884. He remained with Gilbert for more than twenty years. At one point, Gilbert paid for Holyoke to study at the Atelier Duray in Paris for a year. Holyoke eventually became chief draftsman and helped design a number of buildings.

After Gilbert moved to New York City, Holyoke opened his own practice in 1906, specializing in the design of fine residences. Ten years later he joined his nephew, Holyoke Davis, and Magnus Jemne, in partnership. Davis left the firm in 1923 and the business continued until Holyoke's death on March 30, 1925, of appendicitis. In addition to his practice, he founded the Gargoyle Club in St. Paul and served as president of the Minnesota Chapter of the American Institute of Architects.

Notable Buildings
Cornelius Williams residence, 500 Summit Avenue, St. Paul (1904)

George Gardner residence, 301 Summit Avenue, St. Paul (1905)

Unity Unitarian Church, 732 Holly Avenue, St. Paul (1905)

First Methodist Church (now First Trinity United Methodist Church), 1849 Marshall Avenue, St. Paul (1912)

Watson Davidson Sr. residence, 344 Summit Avenue, St. Paul (1915)

Harry Allers residence, 990 Summit Avenue, St. Paul (1916)

St. Paul Academy, 1712 Randolph Avenue, St. Paul (1916)

Winona Armory, Winona (1969) (Bettenburg, Townsend, Stolte & Comb, architects)

Butler Square renovation, 100 N. 6th Street, Minneapolis (1974–76) (Miller, Hanson, Westerbeck & Bell, and Arvid Elness Architects)

YWCA, 1130 Nicollet Mall, Minneapolis (1974) (Freerks, Sperl & Flynn, architects)

Brown County Historical Museum, New Ulm (1980) (Cavin & Rova, architects)

Frank Horner (1923–1980)

Frank Horner was born in Linton, North Dakota, on August 25, 1923. Following military service in World War II, he earned a bachelor's degree in civil engineering at the University of Minnesota in 1949. He worked for two years for a steel fabricating company and a year with a construction company before joining Johnston-Sahlman Company, consulting structural engineers in Minneapolis. Eight years later, Horner formed his own practice as a consulting structural engineer (1960). He was affiliated with many architectural firms in the Twin Cities and consulted on hundreds of projects.

Horner was a major force behind the renovation of the Snelling-Selby neighborhood in St. Paul, where his firm's offices were located. He continued to practice until his death on December 6, 1980, in St. Paul.

Notable Buildings

St. John's University library, Collegeville (1962) (Marcel Breuer, architect)

Shepherd of the Hills Lutheran Church, 500 S. Blake Road, Edina (1965) (SMSQ, architects)

Lawrence Hovik (1903–1958)

Lawrence E. Hovik was born in Minneapolis on March 27, 1903. He graduated from the University of Minnesota with his bachelor's degree in architecture in 1929, and from the Massachusetts Institute of Technology with his master's degree in the same subject in 1935.

Hovik received a traveling scholarship to study city planning in London, where he studied under Sir Raymond Unwin and worked on projects in Hampstead, Letchworth, and Welwyn Garden City. During World War II, he was a project advisor to the U.S. government on war housing.

After the war, he moved to Lincoln, Nebraska, and joined the Chamber of Commerce as director of planning. He created a master city plan for Lincoln, and then moved to Minneapolis to enter the firm of Ellerbe Architects, where he remained the rest of his career as a planner and architect. It is not known what buildings he designed while with Ellerbe.

Hovik died in St. Paul on March 27, 1958.

Notable Buildings
No buildings attributable to Hovik have been found.

John Howe (1913–1997)
John Henry Howe was born in Evanston, Illinois, on May 17, 1913. Early on, he developed a love for architecture, especially the work of Frank Lloyd Wright, which he saw while bicycling around Oak Park and other Chicago suburbs. Upon graduating from high school, he applied for a fellowship at Taliesin, Wright's school and studio in Spring Green, Wisconsin. He was accepted and became an apprentice in 1932. Howe remained with Wright for the next thirty-two years, much of that time serving as chief draftsman, working with such well-known figures as Wesley Peters and Edgar Tafel. During World War II, Howe was incarcerated in the federal prison at Sandstone, Minnesota, for refusing to comply with conscription. He was released in 1946 and resumed his career with Wright.

In 1964, Howe moved to San Francisco where he worked for three years with Aaron Green, another former Wright apprentice. Howe relocated to Minneapolis in 1967 and opened a private practice, which he maintained until his retirement in 1992.

He died in Novato, California, on September 21, 1997.

Notable Buildings
Walter Schmidt residence, Credit River Township, Savage (1968)
Wesley Libbey residence, Grand Rapids (1968)
H. L. Jerpbak residence, Edina (1969)
Howe residence ("Sankoku"), Burnsville (1970–71)
First Church of Christ Scientist, New Brighton (1970–72)
Public Library, Menomonie, Wisconsin (1979)

Wesley Libbey residence, Grand Rapids, 1968 (John Howe). *Photograph courtesy of Northwest Architectural Archives, University of Minnesota.*

Karl Humphrey Jr. (1914–1974)
Karl Eastman Humphrey Jr. was born in El Reno, Oklahoma, on January 25, 1914. He attended Sacred Heart Academy in El Reno for two years and Loyola Academy in Chicago for another year. He finished his secondary education at Classen High School in Oklahoma City, and then entered the University of Oklahoma for a year before transferring to Yale University, from which he received his bachelor's degree in 1935. He went on to spend another three years at the Yale School of Fine Arts, receiving a bachelor of fine arts degree in 1938. Humphrey moved to Minneapolis that same year and entered the architecture firm of McEnary & Krafft. He remained there as a draftsman and associate until the end of 1942, when he opened his own office which he maintained until forming a partnership with Collis Hardenbergh in 1946. This partnership remained active for almost thirty years, specializing in the design of homes for affluent clients, many of them in the Minnetonka area west of Minneapolis.

Humphrey died in Wayzata, Minnesota, on May 28, 1974.

Notable Buildings

WITH COLLIS HARDENBERGH
Robert Longfellow residence, Alexandria (1953)
Charles Case residence, Red Oaks, Maplewood (1953)
Ruth Bovey Stevens residence, Ferndale (1956)
E. B. Wilson residence, Sunfish Lake (1973)

William Hunt (1859–1930)
William A. Hunt was born in Millcreek, Ohio, in 1859. Nothing is known of his education and early career. He appeared in Minneapolis about 1885 and maintained a private practice until he moved to Duluth a few years later. He worked as a draftsman in the office of Emmet Palmer and Lucien Hall until 1893, when he became a partner in the firm. Hunt remained with Palmer after Hall left the firm in 1904 and the partnership dissolved in either 1905 or 1906. Hunt managed a private practice in Duluth until about 1914. After that, he was employed as an architect with an iron mining company in Stuntz, Minnesota, for a number of years.

Hunt died in Duluth on August 15, 1930.

Notable Buildings
Andrew Davidson residence, Duluth (1902) (Palmer & Hall)
Barnes residence, 25 S. 26th Avenue E., Duluth (1906) (Palmer, Hall & Hunt)
Samuel J. Colter residence, Duluth (1910)
Linna Patterson residence, Duluth (1914)

Dorothy Ingemann (1902–1991)
Dorothy Ryer Brink was born on Christmas Day, 1902, in St. Paul. She grew up in the Merriam Park neighborhood and graduated from the University of Minnesota's School of Architecture in 1925. She joined William Ingemann's firm that same year, and two years later they were married. Dorothy helped design the Lowell Inn in Stillwater and did a great deal of the drafting and design work in the office. She was especially adept at producing fine quality renderings and perspectives. She left the firm when her husband retired in 1961 and they moved to San Miguel de Allende, Mexico, in 1965, where she died on April 2, 1991.

Notable Buildings

WITH WILLIAM INGEMANN

Hugh S. Alexander Alumni House (Macalester College president's residence), 1644 Summit Avenue, St. Paul (1926)

Lowell Inn, Stillwater (1927)

Ingemann residence, 7 Malcolm Court, St. Paul (1928)

Citizen's Fund Insurance Building, Red Wing (1929)

Bovey Village Hall, Bovey (1934–35)

Willmar Auditorium, Willmar (1935–38)

Sverdrup-Oftedal Memorial Hall, Augsburg College, Minneapolis (1938)

William Ingemann (1897–1980)

William M. Ingemann was born in St. Paul on March 4, 1897. His father, Victor Ingemann, was a senior member of Ingemann & Company, contractors. Young Ingemann graduated from Central High School and attended the American Academy in Rome. He worked briefly in 1915 in the office of Frederick Mann in Minneapolis, but when the United States entered World War I, Ingemann enlisted and initially was an ambulance driver and later an aviator. Then he was transferred to the American engineering section, where he worked with American town planner George B. Ford to assist in reconstruction work in Belgium under the auspices of the American Red Cross.

Lowell Inn, Stillwater, 1927 (William and Dorothy Ingemann). *Photograph ca. 1927 by John Runk. Courtesy of Minnesota Historical Society.*

Ingemann returned to the United States following his military service and entered the University of Minnesota, where he received his bachelor's degree in architecture in 1922.

For a year prior to graduation, he worked in the New York office of Cass Gilbert as a draftsman (1921–22), then associated with Electus Litchfield in New York from 1922 to 1926. After graduating from the university, Ingemann set up an office in St. Paul. One of his first completed commissions was for the Lowell Inn in Stillwater (1927). In 1925 he married Dorothy Brink, whom he had employed as a draftsman, and she continued working in the firm.

During World War II, Ingemann rejoined the Army Air Force and served for the duration of the conflict. In his absence, the firm was operated by his partner Milton Bergstedt who had entered the practice in 1941. They dissolved the partnership ten years later, and Ingemann moved his business to Riviera Beach, Florida, where he practiced from 1953 to 1955. He returned to St. Paul in 1958 and was appointed vice president and chief architect for the Walter Butler Company. He remained in this position until his retirement in 1961.

Ingemann died in San Miguel de Allende, Mexico, on February 15, 1980.

Notable Buildings

WITH DOROTHY INGEMANN
Hugh S. Alexander Alumni House (Macalester College president's residence), 1644 Summit Avenue, St. Paul (1926)
Lowell Inn, Stillwater (1927)
Ingemann residence, 7 Malcolm Court, St. Paul (1928)
Citizen's Fund Insurance Building, Red Wing (1929)
Bovey Village Hall, Bovey (1934–35)
Willmar Auditorium, Willmar (1935–38)
Sverdrup-Oftedal Memorial Hall, Augsburg College, Minneapolis (1938)

Jerome Jackson (1875–?)
Jerome Paul Jackson was born in Southbridge, Massachusetts, on December 10, 1875. Details of his early life are sketchy, but it is known that he graduated from Amherst College in 1897 and earned a degree in architecture from the Massachusetts Institute of Technology (MIT) in 1899. Following his graduation, Jackson went to work in the office of Shepley, Rutan & Coolidge in Boston. They sent him to Minneapolis to serve as local supervising architect on the construction of Plymouth Congregational Church from 1907 to 1909. Jackson stayed on in Minneapolis and in 1909 established a flourishing practice with Jacob Stone, a fellow student at MIT and coworker at Shepley, Rutan & Coolidge. Both Jackson and Stone were in the army during World War I. Jackson was sent overseas in November 1917 and served with an engineering unit assigned to construct hospital facilities.

Walker Branch Library (now a commercial building), Minneapolis, 1910 (Jerome Jackson and Jacob Stone). *Photograph courtesy of Minneapolis Public Library, James K. Hosmer Special Collection, MPL0065.*

After the war, the partnership was not resumed and both men set up private practices. Jackson moved to New York City in 1927 to work for architect Roger H. Bullard. Sometime between then and 1932, however, he relocated to Mount Vernon, New York, and opened his own office. But, sadly, he, like so many other architects at the time, suffered from a drastic drop in business during the Depression, and was last heard of in Sandy Hook, Connecticut, in 1934, when he contacted the American Institute of Architects (AIA) to say that "every penny counts with me now and I cannot see any prospect for improvement in the near future" and that he therefore was resigning from the Institute. Afterward, he drops out of sight. Stone moved on to California in 1943 to work as an engineer in the Kaiser shipyards, but it is not known what Jackson did during World War II or later.

His place and date of death are unknown.

Notable Buildings
Walker Branch Library (now a commercial building), Minneapolis (1910) (with Jacob Stone)
Seven Corners Branch Library, Minneapolis (1911) (razed 1965) (with Jacob Stone)
East Lake Branch Library, 2916 E. Lake Street, Minneapolis (1924) (now Northern Sun Merchandising)
Roosevelt Community Library, 4026 28th Avenue S., Minneapolis (1927)

Silas Jacobson (1880–1943)
Silas Jacobson was born in Minneapolis on October 11, 1880. His education and training are unknown. He began practicing in St. Paul in 1910 and was in partnership with Ernest Hartford until 1914. For many years, starting about 1916, Jacobson was a senior draftsman in the Minnesota state architect's office. He moved to Madison, Wisconsin, in 1929 where he assumed a similar position in the Wisconsin state architect's office.

Jacobson died in Madison on November 1, 1943.

Notable Buildings
St. Paul Fire Station, 9th Street between Jackson and Robert Streets, St. Paul (1915)

John Jager (1871–1959)
John Jager was born in Carniola, Austria, on May 16, 1871. He received his architectural and engineering training in the Imperial and Royal Polytechnicum in Vienna from 1892 to 1899. Starting in 1898 he worked for two and a half years as professional assistant to Professors Karl Mayreder and Oswald Gruber, during which time Jager drew up a city plan for Ljubljana, Slovenia, then part of the Austro-Hungarian Empire. In 1901 he was sent to Peking, China, as a captain of engineers in the Imperial and Royal Government Service of Austria. He designed a number of buildings for the military services to occupy in the Chinese capital while the Austrians were garrisoning the country following the Boxer Rebellion.

In 1902, Jager came to the United States and settled in Minneapolis. He opened an architectural practice and drew up a plan for the beautification of the city. The drawing was exhibited at the Louisiana Purchase Exposition in St. Louis in 1904. The next year Jager formed a partnership with Carl Stravs that lasted until

St. Bernard's Catholic Church, St. Paul, 1905–06 (John Jager). *Photograph ca. 1910 by Charles P. Gibson. Courtesy of Minnesota Historical Society.*

1909, when he became a draftsman and planner with Hewitt & Brown in Minneapolis; he remained in the firm while working simultaneously as an inspector for the Minneapolis agricultural unit of the American Red Cross, until 1933. Except for service in World War I, he then took the position of supervisor of public works in the Minneapolis City Planning Department.

Jager retired in 1943 and died in Minneapolis on October 31, 1959.

Notable Buildings
St. Stephen's Church, Brockway (1903)
St. Bernard's Catholic Church, Geranium and Albemarle Streets, St. Paul (1905–06)

St. Joseph's Catholic Church, Rosen (1906)

Vincent James (B. 1952)
Vincent James was born on July 14, 1952, in Minneapolis. He graduated from the University of Wisconsin–Milwaukee with his master's degree in architecture in 1978. He worked first in the offices of Hardy Holtzmann Pfeiffer in New York and then, in 1980, became a project architect for Chrysalis Corporation in Valdosta, Georgia. In 1984, James joined Hammel, Green and Abrahamson in Minneapolis where he was an associate vice president. He left the firm in 1990 to open his own office, becoming a partner with Julie Snow the following year. The partnership

was dissolved in 1995 and James resumed private practice as VJAA. His firm has been very successful, winning numerous design awards for projects throughout the United States and abroad. James has also held teaching positions at the University of Wisconsin–Milwaukee (1980–83), the University of Minnesota (1993–2000), Tulane University in New Orleans (1998–99), and Harvard University (beginning in 2001).

Notable Buildings

Kenneth and Judy Dayton residence, 1719 Franklin Avenue W., Minneapolis (1997)

Rapson Hall (addition), University of Minnesota, Minneapolis (2000–02) (with Stephen Holl)

Minneapolis Rowing Club Boathouse, W. River Parkway and Lake Street, Minneapolis (2001)

Charles W. Hostler Student Center and Corniche Frontage, American University, Beirut, Lebanon (2002)

Magnus Jemne (1882–1967)

Magnus Jemne was born in Batnfjordsora, Norway, on March 31, 1882. He came to the United States at the age of seventeen, living first in St. Paul, where he worked in Cass Gilbert's office. He studied architecture at the University of Pennsylvania as a pupil of noted architect Paul Cret, and after graduating about 1903 returned to St. Paul and became an associate of Thomas Holyoke. He and Holyoke formed

Kenneth and Judy Dayton residence, Minneapolis, 1997 (Vincent James). *Photograph by Bill Jolitz. Courtesy of Minnesota Historical Society.*

MINNESOTA ARCHITECTS :: A BIOGRAPHICAL DICTIONARY ▶ 113

Women's City Club (now Wold Architects), St. Paul, 1931 (Magnus Jemne). *Photograph ca. 1935 by Stanley J. McComb. Courtesy of Minnesota Historical Society.*

a partnership in 1916 which they maintained until the latter's death in 1925. Jemne then had a private practice in St. Paul for many years afterward, specializing in the design of stately homes.

He died in St. Paul on February 7, 1967.

Notable Buildings

Women's City Club (formerly Minnesota Museum of Art; now Wold Architects), Kellogg Boulevard and St. Peter Street, St. Paul (1931)

Robert and Freda Ahrens residence, 1565 Edgcumbe Road, St. Paul (1938)

Lemuel Jepson (1847–1929)
Lemuel Jepson was born in Connecticut on July 17, 1847. He began his career by working as a woodworker in Westfield, Massachusetts, running his own cigar box manufacturing business (1875). Two years later, he was residing in Meriden, Connecticut, where he was employed as a carpenter, and by 1880 was in Springfield, Massachusetts, in the same line of work.

What brought him to Minneapolis is unknown, but he was residing there by 1885 and managing his own architectural firm. Jepson remained in Minnesota for the next forty-five years, practicing architecture part of that time. He worked briefly as a draftsman at Barnett and Record (1893–94) and had a partner for a short time, George Kneisly, in 1896–1897, a practice advertising itself as builders of grain elevators. About 1900, he moved to Richfield and by 1908 was employed as a gardener. Nothing further is known of his life and employment.

In 1885, Jepson designed and built several houses of concrete block in north Minneapolis for the Union Stone Building Company. This was a truly innovative approach to construction at the time, and it is not certain if Jepson owned or had any monetary interest in the company.

He died in Minneapolis on February 10, 1929.

Notable Buildings
Concrete block residences, 2705–2707 and 2729 N. 3rd Street, Minneapolis (1885)
Concrete block residences, 2826 and 2828 N. 4th Street, Minneapolis (1885)
Townhouses, 24th Street and Fremont Avenue N., Minneapolis (1891)
Rappahannock Apartments, 601–609 9th Street S., Minneapolis (1895)
Stores and flats, 3103 Irving Avenue S., Minneapolis (1905)

Harley Johnson (1918–1980)
Harley Hovey Johnson was born in Houston, Minnesota, on May 22, 1918. He began training for his career in architecture by working first as a carpenter and bricklayer in Winona with the Nels Johnson Construction Company. He became an office boy in the firm of Magney, Tusler & Setter in Minneapolis in the summer of 1939 while attending the University of Minnesota, from which he graduated with a bachelor's degree in architecture in 1942. He also worked for Holabird & Root in Chicago as job captain during the summer of 1940. Johnson entered the U.S. Navy in 1943, serving until early 1946 in various naval shipyards and in the Office of Naval Intelligence.

After the war, he returned to Magney, Tusler & Setter from February to July 1946, then moved to Cambridge, Massachusetts, and entered Harvard University to earn a master's degree in architecture. At the same time, he worked in the offices of William Galvin in Cambridge and Carl Koch in Belmont, Massachusetts.

After graduation from Harvard in 1947, Johnson returned to St. Paul and was employed in Brooks Cavin's firm as a designer from June to September 1947, then went to work for McEnary & Krafft in Minneapolis as a designer starting in January 1948. He was employed to direct construction of Mount Sinai Hospital in Minneapolis (1948) and Mount Sinai Temple in St. Paul (1949). In 1950, he opened his own firm and remained in private practice until merging with Frank Kerr in 1957. The partnership remained

Summit Terrace, St. Paul, 1889–90 (Clarence Johnston and William Willcox). *Photograph 1891. Courtesy of Minnesota Historical Society.*

active until 1960, when Johnson resumed private practice.

He died in Minneapolis on July 15, 1980.

Notable Buildings
Upsala High School, Upsala (1954)
Winona Daily News publishing plant, Winona (1955)
Albinson Inc., 1401 Glenwood Avenue, Minneapolis (1956)
John Paul residence, 60th Street and James Avenue S., Minneapolis (1956)
Chisago City Fire and Village Hall, Chisago City (1957–60) (with Frank Kerr)

Clarence Johnston (1859–1936)
Clarence Howard Johnston was born on August 28, 1859, in Waseca County, Minnesota. As a child, he moved with his family to St. Paul and was educated in the public schools. After completing high school, he worked in the office of Abraham Radcliffe, a prominent St. Paul architect. It was there that he met Cass Gilbert and the two became good friends. They both left in 1878 to attend the Massachusetts Institute of Technology (MIT). Johnston was forced to drop out before completing one year because of financial stringencies, and he returned to St. Paul where he entered the office of Edward P. Bassford. In 1880 his old professor at MIT wrote to offer him a position in Herter Brothers in New York, which he accepted. He worked there for about two years, part of the time on the massive William Vanderbilt mansion then being erected on Fifth Avenue.

Johnston moved back to St. Paul in 1882 and opened his own office, which he maintained the rest of his life. He was joined in partnership by William Willcox in 1885; Willcox left in 1889. After the partnership was dissolved, Johnston practiced privately, building the business into one of the most successful in the state.

Johnston died on December 31, 1936, in St. Paul.

Notable Buildings
Shumway Hall, Shattuck School, Faribault (1887) (with William Willcox)
Summit Terrace, 596–604 Summit Avenue, St. Paul (1889–90) (with William Willcox)
Church of the Holy Trinity, Veseli (1905)
Chester Congdon residence, Duluth (1907–08)
Samuel and Madeline Dittenhofer residence, 807 Summit Avenue, St. Paul (1908)
Minnesota Historical Society (now Judicial Center), 690 Cedar Street, St. Paul (1916–17)
Walter Library, University of Minnesota, Minneapolis (1925)
Northrop Auditorium, University of Minnesota, Minneapolis (1930)
Tri-State Telephone Building (later Northwestern Bell Telephone building), 70 W. 4th Street, St. Paul (1940)

Harry Jones (1859–1935)
Harry Wild Jones was born near Kalamazoo, Michigan, on June 9, 1859. He was the grandson of Dr. S. F. Smith, who wrote the lyrics to "My Country 'Tis of

Lakewood Cemetery Chapel, Minneapolis, 1908 (Harry Jones). *Photograph 1912. Courtesy of Minnesota Historical Society.*

Thee." Jones was educated at University Grammar School in Providence, Rhode Island, and at Brown University (graduated 1880), and the Massachusetts Institute of Technology, where he received his bachelor's degree in architecture (1882). He worked in the office of the famous architect H. H. Richardson in Boston for a year and in 1883 married Bertha Tucker, niece of the sewing machine inventor Elias Howe. The couple honeymooned in Minneapolis and Jones decided to accept employment in the architectural firm of Plant and Whitney. A year later, Jones traveled to Europe to study and returned to Minneapolis in 1885. He opened his own office, which he maintained until his retirement in 1918.

Jones died in Minneapolis on September 25, 1935.

Notable Buildings

Harry Jones residence, 5101 Nicollet Avenue, Minneapolis (1887)

National Bank of Commerce (later Civic and Commerce Association Building), Minneapolis (1888) (razed 1958–59)

Scottish Rite Temple addition, Dupont and Franklin Avenues, Minneapolis (1904)

Butler Brothers warehouse, 100 N. 6th Street, Minneapolis (1906)

Lakewood Cemetery Chapel, 3600 Hennepin Avenue, Minneapolis (1908)

Hamm Building, St. Paul, 1919–20 (Roy Jones and Beaver Wade Day). *Photograph courtesy of Northwest Architectural Archives, University of Minnesota.*

Roy Jones (1885–1963)
Roy Childs Jones was born in Kendallville, Indiana, on June 22, 1885. He was educated at Purdue University and the University of Pennsylvania, receiving his bachelor's and master's degrees in architecture from the latter in 1908 and 1914. He worked for the prestigious firms of Holabird & Root in Chicago and McKim, Mead & White in New York, probably while attending school. He came to Minneapolis in 1913 and joined the faculty of the University's School of Architecture. During World War I, Jones served with the U.S. Corps of Engineers in France. He returned to Minneapolis and, in addition to his teaching, worked for a time in association with Frederick Mann and as chief designer and draftsman for Toltz, King & Day of St. Paul, from 1919 to 1928. In 1937, he was appointed head of the School of Architecture at the university, a position he held until his retirement in 1953.

Jones died on October 29, 1963, in Minneapolis.

Notable Buildings

WITH BEAVER WADE DAY
Hamm Building, 408 St. Peter Street, St. Paul (1919–20)
Stearns County Courthouse, St. Cloud (1920)
Spink County Courthouse, Redfield, South Dakota (1926)
Ward County Courthouse, Minot, North Dakota (1928)

Edgar Joralemon (1858–1937)
Edgar Eugene Joralemon was born in Augusta, Illinois, on July 31, 1858. He moved to Minneapolis where his father worked as a carpenter beginning in 1867. Young Joralemon started his career as a draftsman with Leroy Buffington in 1876 and the following year moved to the office of Haglin and Corser. In 1880 he was briefly a partner of Franklin Long and a year later was a draftsman in the office of Abraham Radcliffe in St. Paul. Shortly thereafter he went to work for Edward Bassford in the same city and, in 1883, briefly returned to Buffington's office and then Franklin Long's office in 1884. In either 1885 or 1886 he left Long and formed his own practice, specializing in private residences and apartment houses in Minneapolis. He apparently couldn't make it alone, however, for he was in partnership with Charles Ferrin in 1888. Joralemon rejoined Buffington as a draftsman and delineator until 1892 when he moved to the office of George and Fremont Orff and became a partner a year later. The firm of Orff & Joralemon was very successful, designing many residences and commercial buildings in the Upper Midwest, and for several years, at least, ended Joralemon's office-hopping.

Joralemon left Minneapolis in 1898 for Niagara Falls, New York, and established a practice that became quite successful. At some point, he retired to California, where he died in Los Angeles on September 29, 1937.

Notable Buildings
George Van Dusen residence, 1900 La Salle Avenue, Minneapolis (1892–93) (with Orff Brothers)
Waseca County Courthouse, Waseca (1897) (Orff & Joralemon)
Carnegie Library, Niagara Falls, New York (1903)
Hamilton College Chapel, Toronto, Ontario (1908)

George Van Dusen residence, Minneapolis, 1892–93 (Edgar Joralemon and Orff Brothers). *Photograph ca. 1895. Courtesy of Minnesota Historical Society.*

Charles Joy (1840–1928)

Charles E. Joy was born in New Hampshire in March 1840. Much of his early life is unknown, but it is evident that he worked as a printer in Dover, New Hampshire, for about a decade and that for the last three years of his residence there he also worked as a draftsman for Taylor and Craig, a contractor. He may also have worked for the Burlington Railroad for a time, as well, although it is not certain when or for how long. He came to St. Paul in 1884, and two years later formed a partnership with John A. Teltz for a year, and then became a partner of Mark Fitzpatrick for another year. From 1889 to 1894 Joy was in partnership with Denslow Millard. He formed his own office when the partnership broke up and maintained it until 1898 when he moved to Fargo, North Dakota. About two years later he was back in St. Paul, but then he seems

Bushnell-West residence, St. Paul, 1888 (Charles Joy). *Photograph ca. 1888. Courtesy of Minnesota Historical Society.*

to disappear from the scene. It appears that he moved to northern Minnesota and perhaps practiced there for some years.

Joy died in Detroit Lakes, Minnesota, on April 30, 1928.

Notable Buildings
Ice palace, St. Paul (1887) (razed 1887)
Joy residence, 882 S. Point Douglas Road, St. Paul (1888)
Bushnell-West residence, 91 Crocus Place, St. Paul (1888)

Eino Jyring (1905–1992)
Eino "Jerry" Jyring ws born in Eveleth, Minnesota, on November 7, 1905. He attended public schools in Virginia, Minnnesota, and graduated from Virginia High School. He entered the University of Minnesota and received a bachelor's degree in architecture with honors about 1926. He worked successively for firms

United Methodist Church, Thief River Falls, 1969 (Eino Jyring and Richard Whiteman). *Photograph by Bob Firth.*

in Chicago, New York City, and Hibbing, Minnesota, and served with a U.S. government contractor and in the U.S. Navy's Seabees during World War II. When Jyring returned from military service, he established his own architectural practice in Hibbing. He was in partnership with Steven Philip Jurenes from 1946 until the latter's death in 1953. Richard Whiteman joined the firm in 1952 and

Abbey Church, St. John's University, Collegeville, 1954–61 (Frank Kacmarcik, Marcel Breuer, and Val Michelson). *Photograph by Bob Firth.*

was a partner from 1955 to 1972. The firm remains in business today as Architectural Resources, Inc. Jyring was a Fellow of the American Institute of Architects and served as president of the Minnesota Society of Architects.

He retired in 1990 and died on February 10, 1992, in Hibbing.

Notable Buildings
St. Louis County Courthouse, Hibbing (1954)
First Lutheran Church, Virginia (1956) (with Richard Whiteman)
United Methodist Church, Thief River Falls (1969) (with Richard Whiteman)

Frank Kacmarcik (1920–2004)
Frank Thomas Kacmarcik was born in St. Paul on March 15, 1920. After graduating from high school, he attended the Minnesota College of Art and Design to study painting and book design. He entered St. John's Abbey at Collegeville as a novice in the early 1940s and then left to serve in the U.S. Army Medical Corps in Europe as a chaplain's assistant and medical technician. After the war, he studied at the Academie de la Grande Chaumiere and the Centre d'Art Sacre in Paris, where he was trained in painting, religious art, and church decoration.

Kacmarcik returned to St. John's College in 1950 and became a professor of art. Three years later, he collaborated with Marcel Breuer in the design of the Abbey Church. Kacmarcik was a much-sought-after expert consultant in liturgical art and design for many years. In 1983, after working out of his home (designed by Breuer) in St. Paul, he moved back to St. John's and continued to work as an ecclesiastical consultant and designer.

He died in Collegeville, Minnesota, on February 22, 2004.

Notable Buildings
Abbey Church, St. John's University, Collegeville (1954–61) (with Marcel Breuer)
St. Patrick's Catholic Church, Oklahoma City, Oklahoma (1960) (with Murray-Jones-Murray)
Clare Boothe Luce Library, Mepkin Abbey, Moncks Corner, South Carolina (2000–01) (with Bentz-Thompson-Rietow)

Seeman Kaplan (1895–1963)
Seeman Kaplan was born in Minneapolis on June 5, 1895. He grew up in Minneapolis and graduated from the University of Minnesota with a degree in architecture in 1918. After serving in World War I as an officer in the Engineer Corps, he returned to Minneapolis to form a partnership with his brother-in-law, Jack Liebenberg, and Robert Martin in 1920. Kaplan remained in the firm until his death on November 26, 1963, in Tulsa, Oklahoma.

Notable Buildings
WITH JACK LIEBENBERG
Granada Theater (later Suburban World), 3022 Hennepin Avenue, Minneapolis (1928)
Hollywood Theater, 2815 Johnson Street NE, Minneapolis (1935)
Fargo Theater, Fargo, North Dakota (1936)
Varsity Theater, 1308 4th Street SE, Minneapolis (1938)
NorShor Theater, Duluth (1938)
Uptown Theater, 2906 Hennepin Avenue, Minneapolis (1938)

Grain Exchange, Minneapolis, 1900–1902 (Kees & Colburn). *Photograph ca. 1918 by Charles J. Hibbard. Courtesy of Minnesota Historical Society.*

Frederick Kees (1852–1927)
Frederick G. Kees was born on April 9, 1852, in Baltimore, Maryland. He attended public schools there and early on decided on a career in architecture. He entered the firm of E. G. Lind in Baltimore as an apprentice in 1865 and continued to be employed there until 1878. He moved to Minneapolis that year and worked briefly with Leroy Buffington before entering partnership with Burnham W. Fisk. In 1884 he joined with Franklin Long in a partnership that was to become one of the most successful in the Twin Cities in the nineteenth century. It ended in 1898 when Kees left to try his luck in private practice, but after a couple of years he went into business with Serenus Colburn in another highly successful venture. Colburn died in 1927 and Kees formed a relatively brief partnership with Harry G. Bowstead, which ended with Kees' death on March 16, 1927, in Minneapolis. Bowstead maintained the firm until his own death in 1943.

Notable Buildings

KEES & FISK
Syndicate Block (later J.C. Penney), Minneapolis (1882) (razed 1989)
Grand Opera House, Minneapolis (1883) (razed 1897)
James Clark residence, 2119 3rd Avenue S., Minneapolis (1884)

LONG & KEES
Minneapolis Public Library, Minneapolis (1884) (razed 1959)
Lumber Exchange, Hennepin Avenue and S. 5th Street, Minneapolis (1885, 1887)
Donaldson's Glass Block, Minneapolis (1888) (razed 1982)
Hawthorne Terrace Apartments, 20–26 N. 15th Street, Minneapolis (1892)
William Nott residence, 15 Groveland Terrace, Minneapolis (1892)
Minneapolis City Hall and Courthouse, 4th Street and 3rd Avenue S., Minneapolis (1895–1905)

KEES & COLBURN
Grain Exchange (originally Chamber of Commerce Building), 4th Street S. and 4th Avenue S., Minneapolis (1900–02)
Advance Thresher warehouse, 700 S. 3rd Street, Minneapolis (1900–04)
Orpheum Theatre (later the Seventh Street Theater), Minneapolis (1904) (razed 1940)

Walter Keith (1866–1951)
Walter Jewett Keith was born in Minneapolis on August 17, 1866. His early life, including education and career, is rather shadowy. He first surfaces in Minneapolis

architectural circles as a partner in the firm of (Fred H.) Dodge & Keith (1890), and then he went into business with George Bertrand from 1890 to 1894. After that he launched out on his own with a company that eventually became known as The Keith Company. It was a veritable plan factory; Keith's stock-in-trade was the production of building plans, mainly for residences, which could be ordered off the shelf by customers who most likely saw them either in his newspaper column or in *Keith's Magazine,* published by brother Max L. Keith beginning about 1899.

In 1899, Keith's success can be appreciated by the fact that he had 750 commissions that year worth more than $2 million, consisting of churches, schools, residences, and town halls. This volume of business made him a wealthy man, as did his involvement in real estate development. For example, he built and owned the Plaza Hotel in Minneapolis, a fashionable address for a time, adjacent to Loring Park and bordered by Hennepin and Lyndale Avenues. His wealth enabled him to build a fifty-foot launch in which he cruised Lake Minnetonka, and which he planned to take south in the winter.

It is not known when Keith retired. He died in Pasadena, California, on April 5, 1951.

Notable Buildings
Sumner McKnight residence, 2200 Park Avenue, Minneapolis (1891) (with George Bertrand)
George Christian country house, Ferndale, Lake Minnetonka (1899)
Trinity Baptist Church, Bryant and Lincoln Avenues, Minneapolis (1904)
Plaza Hotel, 1700 Hennepin Avenue, Minneapolis (1905) (razed 1960)
Powers Dry Goods Company, 5th Street and Nicollet Avenue, Minneapolis (1906) (razed 1993)
Walter Keith residence, 421 Clifton Avenue, Minneapolis (1911)

Powers Dry Goods Company, Minneapolis, 1906 (Walter Keith). *Photograph 1937 by Minneapolis Star Journal. Courtesy of Minnesota Historical Society.*

Ernest Kennedy (1864–1938)

Ernest J. Kennedy was born in Mankato, Minnesota, in 1864, the son of James Kennedy, a lawyer. He moved to Minneapolis with his family ten years later and attended the University of Minnesota for an undetermined number of years beginning in 1888, but he did not graduate. He then entered the Sorbonne in Paris and later studied at Berlin Polytechnic and Munich Polytechnic, and is said to have also studied in Italy, Spain, and Russia, although it is not known which institutions he attended. He returned to Minneapolis in 1897 and set up what became a very successful practice, specializing in the design of large and prestigious residences for the city's wealthier citizens.

Kennedy died suddenly in Minneapolis on January 11, 1938, collapsing in front of the Minneapolis Athletic Club. His practice was continued by Hiram Livingston until the early 1970s.

Notable Buildings
Alfred Pillsbury residence, 116 E. 22nd Street, Minneapolis (1905)
Shevlin Hall, University of Minnesota, Minneapolis (1905)
Essex Building, 10th Street and Nicollet Avenue, Minneapolis (1911)
E. C. Gale residence (now American Association of University Women), 2115 Stevens Avenue S., Minneapolis (1911)
Rufus Rand residence, 4551 E. Lake Harriet Boulevard, Minneapolis (1915)
Howard McMillan residence, 1821 James Avenue S., Minneapolis (1929)
Lakewood Cemetery administration building, 3600 Hennepin Avenue, Minneapolis (1929)

William Kenyon (1863–1940)

William Marsh Kenyon was born in Hudson Falls, New York, on April 3, 1863. He graduated from Boston Normal School in 1884 and came to Minneapolis in 1893. He worked in private practice until 1913, and then formed a partnership with Maurice Maine that lasted until 1929. Kenyon and Maine were appointed architects of the New Carnelia Company to develop the mining town of Ajo, Arizona, in 1914. Kenyon was also chief architect of the Soo Line Railroad for twenty years and served on the advisory board for the Greater University (of Minnesota) Campus in 1909. After the partnership with Maine ended, Kenyon continued in private practice until his retirement in 1935.

He died in La Jolla, California, on February 4, 1940.

Notable Buildings
John G. Glueck residence, 2447 Bryant Avenue S., Minneapolis (1902)
Lyman Court apartments, Minneapolis (1905) (razed 1978)

Shevlin Hall, University of Minnesota, Minneapolis, 1905 (Ernest Kennedy). *Photograph ca. 1907 by Sweet. Courtesy of Minnesota Historical Society.*

John G. Glueck residence, Minneapolis, 1902 (William Kenyon and Maurice Maine). *Photograph by David Gebhard. Courtesy of Northwest Architectural Archives, University of Minnesota.*

George Lyman warehouse (later Warner Hardware Company), Minneapolis (1906) (razed 1979)
Amphitheatre, Minnesota State Fair Grounds, St. Paul (1906) (razed 1948)
Soo Line building, 5th Street and Marquette Avenue (1924) (with Mauria Maine and Robert Gibson)

Frank Kerr (B. 1914)

Francis Kenneth Kerr was born on May 22, 1914, in Montreal, Quebec. He graduated from high school in Washington, D.C., in 1929 and received a bachelor's degree (1933) and a master's degree (1938) in architecture, both from George Washington University in Washington, D.C. He worked in the Federal Housing Administration (FHA) from 1938 to 1941 and then as a cost engineer in the Underwriter Division of the FHA from 1941 to 1946. Kerr also served briefly in the U.S. Coast Guard in 1942.

His first job as an architect was with the architectural firm of Weihe and Gibbs in Washington, D.C., as a designer (1946). The next year he moved to Minneapolis and was employed with Hills, Gilbertson and Hayes. In 1948 he joined Shifflet, Backstrom and Carter and then left to form his own practice in 1950. He entered partnership with Harlan McClure in 1952, which dissolved in 1955. Kerr then merged his practice with that of Harley Johnson in 1957. The partnership split up in 1960 and formally ended in 1962.

Kerr was employed as a draftsman and project manager with Baker-Lange, Inc., in Minnneapolis in 1967 and then moved to the office of Bettenburg, Townsend, Stolte and Comb in St. Paul as chief architect in 1968. Around 1971 he and Jay Tyson established a practice in Minneapolis, which ended in 1977 and both men resumed private practice. Kerr retired in the 1990s.

Grace Lutheran Church, St. Paul, 1957 (Frank Kerr and Harley Johnson). *Photograph 1961 by C. J. Larson. Courtesy of Minnesota Historical Society.*

Notable Buildings
Grace Lutheran Church, 1730 Old Hudson Road, St. Paul (1957) (with Harley Johnson)
Greyhound Bus Depot, Mankato (1957–58) (with Harley Johnson)
Stan Clinton residence, Essex Road, Minneapolis (1958) (with Harley Johnson)

Robert Kilgore (B. 1923)
Robert Austin Kilgore was born in Minneapolis on January 20, 1923. He attended public schools in the city and graduated from Washburn High School in 1941. In 1949 he received a bachelor's degree in architecture from the University of Minnesota and subsequently began working as a draftsman in the contracting firm of James Leck in Minneapolis. About 1950 he joined McEnary and Krafft, architects, where he remained for the rest of his career, becoming a partner in 1963. He retired from practice about 2004.

Notable Buildings

WITH MERRILL BIRCH, EDWIN KRAFFT, AND DALE MCENARY
Farmers and Mechanics National Bank (now Westin Hotel), 88 S. 6th Street, Minneapolis (1940, adds. 1955, 1961)

Aldersgate Methodist Church, 3801 Wooddale Avenue, St. Louis Park (1951)
Valleyview Hospital and Sanitarium, Jordan (1956)
Peace Presbyterian Church, 7624 Cedar Lake Road, St. Louis Park (1957)
Minneapolis Public Library, Minneapolis (1959) (with Lang & Raugland) (razed 2003)

Wesley King (1879–1959)
Wesley Eugene King was born in Monticello, Minnesota, on July 12, 1879. He attended the University of Minnesoa and received a degree in civil engineering in 1905. King worked for the Bridge Department of the Great Northern Railroad before joining Toltz Engineering Company in 1910. He remained in the company and assumed charge after the deaths of Max Toltz and Beaver Wade Day.
King died in St. Paul on June 4, 1959.

Notable Buildings

WITH MAX TOLTZ
West Publishing Company (now Ramsey County Government Center West), 50 Kellogg Boulevard, St. Paul (1910–11) (Reed & Stem, architects)
Sanitary Foods Manufacturing Company (now Griggs Midway building), 1821 University Avenue, St. Paul (1912)

WITH MAX TOLTZ AND BEAVER DAY
Hamm Building, 408 St. Peter Street, St. Paul (1919)
St. Paul Gas Light Company Service Building (now Xcel Energy), 825 Rice Street, St. Paul (1924)
Robert Street Bridge, St. Paul (1926)

Frank Kinney (1857–1929)
Frank W. Kinney was born in Canada in 1857. His early life and career is unknown. He came to Minnesota and worked as a contractor and, in 1886, settled in Austin where he set up shop as an architect. A decade later he became a partner of Henry Orth and they moved their practice to Minneapolis in 1902. He then became a partner of Menno Detwiler until 1904. Kinney practiced privately for a few years before joining Frank E. Halden in partnership in 1909. The following year he was in business with Joseph Jogerst and then, in 1915, became a partner of William Macomber for about a year. After that, it appears he resumed private practice.
Kinney appears to have worked almost up to his death on June 6, 1929, in Minneapolis.

Notable Buildings
Winneshiek County Courthouse, Decorah, Iowa (1902) (with Menno Detwiler)
Brown County Courthouse, Aberdeen, South Dakota (ca. 1904) (with Menno Detwiler)
Langlade County Courthouse, Antigo, Wisconsin (1904–05) (with Menno Detwiler)
Lafayette County Courthouse, Darlington, Wisconsin (1905)
High School, Northfield (1910) (possibly with Joseph Jogerst)
Calhoun Commercial Club, 705–711 W. Lake Street, Minneapolis (1913)

C. LeRoy Kinports (CA. 1884–1956)
Charles LeRoy Kinports was born in Pennsylvania about 1884. Nothing is known of his early life or where he lived and worked before coming to Minneapolis about

1900. He first appears as a draftsman in Edwin Overmire's office in 1902, where he stayed for about two years. By 1910 he had joined the firm of Long, Lamoreaux & Long, and then he opened his own office in 1916. Kinports formed a partnership with Charles Bell about 1920, but it seems to have been dissolved within a year or so, and Kinports was on his own again until around 1925. He moved to Florida and established a practice with a partner named Blohm. Together they designed some of the famous Streamline Moderne apartment houses in Miami Beach.

Kinports died in Coconut Grove, Florida, on January 12, 1956.

Notable Buildings
Ironwood Memorial Building, Ironwood, Michigan (1922) (with Charles Bell)
Brisa Del Mar Apartments, Miami Beach, Florida (1929) (with Blohm)
Chevy Chase Apartments, Miami Beach, Florida (1936) (with Blohm)

George Klein Jr. (B. 1923)
George Frederick Klein Jr. was born on September 15, 1923, in Minneapolis. He was educated at Ravenscourt High School in Winnipeg, Manitoba, graduating in 1939. He then attended the University of Manitoba for two years before transferring to the University of Minnesota where he received a bachelor's degree in architecture in March 1949.

Klein first worked part-time as a draftsman in the office of Magney, Tusler and Setter in Minneapolis (1947–49), becoming a full-time employee in the firm after graduation. He joined Haarstick and Lundgren in St. Paul in 1950 and was made an associate in 1953. He left for employment with Hammel and Green about a year later and was elected vice president in 1956. In 1968, he became a partner of Leonard Parker in Minneapolis, which dissolved when Klein bought out Parker's interest in 1977. Klein then set up a new practice with Richard J. McCarthy. He retired about 1993. The firm continued as Klein McCarthy and Company, Ltd.

Notable Buildings
Salem Baptist Church, 1995 Silver Lake Road, New Brighton (1966) (with Hammel Green and Abrahamson)

WITH LEONARD PARKER
Student housing, Southwest State University, Marshall (1968–72)
Elliott Hall, University of Minnesota, Minneapolis (1973–74)
Minneapolis Institute of Arts addition, 2400 3rd Avenue S., Minneapolis (1973–74) (with Kenzo Tange)
Law School (now Walter F. Mondale Hall), University of Minnesota, Minneapolis (1977)

Marvin Kline (1903–1974)
Marvin L. Kline was born in Brunswick, Nebraska, on August 9, 1903. He was educated at the University of Minnesota, where he received his degree in architectural engineering in 1929. He was employed from 1928 to 1929 by Northern States Power Company on transmission line work and in steam stations, and he also worked on drainage projects and did townsite work for the Chicago and Northwestern Railroad. From 1929 to 1934 Kline was office and field manager of the Riverside steam station in Minneapolis and the Granite Falls (Minn.) station. He was also a highway engineer for the state of Minnesota. In 1934, he joined Wessel & Brunet as a partner and continued in the firm while serving as mayor of

Washington County Courthouse, Stillwater, 1869 (Augustus Knight). *Photograph 1914 by John Runk. Courtesy of Minnesota Historical Society.*

Minneapolis (1941–44) and as executive director of the Sister Kenny Foundation. At some unknown date, he left architectural practice. In 1963, he went on trial on charges of mail fraud and grand larceny in connection with fund-raising for the Sister Kenny Foundation. He was found guilty and served three years in the Minnesota State Penitentiary.

Kline died in Ventura, California, on April 9, 1974.

Notable Buildings
Flame Bar and Café, 1521 Nicollet Avenue, Minneapolis (1938) (razed 1978) (with Hans Wessel)

Augustus Knight (1831–1914)
Augustus F. Knight was born on November 22, 1831, in Warren, New York. His father was a professor at Harvard College. As a youth, he worked as a laborer on farms and learned the carpentry trade. Knight attended Polytechnic School (later Rensselaer Polytechnic Institute) in Troy, New York. In 1844, he moved with his parents to Buffalo, New York, where he obtained an apprenticeship as a draftsman in the architectural office of Sage, Wilcox & Rush. He remained there until 1857, then moved to Chicago where he stayed two months before moving on to St. Anthony

Farmers and Mechanics National Bank (now Westin Hotel), Minneapolis, 1940, 1955, 1961 (Edwin Krafft, Dale McEnary, Merrill Birch, and Robert Kilgore). *Photograph 1963 by Norton & Peel. Courtesy of Minnesota Historical Society.*

and subsequently St. Paul with a fellow student from his days in Buffalo, H. P. Thompson. Except for a two-year sojourn in St. Louis (1859–61) and brief service in the army during the Sioux uprising of 1862, Knight lived in St. Paul the rest of his life. He set up a private practice in 1861 and maintained it until 1912, with the exception of a short period in the 1880s when he was in partnership with William Castner. He once said that he built no buildings of which, from an artistic standpoint, he was very proud, but at the same time, he was not ashamed of any of them, either.

Knight died in St. Paul on April 17, 1914.

Notable Buildings
William Le Duc residence, Hastings (1861)
St. Mary's Catholic Church, St. Paul (1866–67) (razed ca. 1938)
Washington County Courthouse, Stillwater (1869)

Edwin Krafft (1901–1986)
Edwin W. Krafft was born in Minneapolis on September 26, 1901. He was the great-grandson of Samuel Pond, a pioneer missionary who came to the area in 1834. Krafft graduated from West High School and attended Dartmouth College and the University of Minnesota, where he received his degree in architecture in 1924. He traveled to Europe following graduation and then returned to Minneapolis to become an instructor in the University's School of Architecture (1925–27). Krafft worked at the same time for Magney & Tusler before joining Dale McEnary as an associate in 1931. In 1934 they became partners.

Krafft served as chairman of the Edina Planning Commission from 1943 to 1956 and as president of the Minnesota chapter of the American Institute of Architects. He retired in 1969 and continued to be active in various civic and religious groups until suffering a stroke in 1976.

Angus Hotel (now Blair Apartments), St. Paul, 1887 (Hermann Kretz and William Thomas), St. Paul. Photograph ca. 1930 by Charles P. Gibson. Courtesy of Minnesota Historical Society.

He died in Bloomington, Minnesota, on November 25, 1986.

Notable Buildings
Rufus Rand residence (now Cargill Inc. headquarters), 15407 W. McGinty Road, Minnetonka (1934) (with Dale McEnary)
Farmers and Mechanics National Bank (now Westin Hotel), 88 S. 6th Street, Minneapolis (1940, adds. 1955, 1961) (with Dale McEnary, Merrill Birch and Robert Kilgore)
Minneapolis Public Library, Minneapolis (1959) (razed 2003) (McEnary, Krafft & Birch with Lang & Raugland)

Hermann Kretz (1860–1931)
Hermann Kretz was born in Essen, Germany, on May 20, 1860. At the age of nineteen, Kretz went to work for his uncle as an architect, after completing his education at the University of Essen and the Technical School at Holzminden. About 1880 he immigrated to the United States and worked in New York City, Chicago, Winnipeg, and various other cities before settling in St. Paul in 1886. Kretz became wealthy not only from his highly successful architectural practice but also from real estate investments, including the Commerce building in downtown St. Paul which he designed and built in 1912.

Kretz died in St. Paul on May 10, 1931.

Notable Buildings
Angus Hotel (now Blair Apartments), 165 N. Western Avenue, St. Paul (1887) (with William Thomas)
St. Boniface Catholic Church, Hastings (1893) (dismantled and rebuilt on another site 1996)
St. John Cantius Catholic Church, Wilno (1901)
Church of St. Wenceslaus, New Prague (1906–07)
Commerce building, 4th and Wabasha Streets, St. Paul (1912)

Central YMCA, Minneapolis, 1917 (Lowell Lamoreaux, Louis Long, and Olaf Thorshov). *Photograph 1937 by Norton & Peel. Courtesy of Minnesota Historical Society.*

Lowell Lamoreaux (1861–1922)
Lowell A. Lamoreaux was born in Lansing, Minnesota, on December 23, 1861. At the age of seven, he and his family moved to Minneapolis, where he attended the public schools and graduated from Central High School. He attended the University of Minnesota, from which he graduated in 1887, and after working in Chicago for a short time, was employed

in Cass Gilbert's office in St. Paul about 1892. He became a partner of James McLeod in 1895, and in 1899 joined the firm of Long & Long as an associate. He became a full partner in 1909, the firm then being renamed as Long, Lamoreaux & Long. After Franklin Long's death in 1912, Lamoreaux continued as a partner of Louis Long, Franklin's son, and of Olaf Thorshov, who became a partner in 1920. Lamoreaux moved to Los Angeles, California, in 1921 and returned to Minneapolis for surgery about a year later. He died on February 1, 1922, of pneumonia following surgery.

Notable Buildings
Lamoreaux residence, 39 Seymour Street SE, Minneapolis (1888)
M. H. Boutell residence, 1123 Mt. Curve Avenue, Minneapolis (1895)

WITH FRANKLIN LONG AND LOUIS LONG
Minneapolis City Hospital, Minneapolis (1906) (razed 1977)
Minneapolis Gas and Light Company, Minneapolis (1910–11) (razed 1981)

WITH LOUIS LONG AND OLAF THORSHOV
Central YMCA, (now Oakwood Minneapolis) 9th Street and La Salle Avenue, Minneapolis (1917)
Curtis Hotel, Minneapolis (1922) (razed 1984)

Oscar Lang (1888–1960)
Oscar Theodore Lang was born on August 25, 1888, in Minneapolis, and spent almost his entire life and career in the city. He received his early education in Sweden, where he traveled with his mother for three years. He was awarded a bachelor's degree in architecture from the University of Pennsylvania. From 1915 to 1922 he worked as a designer and chief draftsman in the firms of Cecil Chapman (1908), Hewitt and Brown (1912–20), and Long, Lamoreaux and Long (1920–21) in Minneapolis. He worked briefly for the Board of Education as a designer, and then became a partner of Arnold L. Raugland and Carroll E. Lewis in 1922, a partnership that lasted the rest of his career.

Lang & Raugland (Lewis left the firm in 1930) was noted for its large corporate and institutional designs, such as banks, factories, office buildings, and churches. With the demise of the original partners in the 1960s, the firm became known as Entrikin, Domholt & King and continued in business until the 1980s.

Lang died on December 10, 1960, in Minneapolis.

Notable Buildings

LANG, RAUGLAND & LEWIS
Frank Griswold residence, 56 Russell Avenue, Minneapolis (1926)
Bethlehem Lutheran Church, 4100 Lyndale Avenue S., Minneapolis (1928)
St. Andrew's Episcopal Church, 1832 James Avenue N., Minneapolis (1928)

LANG & RAUGLAND
Greyhound Bus Depot (now First Avenue), 701 1st Avenue N., Minneapolis (1936)
Alpha Kappa Psi fraternity house, 1116 5th Street SE, Minneapolis (1950–52)
Aldrich Avenue Presbyterian Church, 3501 Aldrich Avenue S., Minneapolis (1952)
First Presbyterian Church, Minot, North Dakota (1956)
Winona State College classroom building, Winona (1963–64)

Greyhound Bus Depot (now First Avenue and 7th Street Entry), Minneapolis, 1936 (Lang & Raugland). *Photograph by Charles W. Howson Company. Courtesy of Minnesota Historical Society.*

Ananias Langdon (1812–1893)
Ananias Langdon was born in Saratoga County, New York, in 1812. He moved to Troy, New York, to practice architecture and resided there until 1855, when he relocated to Winona, Minnesota, and opened an office in the young community. His obituary noted that he used crutches as a result of an accident that occurred about 1883, and that his life in Winona was "quiet and uneventful"—so much so that little is known of his life and work.

Langdon died in Rochester, Minnesota, on July 8, 1893.

Notable Buildings
St. Paul's Episcopal Church, Winona (1873)

Austin Lange (1910–1978)
Knowledge of many details of Austin H. Lange's life is lacking. He was born in La Crosse, Wisconsin, on April 5, 1910. It is not known where he received his education. He served in the U.S. Navy from 1942 to 1945, was a partner of Edward Baker in Minneapolis from 1964 to 1973 and was a stained glass designer in addition to being an architect.

Lange died on June 22, 1978, in Minneapolis, and is buried in Fort Snelling National Cemetery.

Notable Buildings
L'Hotel Sofitel, 5600 W. 78th Street, Bloomington (1970) (with Edward Baker)

IDS Center, 80 S. 8th Street, Minneapolis (1970–74) (Baker-Lange Associates with Johnson and Burgee, New York)

Albert Larson (1893–1974)
Albert Oliver Larson was born in St. Paul on August 24, 1893. He received his professional training at the University of Pennsylvania where he studied architecture from 1912 to 1915. He returned to St. Paul and studied in the Atelier Masqueray in 1916, a studio operated by Emmanuel Masqueray. He was also employed as a draftsman from 1912 to 1917 by Allen Stem. Larson worked briefly for Clarence H. Johnston in 1917 and for Toltz, King & Day in 1919. From 1919 to 1922 he was in the firm of Magney & Tusler of Minneapolis. In 1922 he and Donald McLaren formed a partnership that lasted the rest of their lives. The firm survived them and finally went out of business in 1980.

Larson died in Boca Raton, Florida, on October 28, 1974.

Notable Buildings

LARSON & MCLAREN
Baker Block, 706 2nd Avenue S., Minneapolis (1927)
Groveland Apartment Hotel (now 510 Groveland), 510 Groveland Avenue, Minneapolis (1929)
Plymouth Building (refacing), 12 S. 6th Street, Minneapolis (1936)
Minneapolis Star Journal and Tribune Building, 425 Portland Avenue, Minneapolis (1940, 1944–45)
Radisson Hotel (refacing), Minneapolis (1947) (razed 1982)

Stowell Leach (1906–1994)
Stowell Douglas Leach was born on December 19, 1906, in Faribault, Minnesota. He attended public schools and graduated from Faribault High School in 1925. He entered the University of Minnesota and graduated with a bachelor's degree in architecture in 1929. From 1929

Groveland Apartment Hotel (now 510 Groveland), Minneapolis, 1929 (Larson & McLaren). *Photograph courtesy of Northwest Architectural Archives, University of Minnesota.*

to 1930 he worked in the office of J. C. Pendergast, Minneapolis architect, as a junior draftsman, and then was employed by General Bronze Corporation in Minneapolis (part of Flour City Ornamental Iron Works) from 1930 to 1932. Leach moved to Niles, Michigan, and worked for the Kawneer Company from 1934 to 1936 as senior draftsman and squad leader.

In 1936 he returned to Minneapolis and joined McEnary & Krafft as draftsman, designer, and specifications writer. He remained with them until 1941, then moved to Great Falls, Montana, where he was a member of the firm of Shanley, Van Teylingen & Henningston, architects & engineers. It is likely that he met John Lindstrom there, and the two followed the same track through a series of wartime construction firms. Later that same year he joined Sanderson & Porter in Pine Bluff, Arkansas, as a specifications writer and head of the production department. In 1943, Leach moved yet again, to Edmonton, Alberta, to work for Metcalfe-Hamilton-Kansas City Bridge Company. The following year he returned to Minneapolis and entered the firm of Magney, Tusler & Setter, where he remained for the rest of his career, eventually becoming a partner (Setter, Leach & Lindstrom, now Leo A. Daly).

It is not known when Leach retired. He died in Minneapolis on September 29, 1994.

Notable Buildings

SETTER, LEACH & LINDSTROM
Christ Chapel, Gustavus Adolphus College, St. Peter (1961)
Entomology, Fisheries and Wildlife Building (Hodson Hall), University of Minnesota, St. Paul (1969)
Normandale Office Park, Normandale Boulevard and 82nd Street, Bloomington (1972)
Folke Bernadotte Memorial Library, Gustavus Adolphus College, St. Peter (1972)
Richfield Bank and Trust Company, 6625 Lyndale Avenue S., Richfield (1972)

Charles Leonard (1815–?)
Charles S. Leonard was born in either Rochester or Springfield, Massachusetts, in 1815. Nothing is known of his life and career until he emerged in St. Paul in 1860, working as a master carpenter. By then he was married and had five children. About 1868 he became a partner of Monroe and Romaine Sheire in an architecture and contracting company. Four years later he joined John Seeger in a similar business that lasted until about 1877. It is possible that he left the city in the early 1880s and moved to South Dakota for a few years, probably working as an architect and builder, but by 1890 he was in Albert Lea.

His place and date of death are unknown.

Notable Buildings

WITH MONROE SHEIRE
Alexander Ramsey residence, 265 Exchange Street, St. Paul (1868–72)
Church of St. Joseph, St. Joseph (1871)

Jack Liebenberg (1893–1985)
Jacob J. "Jack" Liebenberg was born in Milwaukee, Wisconsin, on July 4, 1893. He attended the University of Minnesota and graduated in the first class from the newly formed School of Architecture in 1916. He received a scholarship to Harvard

Hollywood Theater, Minneapolis, 1935 (Liebenberg & Kaplan). Photograph courtesy of Northwest Architectural Archives, University of Minnesota.

University and took his master's degree from there the following year. Liebenberg served in the Army Air Corps in World War I, part of that time in an aircraft engine factory in St. Paul. He returned to Minneapolis after the war and worked for a short time with D. C. Bennett's firm while teaching at the university's School of Architecture. He then formed a partnership in 1920 with Robert C. Martin and, a year or so later, with one of his former students, Seeman Kaplan (whose sister Liebenberg married). From 1923 on, the firm was known as Liebenberg & Kaplan and became one of the most successful in the Twin Cities.

Liebenberg & Kaplan made a specialty of designing prestigious homes, Jewish temples, and movie theaters. Several of the latter were in the Art Deco style. They also operated a contracting company, Cardell, which built many of their buildings and which was terminated about 1960.

After Kaplan died in 1963, Liebenberg remained in business with partners Saul Smiley and Joel Glotter. He left the partnership in 1973 and set up a small private practice, which he maintained until his retirement in 1980.

Liebenberg died in Edina, Minnesota, on March 23, 1985.

Notable Buildings

LIEBENBERG & KAPLAN

Granada Theater (later Suburban World), 3022 Hennepin Avenue, Minneapolis (1928)

Hollywood Theater, 2815 Johnson Street NE, Minneapolis (1935)

Fargo Theater, Fargo, North Dakota (1936)

Varsity Theater, 1308 4th Street SE, Minneapolis (1938)

NorShor Theater, Duluth (1938)

Uptown Theater, 2906 Hennepin Avenue, Minneapolis (1938)

John Lindstrom (1915–1995)

Lester John Lindstrom was born in Minneapolis on April 17, 1915. He graduated from North High School in 1932 and attended the University of Minnesota, where he spent three years in the College of Science, Literature, and the Arts before taking a degree in architecture after another four years of study, in 1940. He received his master's degree in architecture from the Massachusetts Institute of Technology the following year.

From March to September 1940, he was a junior draftsman in the Minneapolis firm of Wessel, Brunet & Kline. A year later, with the onset of World War II, he began a series of defense industry jobs with several architects and engineers. He moved to Great Falls, Montana, and worked for Shanley, Van Teylingen & Henningston as a senior draftsman from September to December 1941, where he probably met Stowell Leach. He next joined Sanderson & Porter Construction Company in New York City as senior draftsman and architectural designer, remaining there until January 1943. Lindstrom relocated to Edmonton, Alberta, to work for Metcalfe-Hamilton-Kansas City Bridge Company as a senior draftsman and architectural designer through 1943. He returned to Minneapolis in August 1945 and joined Magney, Tusler & Setter as a designer. He remained with that firm for the rest of his career. He became a partner in 1952.

Lindstrom died on March 14, 1995, in Fountain Hills, Arizona.

Notable Buildings

SETTER LEACH & LINDSTROM
Christ Chapel, Gustavus Adolphus College, St. Peter (1961)
Entomology, Fisheries and Wildlife Building (Hodson Hall), University of Minnesota, St. Paul (1969)
Normandale Office Park, Normandale Boulevard and 82nd Street, Bloomington (1972)
Folke Bernadotte Memorial Library, Gustavus Adolphus College, St. Peter (1972)
Richfield Bank and Trust Company, 6625 Lyndale Avenue S., Richfield (1972)

John W. Lindstrom (1874–1962)

John W. Lindstrom was born in Gottenburg, Sweden, in 1874. He came to the United States at an early age. Nothing is known of his training and experience prior to settling in Minneapolis as a cabinetmaker in 1902. The following year he was employed as a draftsman by Fremont Orff. He then opened an architectural practice, partnering first with Ora W. Williams (1906) and then Joseph Almars (1907–16). He established a private practice in 1916 and continued to operate it for many years. He became quite successful, designing many residences and commercial buildings.

Lindstrom retired in 1956 and died in Minneapolis on January 18, 1962.

Notable Buildings
Adirondack Apartments, 608–610 S. 9th Street, Minneapolis (1911)
Franklin Theater, 1021 E. Franklin Avenue, Minneapolis (1915)
Fred Soderberg residence, 112 W. Minnehaha Parkway, Minneapolis (1924)
Oscar Peterson residence, 5049 Belmont Avenue S., Minneapolis (1926)
Delta Zeta sorority house, 1100 4th Street SE, Minneapolis (1927)

Peter Linhoff (1876–1954)

Peter J. Linhoff was born in Shakopee, Minnesota, on July 21, 1876. The facts of his life are very sketchy. Nothing is known of his education or early career. He appeared in St. Paul about 1899 as a draftsman with Louis Lockwood and remained in the firm to succeed the latter after his death in 1907. Linhoff continued in practice until his retirement in 1940.

He died in St. Paul on January 24, 1954.

Notable Buildings
C. P. Waldon residence, 942 Summit Avenue, St. Paul (1908)
Van Slyke residence, 1180 Summit Avenue, St. Paul (1909)
Robert S. Waddell residence, 693 Goodrich Avenue, St. Paul (1915)

Hiram Livingston (1889–1981)

Hiram Harold Livingston was born in Walcott, Minnesota, on May 13, 1889. He studied for two years at the Armour Institute (now Illinois Institute of Technology) in Chicago and in 1914 at the Art Institute of Chicago. Little is known of his professional career except that he spent fifteen and a half years as a draftsman in several firms, and was in private practice for three and a half years up to 1930. He joined Ernest Kennedy in Minneapolis for the last two years of Kennedy's life (1936–38) and assumed the latter's business after his death in 1938.

Livingston retired about 1972 and died in Sun City, California, on February 16, 1981.

Notable Buildings
Ruth Boynton residence, 2738 W. River Road, Minneapolis (1939)
Bernice Gestie residence, 15 Melbourne Avenue SE, Minneapolis (1940)

Louis Lockwood (1865–1907)

Louis F. Lockwood was born in London, England, in 1865. His father, Francis Lockwood, was an artist. Young Lockwood graduated from Kings College, Cambridge, in 1885 and studied architecture in architects' offices in London for a year after graduation. He came to the United States in 1889 and settled first in Portland, Oregon. After working there for a brief time, he moved successively to Seattle, Washington, and San Francisco, California, before coming to St. Paul about 1892. He set up a practice that soon became extremely busy and very successful, so much so that he died of pernicious anemia brought on from overwork.

Lockwood's sobering obituary in the St. Paul *Pioneer Press* summed up the intensity with which he lived his life: "[His] earnestness and devotion [to the profession] seems to have carried him too far. He was the victim of his own professional zeal. With success he did not learn to shift enough of the burden of details to others... As long as there was anything to be done, rest meant nothing to him. In his enthusiasm he burned the candle at both ends and died, to all intents, a victim of too intense devotion to his profession. Had he learned to spare himself and to husband his strength, had he learned the real economy of recreation and of moderation in work, he would perhaps have lived for many years and the city in which he lived would have been the gainer."

His death occurred the day after the first anniversary of his marriage to his wife, Elizabeth. At the time of his death, on November 28, 1907, Lockwood was in partnership with Peter Linhoff, who assumed the practice.

Notable Buildings
Winsted City Hall, Winsted (1895)
Charles Straus residence, 842 Summit Avenue, St. Paul (1898)
William Bannon residence, 1009 Summit Avenue, St. Paul (1901)
C. F. Arral residence, 726 Summit Avenue, St. Paul (1903)
J. T. Landers residence, 786 Summit Avenue, St. Paul (1905)
Farwell, Ozmun & Kirk building (Ramsey County Government Center East), 150–160 Kellogg Boulevard E., St. Paul (1905–06)

Franklin Long (1842–1912)
Franklin Bidwell Long was born in South Bainbridge, New York, on March 3, 1842. He attended the public schools and local village academy, and was especially adept in mathematics and mechanical arts. In 1859 the family moved to Woodstock, Illinois, where Long went to work in a variety of jobs. He left the family and relocated to Chicago where he worked as a carpenter and builder, subsequently becoming interested in architecture. He entered the office of J. C. Cochrane as an apprentice draftsman and after a year formed a partnership with a fellow apprentice named Ackerman.

Long moved to Minneapolis in 1868 and opened an office on Bridge Square, subsequently entering partnership with Robert Alden, an architect already established in the city. After the latter's death in 1877, Long went into business with Charles Haglin, while dabbling in real estate on the side. The partnership ended in the early 1880s. Long built the Kasota Block at the corner of 4th Street and Hennepin Avenue in 1884 and joined with Frederick Kees in a very successful

Farwell, Ozmun & Kirk building (now Ramsey County Government Center East), St. Paul, 1905-6 (Louis Lockwood). *Photograph ca. 1907 by Charles P. Gibson. Courtesy of Minnesota Historical Society.*

Masonic Temple (now Hennepin Center for the Arts), Minneapolis, 1888 (Franklin Long & Frederick Kees). *Photograph courtesy of Northwest Architectural Archives, University of Minnesota.*

practice that had offices in the building. When Kees left the firm in 1898, Long formed a partnership with his son, Louis, who continued the practice until the mid-1920s.

Long died at his home in Minneapolis on August 21, 1912.

Notable Buildings

WITH FREDERICK KEES

First Baptist Church, 10th Street and Harmon Place, Minneapolis (1883–85)

Kasota Block, 326–332 Hennepin Avenue, Minneapolis (1884) (razed 1960)

Minneapolis Public Library, 10th Street and Hennepin Avenue, Minneapolis (1884) (razed 1961)

Masonic Temple (now Hennepin Center for the Arts), 6th Street and Hennepin Avenue, Minneapolis (1888)

Long & Kees

In the late 1880s, Franklin Long and Frederick Kees joined in what became one of the most successful architectural practices in the history of Minneapolis. Long, a native of New York, met Kees, a native of Maryland, in 1884 and they set up their partnership. It lasted until 1898 when Kees left to form his own firm. Long made his son, Louis, a partner and then, in 1909, added Louis Lamoreaux, who had been in the firm for some years.

Franklin Long died in 1912, but the firm carried on as Long, Lamoreaux and Long until the early 1920s when, first Lamoreaux, and then a few years later Louis Long, died. By 1926, there was no one in the firm bearing the name of Long. However, it was so well-known that Olaf Thorshov, who was made a partner in 1920, continued the name as Long and Thorshov. His premature death in 1928 led his son, Roy, to assume the practice and he maintained it, with the name intact, until 1942. Then he and his new partner, Robert Cerny, renamed it Thorshov and Cerny. This partnership was dissolved in 1960 and two practices emerged: (Willard) Thorsen and Thorshov, and Cerny and Associates. Thorsen and Thorshov sold their firm to Hammel, Green and Abrahamson in 1987 and retired, and Robert Cerny continued his firm until he retired in 1978 and closed the office, ending a continuous lineage of more than a century.

Plymouth Building, Minneapolis, 1909–10 (Louis Long and Lowell Lamoreaux). *Photograph 1912 by Charles J. Hibbard. Courtesy of Minnesota Historical Society.*

Notable Buildings

WITH LOWELL LAMOREAUX
Radisson Hotel, 41–43 S. 7th Street, Minneapolis (1909) (razed 1982)
Plymouth Building, 12 S. 6th Street, Minneapolis (1909–10)
Central YMCA, 9th Street and La Salle Avenue, Minneapolis (1917)

Louis Lundgren (1919–1991)

Louis Ross Lundgren was born in Leeds, North Dakota, on April 19, 1919. The family moved to St. Paul at an unknown date and he graduated from Johnson High School in 1937. During World War II, he served in a naval construction unit and, after returning from service, graduated from the University of Minnesota with a bachelor's degree in architecture in 1947. Lundgren and Donald Haarstick, along with Grover Dimond Jr., formed a partnership in 1949, which became very successful, specializing in the design of education and public buildings. In the 1960s, Lundgren was a founder and president of the Minnesota Coalition for Affordable Housing, and president of the St. Paul Philharmonic Society. The firm also had an office in San Francisco from about 1957 to 1962.

Haarstick and Lundgren became part of a conglomerate of architects and engineers called Convention Center Architects & Engineers, formed to design the St. Paul Civic Arena and Kellogg Square, both built between 1968 and 1970. The conglomerate was dissolved in 1972 and Haarstick and Lundgren each set up his own practice.

Lundgren continued to maintain his firm in St. Paul until his death on June 17, 1991.

Louis Long (1870–1925)

Louis L. Long, son of Franklin Long, was born in Minneapolis in 1870. He was educated in the Minneapolis public schools and studied architecture at the University of Minnesota, which he attended from 1890 to 1894 without receiving a degree. He entered his father's firm, Long & Kees, and was made a partner after the departure of Kees in 1898. He remained in the practice until his death on May 21, 1925, while en route to California to visit his mother and sister.

Aldrich Arena, Maplewood, 1962 (Haarstick & Lundgren). *Photograph courtesy of Northwest Architectural Archives, University of Minnesota.*

Notable Buildings

HAARSTICK & LUNDGREN

Burnsville High School, 600 Highway 13, Burnsville, (1958)

Aldrich Arena, 1850 White Bear Avenue N., Maplewood (1962)

Harding Senior High School, 1540 E. 6th Street, St. Paul (1965)

John Adams Junior High School, Rochester (1969)

Kellogg Square, 111 E. Kellogg Boulevard, St. Paul (1969-73) (Interpro)

Como Park Senior High School, 740 W. Rose Avenue, St. Paul (1979-80) (Louis Lundgren)

Edwin Lundie (1886-1972)

Edwin Hugh Lundie was born in Cedar Rapids, Iowa, on October 13, 1886. He attended grade school in Cedar Rapids from 1892 to 1899 and continued his education in Salem, North Dakota, after the family moved there while he was in high school. In 1904, Lundie came to St. Paul where he entered the architectural firm of (Cass) Gilbert and (Thomas) Holyoke as an unpaid apprentice. He worked as a stock clerk to make ends meet and in 1907 became a draftsman for Louis Lockwood. Beginning in 1908 Lundie was employed by Holyoke and then in 1913 he joined the office of Emmanuel Masqueray as a draftsman and studied in Masqueray's atelier for a time.

Aberle residence, St. Paul, 1927 (Edwin Lundie). *Photograph 1929. Courtesy of Minnesota Historical Society.*

Lutsen Resort, Lutsen, 1949–60 (Edwin Lundie). *Photograph 1951 by Kenneth Melvin Wright. Courtesy of Minnesota Historical Society.*

Following Masqueray's death in 1917, Lundie, Fred Slifer, and Frank Abrahamson—all former employees—formed a successor firm to finish the uncompleted work on hand in the office. When it was completed, Lundie set up his own practice in St Paul, specializing in prestigious residences, noted for the extremely high quality of workmanship and attention to detail that went into them.

Lundie died in St. Paul on January 8, 1972.

Notable Buildings
Edwin J. Binswanger residence, 73 Otis Lane, St. Paul (1926)
F. E. Weyerhaeuser residence, Manitou Island, White Bear Lake (1926–31)
Aberle residence, 54 Crocus Place, St. Paul (1927)
Thomas Daniels estate, Gem Lake (1930–36)
Lytton J. Shields residence, Dellwood (1938–44)
G. N. Slade house, Birch Bay, Lake County (1940–42)
Lutsen Resort, Lutsen (1949–60)
A. M. Fiterman residence, 2525 Lake of the Isles Parkway E., Minneapolis (1950–53)
Daniel Gainey estate, Owatonna (1960)
Minnesota Landscape Arboretum, Chanhassen (1966–72)

James MacLeod (1870–1912)
James Alan MacLeod was born in Minneapolis on September 27, 1870. He was educated in the public schools and started his career in architecture by working as a student in an architect's office at the age of seventeen. He moved to Denver where he opened a practice and remained until 1893, when he returned to Minneapolis and formed a very busy and prosperous partnership with Lowell Lamoreaux. The partnership dissolved in 1899 when the latter joined Franklin Long, and MacLeod went into private practice. He subsequently moved to St. Paul in 1904 and maintained an office there for about eight years.

MacLeod died in Minneapolis on July 15, 1912.

Notable Buildings
Joyn Dorner residence, 1720 Dupont Avenue S., Minneapolis (1895) (with Lowell Lamoreaux)
Wilbur J. Hartzell residence, 1 Seymour Avenue SE, Minneapolis (1897) (with Lowell Lamoreaux)
Lake County Courthouse, Two Harbors (1906)

William Macomber (1884–1935)
William Kaluna Macomber was born in Hawaii on June 12, 1884. He studied at the University of California and the University of Minnesota. It is not known when he came to Minnesota, but it appears that he started practicing in Minneapolis about 1910. He was a partner of Frank W. Kinney in 1915, and then he associated with James Burner (1916–17). He practiced privately for a number of years before joining Ursa Freed in a brief partnership in 1922. Macomber returned to private practice and then merged with Walter R. Dennis in another partnership in 1930–31.

Macomber died on January 2, 1935, in Minneapolis.

Notable Buildings
Sibley County Courthouse, Gaylord (1917) (with James Burner)

Norman Madson (1918–2007)

Norman Madson was born in Stanhope, Iowa, on May 14, 1918. He graduated from Waldorf College in Forest City, Iowa, in 1941, where he earned an associate of arts degree. He received a bachelor's degree in architecture and engineering from Iowa State College in 1943 and served in the U.S. Navy during World War II. After the war, he spent two years as a partner in a construction company and, in 1953, joined with Edward Sovik and Sewell Mathre to form a partnership in Northfield, Minnesota. Madson left the firm in 1973 to become director of the physical plant and staff architect at St. Olaf College. He retired in 1993 and died in Britt, Iowa, on April 13, 2007.

Notable Buildings

SOVIK, MATHRE & MADSON
Lutheran Social Services Building, 2414 Park Avenue, Minneapolis (1957)
Trinity Lutheran Church, Brainerd (1957)
Calvary Lutheran Church, 6817 Antrim Road, Edina (1959)
Vinje Lutheran Church, Willmar (1962–64)
Lutsen Sea Villas, Lutsen (1968)
St. Leo's Catholic Church, Pipestone (1969)

Gottlieb Magney (1884–1969)

Gottlieb Renatus Magney was born in Hager City, Wisconsin, on April 15, 1884. He attended public schools in Amery, Wisconsin, and Stillwater, before entering the University of Minnesota, from which he received his degree in 1905. Magney worked for about a year for the Board of Education in Seattle, Washington, as a draftsman before moving to San Francisco where he entered the firm of Welch & Casey as a construction engineer helping to rebuild the city after the earthquake of 1906. About 1907 he moved to Duluth and became a partner of P. M. Olson. The partnership was short-lived,

Women's Club, Minneapolis, 1927 (Magney & Tusler). *Photograph by Charles J. Hibbard. Courtesy of Minnesota Historical Society.*

however, for he appeared in Minneapolis in 1908, having joined Edwin Hewitt's practice. In 1912 he became a partner of Cecil Chapman and then, in 1917, entered partnership with Wilbur Tusler in what became one of the most successful firms in Minnesota. He remained in the firm until his retirement in 1954.

Magney died in Minneapolis on May 20, 1969.

Notable Buildings

MAGNEY & TUSLER

Young Quinlan store, 81 S. 9th Street, Minneapolis (1926)

Women's Club, 410 Oak Grove Street, Minneapolis (1927)

Calhoun Beach Club, 2730 W. Lake Street, Minneapolis (1927–28)

Foshay Tower (now W Minneapolis—The Foshay), 9th Street and Marquette Avenue, Minneapolis (1929)

Post Office, 1st Street S. and Nicollet Avenue, Minneapolis (1935) (Leon Arnal, designer)

John Magney (1912–1981)

John Reinhold Magney was born in Duluth on August 14, 1912. A nephew of Gottlieb Magney, he attended the University of Minnesota's School of Architecture, where he received a bachelor's degree in architecture in 1937. He returned to Duluth and was employed by Claude H. Smith for a few years before serving in the U.S. Navy in World War II. After the war, Magney worked in the office of Magney, Tusler and Setter in Minneapolis from 1945 to 1960, becoming an associate in 1950 and then partner in 1952. In 1960, he left to form his own firm in Minneapolis, specializing in hospitals, schools, and commercial structures.

Magney died on January 29, 1981, in Minneapolis.

Notable Buildings

Camp Cassaway (Girl Scouts of America), Cass Lake (1957)

Hospitals in Ely, Bemidji, Grand Marais, and Cloquet (n.d.)

Boiler House and Laundry building, Northwestern Hospital, Minneapolis (n.d.)

Michaela Mahady (B. 1952)

Michaela Maria Mahady was born in Bismarck, North Dakota, in 1952. She received a bachelor's degree in art from Macalester College, St. Paul, in 1973, and a master's degree in architecture from the University of Minnesota in 1986. She joined SALA Architects in Minneapolis the following year, while continuing to work as an art designer and co-owner of Pegasus Studio in Stillwater. Mahady has lectured at the Science Museum of Minnesota and at the University of Minnesota, and has won several design awards.

Notable Buildings

Maple Forest residence, Minnetrista (1994)

Glasgow residence, Minnetonka (1995)

L'Eaubelle residence, Deephaven (1995–96)

Nancekivell residence, North Oaks (1998)

Weiss Haus residence, Minoqua (1999)

Lewis Lake home, Cross Lake (2000)

Maurice Maine (1881–1950)

Maurice Francis Maine was born on February 6, 1881, in Rockland, Maine. He came to Minneapolis at about the age of nineteen and was educated at Hamline University in St. Paul and in art schools in the Twin Cities. He spent his entire career in Minneapolis. From 1913 to 1929 he was in partnership with William Kenyon. Together they designed numerous residences, apartment houses, and stores, as well as depots, shops, and other structures for the Soo Line Railroad, for which Kenyon was chief architect for twenty years. After the breakup of the partnership, Maine continued to practice privately for many years.

He died in Minneapolis on September 10, 1950.

Notable Buildings

WITH WILLIAM KENYON
Soo Line building, 5th Street and Marquette Avenue (1924) (also with Robert Gibson)

Frederick Mann (1868–1959)
Frederick Maynard Mann was born in New York City on May 1, 1868. He moved to Minneapolis as a boy and attended public schools and then the University of Minnesota, where he graduated with a bachelor's degree in civil engineering

Memorial Stadium, University of Minnesota, Minneapolis, 1924 (Frederick Mann, James Forsyth, and Leon Arnal). Photograph ca. 1924. Courtesy of Minneapolis Public Library, James K. Hosmer Special Collection, M0123.

in 1892. He attended the Massachusetts Institute of Technology (MIT), earning a bachelor's degree in architecture (1894) and master's degree in the same subject in 1895. While a student, he worked for the Northern Pacific Railroad as a structural engineer.

Following his training at MIT, Mann became an instructor in architecture at the University of Pennyslvania (1896–1901), Washington University (1902–10), where he founded the architecture school, and the University of Illinois (1910–13), whose architecture school he reorganized. He and Louis Pinault formed a partnership in 1915, which was interrupted for Pinault's service in World War I, resumed after the war, and ended in 1922. In the meantime, Mann had accepted the position as head of the new School of Architecture at the University of Minnesota, a position he held from 1913 until his retirement in 1936. During his tenure, he served as advisory architect to the university and was a member of the Minneapolis planning commission from 1927 to 1936, acting as its president from 1927 to 1931.

Mann moved to his ranch at Healdsburg, California, after he retired and died there on October 27, 1959.

Notable Buildings
Church of St. John the Evangelist, Philadelphia, Pennsylvania (1900)
University Methodist Church, Austin, Texas (1912)
University YMCA, 15th Street and University Avenue SE, Minneapolis (1922)
Memorial Stadium, University of Minnesota, Minneapolis (1924) (razed 1992) (with James Forsyth and Leon Arnal)
C. F. Haglin residence, 4501 E. Lake Harriet Boulevard, Minneapolis (1924)
Alpha Rho Chi fraternity house (now Kappa Sigma fraternity), 315 19th Avenue SE, Minneapolis (1926)
J. K. Shaw residence, 4861 E. Lake Harriet Boulevard, Minneapolis (1926)

Emmanuel Masqueray (1861–1917)
Emmanuel Louis Masqueray was born in Dieppe, France, on September 10, 1861. He studied architecture at the École des Beaux-Arts in Paris from 1879 to 1884, receiving several awards for his designs. He came to the United States in 1887 to work for the firm of Carrere & Hastings in New York City. Five years later, he joined the office of Richard Morris Hunt, where he helped design many notable buildings, including The Breakers for William Vanderbilt in Newport, Rhode Island. In 1897 Masqueray left Hunt's office and went to work for Warren & Wetmore, also in New York City. Four years later, he was

Basilica of St. Mary, Minneapolis, 1905–15 (Emmanuel Masqueray). *Photograph 1958. Courtesy of Minnesota Historical Society.*

Cathedral of St. Paul, St. Paul, 1905–15 (Emmanuel Masqueray). *Photograph 1918 by Charles P. Gibson. Courtesy of Minnesota Historical Society.*

appointed chief of design at the Louisiana Purchase Exposition in St. Louis, a position he held for three years. He resigned shortly after the fair opened in 1904, and was asked by Archbishop John Ireland to come to St. Paul to design the Cathedral of St. Paul.

Masqueray arrived in St. Paul in 1905 and remained there the rest of his life. He designed two dozen parish churches for Catholic and Protestant congregations in the Upper Midwest and three more cathedrals. He also designed a few residences and several parochial schools.

Masqueray died on May 26, 1917, in St. Paul.

Notable Buildings
Cathedral of St. Paul, 250 Summit Avenue, St. Paul (1905–1915)
Basilica of St. Mary, 88 N. 17th Street, Minneapolis (1905–1915)
St. Louis Church, 506 Cedar Street, St. Paul (1909)
John D. Moran House, 1039 Ashland Avenue, St. Paul (1909)
St. Paul's Episcopal Church on the Hill, 1524 Summit Avenue, St. Paul (1912)
Bethlehem Lutheran Church, 655–661 Forest Street, St. Paul (1914)
Paul Doty residence, 422 Portland Avenue, St. Paul (1915)

Ralph Mather (1887–1978)
Ralph Mather's education and early career are largely unknown. He was born in Wisconsin on August 13, 1887, and was residing in St. Paul by 1903. He began practicing in St. Paul about 1915, after becoming a partner of James Burner in Minneapolis from 1913 to 1914. Mather maintained the St. Paul office and Burner ran the Minneapolis facilities. The partnership soon dissolved and, about 1917, Mather joined Alan Fleischbein in a practice in St. Paul. It is not known how long the partnership lasted.

Mather died on April 22, 1978, in St. Paul.

Notable Buildings

George S. McLeod residence, 1770 Summit Avenue, St. Paul (1915)

Roy Molen residence, 3076 Hamline Avenue N., Roseville (1925) (with Alan Fleischbein)

Sewell Mathre (B. 1922)

Sewell Jerome Mathre was born on August 10, 1922, in Vancouver, British Columbia. His family immigrated to the United States while he was still a child and he graduated from high school in Estherville, Iowa, in 1940. Mathre attended Waldorf College in Forest City, Iowa, for two years and received an associate in science degree in 1942. In 1949, he received a bachelor's degree in architecture at Iowa State College in Ames and, three years later, a master's degree from the Cranbrook Academy of Art, Bloomfield Hills, Michigan. He worked for several firms in Alaska, Wisconsin, Iowa, and New York before returning to Minnesota in 1953, where he joined Gerhard Peterson in St. Paul. He left before the year was out to enter practice with Edward Sovik and Norman Madson in Northfield. Mathre retired in 1993.

Notable Buildings

SOVIK, MATHRE & MADSON

Lutheran Social Services Building, 2414 Park Avenue, Minneapolis (1957)

Trinity Lutheran Church, Brainerd (1957)

Calvary Lutheran Church, 6817 Antrim Road, Edina (1959)

Vinje Lutheran Church, Willmar (1962–64)

Lutsen Sea Villas, Lutsen (1968)

St. Leo's Catholic Church, Pipestone (1969)

Charles Maybury (1830–1917)

Charles Granderson Maybury was born on January 13, 1830, in Solon, New York. His father was a stonecutter and farmer, and young Maybury worked on the family farm until he was sixteen. He was educated in the local public schools and, for less than a year, in a private school. Following his education, he was apprenticed to a prominent contractor and builder in central New York State for close to five years, following which he became a partner in the company. After three years the firm dissolved and Maybury went into business for himself as a draftsman and builder. Two years later (1856), he headed west and arrived in Winona that same year. His first structure was the Sanborn building, which he designed and built, the largest structure in the small river settlement. In 1865 Maybury bought the office of Abraham Radcliffe when the latter returned to St. Paul after a three-year hiatus in Winona, and thereafter concentrated solely on design. His son Jefferson became a partner in 1881.

Maybury died on February 9, 1917, in Winona.

Notable Buildings

WITH JEFFERSON MAYBURY

St. John Nepomucene Catholic Church, Winona (1886)

Winona County Courthouse, Winona (1888)

St. Stanislaus Polish Catholic Church, Winona (1894–95)

Central United Methodist Church, Winona (1894–96)

Jefferson Maybury (1858–1928)
Jefferson Nichols Maybury, oldest son of Charles Maybury, was born on March 2, 1858 in Winona, Minnesota. He began working in his father's office as a young man and, after leaving high school, he trained in Edward Bassford's office in St. Paul for one year (1880). Maybury returned to Winona to become his father's partner on January 1, 1881. C. G. Maybury & Son, as it was called, continued well past the turn of the century. In 1903–04, Maybury was appointed as a specifications writer for the Louisiana Purchase Exposition in St. Louis. When he finished his work there, he once again returned to Winona. He moved to Seattle, Washington, in 1904, where he became architect of the Board of Education.

Maybury died in Seattle on May 5, 1928.

Notable Buildings

WITH CHARLES MAYBURY
St. John Nepomucene Catholic Church, Winona (1886)
Winona County Courthouse, Winona (1888)
St. Stanislaus Polish Catholic Church, Winona (1894–95)
Central United Methodist Church, Winona (1894–96)

Harlan McClure (1916–2001)
Harlan Ewart McClure was born in Delaware, Ohio, on October 19, 1916. He attended McKinley School in Washington, D.C., where he obtained a bachelor's degree in architecture in 1933. He also earned a Bachelor of Arts degree from Washington University in 1937. For the next year he was a student of architecture at the Royal Swedish Academy in Stockholm. He returned to the United States and entered the Massachusetts Institute of Technology, where he earned his master's degree in architecture in 1941. McClure worked in the office of Francis Sullivan (1938), as an architectural designer in the National Park Service (1939), and as a project planner in the Federal Housing Administration (1941), all in Washington, D.C.

During World War II, McClure was a student at Princeton University and Harvard University, earning a diploma in civil affairs at the former and a military government diploma at the latter, while serving as an officer in the U.S. Navy (1941–46). While in the navy, he was a project manager in charge of airport construction, an operations officer on aircraft carriers in the Atlantic and Pacific fleets, and a public works officer at the end of the war in Alameda, California.

After World War II, he came to Minneapolis and became an instructor in the School of Architecture at the University of Minnesota. At the same time, he worked as a consulting architect in the office of Long & Thorshov (1946–47) before setting up his own firm with Francis Kerr. The partnership ended in 1955 when McClure moved to Clemson, South Carolina, to become head of the Department of Architecture at Clemson University. He was appointed dean when the department became a college in 1958, and was named a Fellow of the American Institute of Architects in 1962.

McClure died in Clemson, South Carolina, on November 1, 2001.

St. Stanislaus Polish Catholic Church, Winona, 1894–95 (Charles Maybury and Jefferson Maybury). *Photograph by Bob Firth.*

Notable Buildings

Boedeker residence, Marengo, Iowa (1951, 1956) (McClure, Kerr & Fuller)

Lee Hall, Clemson University, Clemson, South Carolina (1958)

St. John's Lutheran Church, Cherryville, North Carolina (n.d.)

McClure residence, Tyrol Hills (n.d.)

Dale McEnary (1890–1964)

Dale Robert McEnary was born in Minneapolis on July 13, 1890. He studied civil engineering at the University of Minnesota from 1908 to 1911, and received a bachelor's degree in architecture from the Massachusetts Institute of Technology in 1914. After graduation, he worked in the office of Charles Frost in Chicago, assisting in the design of railroad stations, warehouses, and other types of commercial and institutional structures. When World War I broke out, McEnary first served in the Quartermaster Corps of the army in Washington, D.C., developing and supervising the construction of buildings for the War Department. He then was assigned to the Field Artillery Officers' Training School at Camp Taylor, Louisville, Kentucky, and finished his military service there. In 1919, he returned to Minneapolis as supervising architect of the St. Paul Union Depot, which was designed by Frost.

McEnary became an associate of Frederick Mann in 1921 and they worked on several buildings at the University of Minnesota, including Memorial Stadium. In 1925 he joined Walter Wheeler, an engineer in Minneapolis, as an associate, and was in charge of architectural work on the Cream of Wheat factory then being built in northeast Minneapolis. He also worked on the University of North Dakota stadium in Grand Forks.

During the 1920s, McEnary was affiliated with several firms, and then he partnered with Edwin Krafft in 1934. In 1942, McEnary was with C. F. Haglin Construction Company in charge of all local building operations. This apparently was at the same time as he continued to work in his own practice.

McEnary died in Minneapolis on February 27, 1964.

Notable Buildings

WITH EDWIN KRAFFT

Miller's Cafeteria, 20 S. 7th Street, Minneapolis (1935) (razed 1964)

Farmers and Mechanics Savings Bank (now Westin Hotel), 88 S. 6th Street, Minneapolis (1940)

Elevator and flour mill, International Milling Company, Hummerstone, Ontario (n.d.)

Donald McLaren (1891–1950)

Donald Andrew McLaren was born in Chippewa Falls, Wisconsin, on April 18, 1891. He attended schools there and then entered Cornell University, where he received a bachelor's degree in architecture in 1916. He served in the U.S. Navy in World War I. Before entering the armed forces, McLaren worked for James Gamble Rogers in New York City from 1916 to 1917. After the war, he returned to Rogers' office and remained there until 1920. That year, he moved to Minneapolis and worked in the firm of Magney & Tusler until 1922, when he formed a partnership with Albert O. Larson. McLaren remained in the firm until his death on November 13, 1950, in Zumbra Heights, Lake Minnetonka.

Notable Buildings

WITH ALBERT LARSON

Baker Block, 706 2nd Avenue S., Minneapolis (1927)

Groveland Apartment Hotel (now 510 Groveland), 510 Groveland Avenue, Minneapolis (1929)

Plymouth Building (refacing), 12 S. 6th Street, Minneapolis (1936)

Minneapolis Star Journal and Tribune Building, 425 Portland Avenue, Minneapolis (1940, 1944–45)

Radisson Hotel (refacing), Minneapolis (1947) (razed 1982)

Rosemary McMonigal (B. 1957)

Rosemary Anne McMonigal was born on October 9, 1957, in Minneapolis. She attended the University of Minnesota, where she earned a bachelor's degree in architecture in 1981. She worked as an architectural intern at Cenex in St. Paul, from 1978 to 1982. After spending a year in Finland, McMonigal returned to Cenex in 1983, and then joined Levine Architects in Minneapolis in 1984. That same year she set up her own successful practice, Rosemary McMonigal Architects, which specializes in residential work.

Notable Buildings

Mt. Airy Community Center, 91 E. Arch Street, St. Paul (1995)

Korba and McMonigal residence, 204 Woodlynne Avenue, St. Paul (1996)

Rieser residence, Stillwater (2000)

Barb and Hans Gasterland residence, 272 Vincent Avenue N., Minneapolis (2002)

Allen and Herman residence, Little Carnelian Lake, Stillwater (2003)

Robert McNicol (CA. 1854–?)

Robert McNicol was born in New York State about 1854. Nothing is known of his life, education, and career until 1880, by which time he was residing in Boston and practicing architecture. He moved to St. Paul in 1887 and joined Charles Mould in a partnership that lasted until 1891. It is possible the two men knew each other previously, possibly as colleagues in the same firm. McNicol appears to have left St. Paul after the partnership with Mould ended and is next heard from living in Queens, New York, in 1910, working as an architect. His life and career after that are unknown.

Notable Buildings

WITH CHARLES MOULD

John Merriam residence (later Science Museum of Minnesota), St. Paul (1887) (razed 1964)

Elizabeth Robbins residence, 40 Irvine Park, St. Paul (1887)

Schlieman-Kalscheuer residence, 196 Mounds Boulevard, St. Paul (1888)

A. Reinhold Melander (1894–1979)

Albin Reinhold Melander was born in Duluth, Minnesota, on July 16, 1894. He attended Central High School in Duluth and the University of Minnesota, where he received a bachelor's degree in architecture in 1921. His wife, Florence Knox Melander, also graduated from the university with a degree in architecture. Melander went on to enter the University of Besançon in France before returning to Duluth. He was a student draftsman in Anthony Puck's office (1919–21), worked with F. G. German in 1921, and Kees and Colburn in Minneapolis, also in 1921. He taught architecture at North Dakota

Notable Buildings
Lincoln Hotel, Duluth (1926) (with Harold Starin)
G. M. Rockwood residence, Duluth (1936)
Ordean Field stadium, Duluth (1936–38)
Roger Weaver residence, Duluth (1938)
Civic Center, International Falls (1939)
Enger Tower, Duluth (1939)

Val Michelson (1916–2006)

Valerius "Val" Michelson was born in St. Petersburg, Russia, on March 22, 1916. He was trained in the National Academy of Fine Arts in St. Petersburg from 1935 to 1941. Michelson served as an engineer in the Soviet army after the outbreak of World War II and was captured by the Germans in 1942. Because of his training and knowledge of the German language, he was put to work as an interpreter and employed in construction works. He escaped from a prisoner of war camp and eventually made his way to Western Europe, where he met his second wife in a displaced persons camp after the war. Michelson attended the Technische Hochschule in Karlsruhe, Germany, from 1946 to 1948 and helped set up temporary schools and other structures for refugees.

Michelson and his wife came to the United States in 1949 and settled near Ithaca, New York, where he found employment as a waiter and as a draftsman in an architect's office in the evening. He entered Columbia University and studied architecture for a year, receiving his master's degree in 1952. From 1951 to 1953, he worked in the office of Percival Goodman in New York City as a designer and job captain, and then joined Marcel Breuer where he was assigned to supervise the design and construction of Abbey Church at St. John's University in

Enger Tower, Duluth, 1939 (A. Reinhold Melander). Photograph ca. 1945. Courtesy of Minnesota Historical Society.

State College in Fargo from 1921 to 1923 and then entered partnership in Duluth with Harold St. Clair Starin in 1924. The partnership lasted until 1930 when Melander started a private practice. When he retired in 1972, he was replaced by Richard Whiteman as a partner. The firm continues to the present day as Melander, Melander and Schilling with Melander's son, Donald, as one of the partners.

Melander died in Duluth on April 15, 1979.

St. John's Preparatory School, Collegeville, 1961–62 (with Edward Hanson). *Photograph ca. 1965 by Shin Koyama. Courtesy of Minnesota Historical Society.*

Collegeville, Minnesota. Michelson moved to Minnesota to carry out this project and, when it was finished, left Breuer to establish a partnership in St. Paul with Edward Hanson. The partnership dissolved in 1963 and Michelson formed Val Michelson and Associates, which continued until his retirement in the 1990s. He also taught at the University of Minnesota's School of Architecture from 1964 to 1986.

Michelson died on August 3, 2006, in Minneapolis.

Notable Buildings
Abbey Church, St. John's University, Collegeville (1954–61) (with Marcel Breuer and Frank Kacmarcik)
St. John's Preparatory School, Collegeville (1961–62) (with Edward Hanson)
St. Paul Priory (for Sisters of St. Benedict), Maplewood (1962–69)
Itasca Community College, Grand Rapids (1986–89)

William Milbrath (1915–2000)
William Milbrath was born in Austin, Minnesota, on February 8, 1915. He graduated from the University of Minnesota in 1941, receiving a bachelor's degree in architecture. Following service in the U.S. Army Air Corps during World War II, for which he worked on the design, construction, and administration of Air Force facilities in the Pacific, he returned to Minnesota and was employed by Green Giant Canning Company in Le Sueur designing new offices and plant facilities.

In 1948, Milbrath moved to Osage, Iowa, to enter the office of Plan Associates, and then, in 1950, he relocated to Austin and spent the remainder of his life and career there in private practice, specializing in the design of church buildings and residences.

Milbrath died in Austin on June 1, 2000.

Notable Buildings
Holy Cross Evangelical Lutheran Church, Austin (1950)

Zion E.U.B. Church, Sargeant (1956)
Austin Daily Herald building, Austin (1971)
Austin Fire Station, Austin (1976)

Denslow Millard (1841–CA. 1910)
Denslow Webster Millard was born in Blair County, Pennsylvania, on January 5, 1841. Much of his early life and career is cloaked in mystery, but it appears that he moved with his family to Lockport, Michigan, and lived there until about 1880. He began working in St. Paul around 1880 or 1881 as a draftsman in Abraham Radcliffe's office. Millard left two years later and opened his own practice, which he maintained until entering a brief partnership with Emil Ulrici in 1887. He and Charles Joy went into business together about three years later and remained partners until 1894. Sometime between 1895 and 1900 Millard left St. Paul and apparently returned to Pennsylvania because by 1910 he was living with his son, Julian, in Altoona. His place and date of death remain unknown.

Notable Buildings
First National Bank (later Hackney Building), St. Paul (ca. 1885) (razed 1941)
Capital City Panorama, St. Paul (1887–89) (razed 1890) (with Emil Ulrici)

William Miller (1923–1993)
William Jerome Miller was born in Rochester, Minnesota, on August 30, 1923. He attended Rochester Junior College in 1941–43, then entered the U.S. Army during World War II (1943–46). While in the army, he studied civil engineering at North Carolina State College and St. John's University in Collegeville. After the war, Miller entered the University of Minnesota and received a bachelor's degree in architecture in 1950. He worked as a draftsman in the firms of McGhie & Armstrong in 1947 and in Peter P. Bross in 1948, both in Rochester. In 1948–49 he was employed as a draftsman in Magney, Tusler & Setter, Minneapolis, and then joined Long & Thorshov in 1950 as draftsman and job captain. He became an associate in the same firm in 1956 and vice president in Cerny Associates from 1959 to 1963. In 1963, Miller formed a partnership with Foster W. Dunwiddie. He remained in the firm until his retirement about 1990. The firm continues to the present time.

Miller died in Edina, Minnesota, on March 20, 1993.

Notable Buildings

WITH FOSTER DUNWIDDIE
Metropolitan Stadium east grandstand, Bloomington (1964) (razed 1985)
Rosedale Shopping Center renovation, Roseville (1970–72)
Minneapolis–St. Paul International Airport Green Concourse, Bloomington (1978–80)
Hubert Humphrey Charter Terminal, Minneapolis–St. Paul International Airport, Bloomington (n.d.)

E. Townsend Mix (1831–1890)
Technically, Edward Townsend Mix should not be included in this book because he lived in Minnesota a scant two years instead of the required three. On the other hand, he started designing buildings in the state in the early 1870s and it is possible he had an office here at least by the mid-1880s. His list of Notable Buildings bespeaks his ability to design

Guaranty Loan building (later the Metropolitan building), Minneapolis, 1888–90 (E. Townsend Mix). *Photograph ca. 1892. Courtesy of Minnesota Historical Society.*

structures of quality and distinction, and several of them are in Minneapolis.

Mix was born in New Haven, Connecticut, on May 13, 1831. His family was involved in the whaling industry. He received his education in New Haven schools but probably did not attend college. In 1852, he was working for W. W. Boyington in Chicago. Mix relocated to Milwaukee in 1856 and spent the next thirty years there in architectural practice. He moved to Minneapolis in 1888, most likely to supervise construction of the Guaranty Loan (Metropolitan) building.

He died at his residence in the West Hotel in Minneapolis on September 2, 1890.

Notable Buildings
Dodge County Courthouse, Mantorville (1871)
William Washburn residence ("Fairoaks"), Minneapolis (1883) (razed 1924)
Temple Court office building, Minneapolis (1886) (razed 1953)

Globe Printing Company, 20 S. 4th Street, Minneapolis (1888–89) (razed 1958)
Guaranty Loan building (later Metropolitan building), 3rd Street and 2nd Avenue S., Minneapolis (1888–90) (razed 1962)

Anthony Morell (1875–1924)
Anthony Urbanski Morell was born Anthony Urbanski in France in 1875. He attended schools there, and about 1902 came to the United States and changed his name to Morell, his mother's maiden name. Morell worked for a time in New York City in the office of Charles W. Leavitt Jr., where he met Arthur Nichols. In 1909 they formed a partnership and moved to Minneapolis. Morell, characterized as artistic, creative, and possessed of high ideals and a hot temper, worked as a consultant to the Minneapolis City Planning department and served as a member and secretary of the Minneapolis Planning Commission. He assisted with the preparation of a new civic center development and designed civic center plans for other cities.

Morell died suddenly of heart failure on October 7, 1924, in Minneapolis.

Notable Buildings

WITH ARTHUR NICHOLS
Morgan Park, Duluth (1914)

Charles Mould (1854–?)
Charles T. Mould was born in New York State in 1854. Details of his early life, education, and career are lacking. He worked as an architect in Utica, New York, for a period around 1880 and moved to St. Paul about 1883, where he opened an office in the Mannheimer Block. In 1885 he was joined by Harvey Ellis, who may have been an associate or even partner, but most likely was a chief draftsman and designer. Mould and Robert McNicol became partners in 1887, after the departure of Ellis, and remained together until 1891. After that, both men left the city. Mould next turns up in Pottsville, Pennsylvania, in 1910, working as an architect. His later life and career remain unknown.

Notable Buildings

WITH ROBERT MCNICHOL
John Merriam residence (later Science Museum of Minnesota), St. Paul (1887) (razed 1964)
Elizabeth Robbins residence, 40 Irvine Park, St. Paul (1887)
Schlieman-Kalscheuer residence, 196 Mounds Boulevard, St. Paul (1888)

Dale Mulfinger (B. 1943)
Dale Merlin Mulfinger was born in Washington County, Minnesota, on July 14, 1943. He received a bachelor's degree in architecture at the University of Minnesota in 1967. He worked with the Architects Collaborative in Cambridge, Massachusetts, and with Brown Daltus in Rome, Italy, before returning to Minneapolis to establish a partnership with Sarah Susanka in 1983. Mulfinger has been an adjunct professor in the College of Architecture and Landscape Architecture at the University of Minnesota for a number of years and is the author of two notable books, *The Architecture of Edwin Lundie* (1995) and (with Susan Davis) *The Cabin* (2001).

Notable Buildings
Dittmar-Mulfinger cabin, Lake Vermillion (with Gunter Dittmar) (1999)

State Capitol Approach, St. Paul, 1944 (Arthur Nichols). *Photograph 1954 by Kenneth Melvin Wright. Courtesy of Minnesota Historical Society.*

WITH SARAH SUSANKA
Abramovitz residence, Buenos Aires, Argentina (2000)
Kohlstedt cabin, Tucker Lake, Gunflint Trail (2000)
Ludlow cabin, Lake Vermillion (2003)
Works Brothers lodge, Madge Township (2003)

WITH RAFFERTY RAFFERTY AND TOLLEFSON
University of Minnesota Landscape Arboretum Visitor Center, Chanhassen (2004)

Arthur Nichols (1881–1970)
Arthur Richardson Nichols was born in Springfield, Massachusetts, on April 15, 1881. He was the first graduate in landscape architecture from the Massachusetts Institute of Technology (1902). He worked in the office of New York landscape architect Charles W. Leavitt for seven years, where he met Anthony Morell. The two formed a partnership and came to Minneapolis in 1909 to set up their office. While working with Morell, Nichols served as a consulting landscape architect for the University of Minnesota (1912–44). He also was consulting

landscape architect for the Minnesota Highway Department (1932–40) and the Minnesota State Parks Department (1950–60). He designed the site plan for the Capitol Approach in St. Paul (1944), the University's Northrop Mall, and numerous colleges in the area. The firm continues today as Sanders, Wacker & Bagley.

Nichols retired in 1953 but came out of retirement to prepare plans and site studies for virtually every new or existing state park in the state. He retired for good in the early 1960s and died in Rochester, Minnesota, on January 23, 1970.

Notable Buildings
Morgan Park, Duluth (1914) (with Anthony Morell)
Sunset Memorial Park Cemetery, Minneapolis (1927–29)
State Capitol Approach, St. Paul (1944)

James Niemeyer (1890–1957)
James Charles Niemeyer was born in St. Paul on August 1, 1890, son of John Niemeyer, an interior decorator and painter who worked for the Minnesota Linseed Oil Company of Minneapolis.

Niemeyer was educated in the parochial schools of St. Paul, graduating from Cretin High School and St. Thomas College, receiving a degree in mechanical engineering. He studied at the Royal Academy of Rome and returned to St. Paul about 1916 to practice architecture. He served in the U.S. Army's Ordnance Department during World War I, and in 1929 was appointed city architect for a year, before resuming private practice. Niemeyer designed churches, residences, commercial buildings, and warehouses, only a few of which are known.

He died in St. Paul on October 28, 1957.

Notable Buildings
Glenn Walding house, 709 Linwood Avenue, St. Paul (1916)
Charles Pomeroy residence, 1756 Wellesley Avenue, St. Paul (n.d.)

Carl Nystrom (1867–1944).
Carl Edward Nystrom was born in Sweden in 1867. He came to the United States in 1889 and worked in architectural offices in Ironwood, Michigan, and Ashland, Wisconsin, before settling in Duluth in 1892. He moved to Hancock, Michigan, later in the same decade and then, in 1900, to Laurium, Michigan. He was back in Duluth as a partner of Frank L. Young from 1902 to 1905 and William Bray from 1906 to 1914. After that he practiced alone, sometimes teaming up with Peter Olsen to conduct work on several houses he had designed with Bray.

Nystrom died in Duluth on August 3, 1944.

Notable Buildings
WITH WILLIAM T. BRAY
Julia Duncan residence, 2221 E. 2nd Street, Duluth (1906)
A. W. Frick residence, 2231 E. 2nd Street, Duluth (1906)
Ward Ames Jr., residence, 2216 E. 2nd Street, Duluth (1908)
N. C. Clark residence, 2423 E. 2nd Street, Duluth (1910)
Alexander McDougall residence, 2201 E. 1st Street, Duluth (1910)

Didrik Omeyer (1851–1907)
Few details are available about the life of Didrik A. Omeyer. He was born in Norway, but his education and training is unknown. He worked in the office

Cottonwood County Courthouse, Windom, 1904 (Didrik Omeyer). *Photograph ca. 1925 by Moen Photo Service. Courtesy of Minnesota Historical Society.*

of Abraham Radcliffe for about a year around 1883, and with Augustus Gauger for about three years, before forming a partnership with Martin P. Thori in 1888. They had a thriving business for at least a decade, and then parted company around 1900. Omeyer went into business for himself and Thori formed a partnership with William Alban. Omeyer and Thori produced a book of stock house plans in 1893, titled *Homes for All*.

Omeyer died in St. Paul on February 13, 1907.

Notable Buildings
Thomas Swem residence, 775–777 W. Fairmount Avenue, St. Paul (1890) (with Martin Thori)
Union Opera House, Leroy (ca. 1895) (with Martin Thori)
E. J. Webber residence, Fergus Falls (1896) (with Martin Thori)
Ada City Hall, Ada (1903–04)
Cottonwood County Courthouse, Windom (1904)

Fremont Orff (1856–1914)

Fremont D. Orff was born in Bangor, Maine, in 1856. It is not known how or where he was educated. In the 1870s he worked as a draftsman for his older brother, George, but where this occurred is not known. He came to Minneapolis around 1880 and worked briefly as a draftsman for Haglin & Corser, and then a year later joined his brother, who had moved there in 1878, in partnership. They maintained one of the most successful firms in the city until 1892. The partnership ended when George was appointed supervisor of construction for the Minneapolis Public Schools. Fremont continued in practice with successive partners in the 1890s, the most notable being Edgar Joralemon from 1893 to 1898. After the latter moved to Buffalo, New York, Orff was briefly a partner of Ernest Guilbert. When Guilbert left for New York City in November 1899, Orff continued in single practice in Minneapolis for the rest of his life.

He died in Rochester, Minnesota, on February 16, 1914.

Notable Buildings
Mutual Block (Janney, Semple, Hill & Company), Minneapolis (1887–88) (razed 1965) (Orff and Orff)
George Van Dusen residence, 1900 La Salle Avenue, Minneapolis (1892–93) (Orff and Orff with Edgar Joralemon)
E. G. Welton residence, Minneapolis (1893) (razed 1959) (Orff and Joralemon)
Big Stone County Courthouse, Ortonville (1901–02)
Renville County Courthouse, Olivia (1902)
Carnegie City Library, Little Falls (1905)

George Orff (1835–1908)
George Orff was born in Bangor, Maine, in 1835. He worked as a carpenter in his teens and early twenties in Bangor, then went to Boston in 1861 and studied architecture with various firms for the next decade, among them Calvin Ryder, an architect from Maine. He returned to Bangor in 1870 and set up a practice in which his brother Fremont was employed for a time as a draftsman. Orff moved to Minneapolis in 1878 and practiced alone until about 1881 when he formed a partnership with Fremont. This continued until 1892 when Orff was appointed supervisor of construction for the Minneapolis public schools. During his tenure in this position, he oversaw the construction of East High School at University and East Hennepin Avenues. Orff then became a building inspector for the city before retiring in 1905. He left Minneapolis and went back to Boston. Eventually he returned to Maine, where he died on March 11, 1908, in Skowhegan.

Notable Buildings

WITH FREMONT ORFF
J. A. Fagan residence, 2300 Portland Avenue S., Minneapolis (1889) (razed ca. 1966)
Dr. A. H. Lindley residence, 1920 Stevens Avenue S., Minneapolis (1890)
M. A. Pratt residence, Minneapolis (1891) (razed 1959)

Henry Orth (1866–1946)
Henry W. Orth was born in Norway on April 14, 1866. He came to the United States with his family at the age of two. It is not known where they settled at first, but he attended a business college. In 1891 he was in Minneapolis and had a brief partnership with Edwin Overmire. He relocated to Austin, Minnesota, in 1896 where he formed a partnership with Frank W. Kinney. The partners moved their practice to St. Paul shortly thereafter and it ended in 1902. Orth became a partner of Charles Buechner in a successful firm that lasted until the latter's death in 1924. During part of this time Orth served as

president of the Minneapolis Brewing Company (later, Grain Belt Brewing Company). Orth continued the architectural firm for a number of years and associated with Philip Bettenburg for an unknown period of time. In 1938 he resumed a private practice until his death on March 5, 1946, in St. Paul.

Notable Buildings
Norwegian Evangelical Lutheran Church (now Christ Lutheran Church), University Avenue and Park Street, St. Paul (1913) (with Charles Buechner)

Edwin Overmire (1864–1905)
Edwin P. Overmire was born in Matoon, Illinois, in 1864. He and his family moved to Minneapolis in 1882 and young Edwin began working as a stenographer. He was employed by the firm of Plant & Whitney about two years later and continued with Whitney when the partnership dissolved. Perhaps at the urging of Whitney, who was a native of Massachusetts, Overmire went to Boston and studied and worked there for five years, part of the time with H. H. Richardson. He returned to Minneapolis in 1891 and had a brief partnership with Henry Orth before joining Frederick Clarke's firm at some point, and then assumed Clarke's practice when the latter left town in the late 1890s. Overmire opened an office in the Sykes Block in downtown Minneapolis, specializing in large residences. He may have suffered from tuberculosis, because his obituary mentions that he had gone to a sanatorium in northern Wisconsin for treatment.

Overmire died in Minneapolis on September 7, 1905, at the age of forty-one, leaving a wife and three children.

Notable Buildings
Gruman residence, 1942 Irving Avenue S., Minneapolis (1900)
W. J. Jennison residence, 2546 Portland Avenue S., Minneapolis (1900)
Lindsay residence, 2722 Park Avenue S., Minneapolis (1901)
F. J. Pray residence, 1931 1st Avenue S., Minneapolis (1901)
W. D. Lowry residence, 1906 Emerson Avenue S., Minneapolis (1901)
Asbury Methodist Hospital (now I. O. Miller Hall), 910 Elliot Avenue S., Minneapolis (1905–06)

Clayton Page (1920–1969)
Clayton Meredith Page was born on March 17, 1920, in Minneapolis. He graduated from the University of Minnesota in 1946 with his bachelor's degree in architecture, and received a master's degree from Harvard University. He served as an instructor in architecture at the University of Idaho and Clemson University. He joined Brooks Cavin Jr. in partnership in 1960 and remained in the firm until his death in Minneapolis on February 6, 1969.

Notable Buildings
Richard Lange residence, Lake Gervaise, Little Canada (1956–61)

WITH BROOKS CAVIN JR.
J. B. Coleman residence, St. Croix Cove, Wisconsin (1963)
Kate Dunwoody Hall, Minneapolis (1964) (razed ca. 2000)
Lewis Paper residence, 1944 Bayard Avenue, St. Paul (1967)
Washburn Branch Library, 53rd Street and Lyndale Avenue S., Minneapolis (1968–70)

Emmet Palmer (1847–1935)
Emmet S. Palmer was born in La Porte, Indiana, on September 26, 1847, but little else is known of his early life and career, including when he came to Minnesota. He was working as a carpenter in Duluth by 1886, and about 1890 formed an architecture practice with Lucien Hall. In 1893 William Hunt became a partner and the firm of Palmer, Hall & Hunt became one of the most successful in the city during the 1890s. The firm was responsible for the design of many residences, schools, and other structures in Duluth during the 1890s and early 1900s.

Palmer's whereabouts after the early 1900s is mainly unknown, although there is evidence that he was working in Seattle, Washington, from about 1906 to 1909. Where he went after that is not clear, but it appears he drifted south to California.

Palmer died in Fresno, California, on July 25, 1935.

Notable Buildings

WITH LUCIEN HALL
Central High School, Lake Avenue and 2nd Street, Duluth (1891–92)
Charles Lovett residence, 1728 E. 3rd Street, Duluth (1892)

PALMER, HALL & HUNT
Irving School, 101 N. 56th Avenue W., Duluth (1894)
Joseph Sellwood residence, 16 E. 18th Avenue, Duluth (1902)
Andrew Davidson residence, 1525 E. Superior Street, Duluth (1902)

Walter Pardee (1852–1925)
Walter Stone Pardee was born in New Haven, Connecticut, in August 1852. He moved with his parents to St. Anthony in 1856 and graduated from the University of Minnesota in 1877, where he studied architecture. He spent four years in the office of Leroy Buffington, and then became the first building inspector for the city of Minneapolis (1884–87). Pardee was the architect for the Minneapolis Board of Education from 1887 to 1891, designing several schools during his tenure. He then set up a private practice for the next seven years, ending his career by working in the city engineer's office from 1898 to 1910 while also maintaining his office.

He retired in 1910 and died in Minneapolis on May 24, 1925.

Notable Buildings
Frederika Bremer School (now Bremer Way Condominiums), 1214 Lowry Avenue N., Minneapolis (1887)
Greeley School, Minneapolis (1888) (razed 1976)

Irving School, Duluth, 1894 (Palmer, Hall & Hunt). *Photograph by Hugh McKenzie. Courtesy of Northeast Minnesota Historical Center, Duluth.*

Frederika Bremer School (now Bremer Way Condominiums), Minneapolis, 1887 (Walter Pardee). *Photograph ca. 1915. Courtesy of Minnesota Historical Society.*

Madison School (now Madison Apartments), 501 15th Street E., Minneapolis (1889)

Leonard Parker (B. 1923)
Leonard S. Parker was born in a small village near Warsaw, Poland, on January 16, 1923. His family immigrated to the United States the same year and settled in Milwaukee, where Parker grew up. He served in the army in World War II and following the war studied architecture at the University of Wisconsin, where he received a bachelor's degree (1948). He earned a master's degree the following year from the Massachusetts Institute of Technology and then spent six years as senior designer/project manager with Eero Saarinen and Associates at Bloomfield Hills, Michigan. In 1956, Parker moved to Minneapolis and became an

Rochester Public Library, Rochester, 1995 (Leonard Parker & Associates). *Photograph courtesy of Rochester Public Library.*

associate in the firm of Saul C. Smiley and Associates. The next year he established his own practice, Leonard Parker Associates, which became Parker Klein Associates when George Klein was added as a partner in 1968. In 1977, Klein bought out Parker's interest in the firm and Parker set up another practice. In 2004 it merged with Durrant of Des Moines, Iowa, forming Parker Durrant, and in 2005 Parker left the company to once again establish a private practice. Parker taught for many years in the School of Architecture at the University of Minnesota, and was awarded a Gold Medal from the AIA Minnesota in 1986.

Notable Buildings
Law School (now Walter F. Mondale Hall), University of Minnesota, Minneapolis (1977) (with George Klein)

LEONARD PARKER & ASSOCIATES
Minnesota Public Radio building, 45 E. 7th Street, St. Paul (1980)
Hubert H. Humphrey Institute, University of Minnesota, Minneapolis (1984)
Minneapolis Convention Center, 1301 2nd Avenue S., Minneapolis (1988–90) (also with Setter Leach and Lindstrom and others)
U.S. Embassy, Santiago, Chile (1993–94)
Rochester Public Library, Rochester (1995)

Marion Parker (1873–1935)
Marion Alice Parker was born in Reading, Massachusetts, on September 6, 1873. She came to Minneapolis before 1890 and entered the University of Minnesota in 1892, from which she graduated in 1896 with a degree in education. Parker taught in Minneapolis public schools from 1897 to 1903, and then went to work as a draftsman with the Keith Company in 1904. Two years later she was studying art at the Minneapolis School of Fine Arts. In 1908 she was employed as a draftsman in the office of Purcell and Feick and remained there until 1916. She was characterized by Purcell as being "dependable, but not brilliant, her knowledge of construction sufficient to follow but not to organize." He wrote that Parker "learned most of what she knew of architecture as a building art" during those years. He also described her as having a "very large dark facial blemish on one cheek," probably a birthmark.

After leaving the firm, she set up her own practice in Minneapolis, which lasted until the mid-1920s. About 1926, Parker moved to Laguna Beach, California, and opened a shop selling handicrafts. While traveling to visit William Purcell, who was then living in Monrovia and recovering from tuberculosis surgery, she fell ill and died on November 18, 1935, at the home of her sister who lived only a few blocks from Purcell.

Notable Buildings
Pi Beta Phi sorority, 1019 University Avenue SE, Minneapolis (1916) (with Ethel Bartholomew)

George Pass (1848–1931)
George W. Pass was born in Pella, Iowa, on July 26, 1848. He was educated in the schools in Pella and worked as a carpenter and contractor for a number of years. He moved to Mankato in 1877 and opened a carpentry shop on Front Street. He soon spread his business into contracting and superintending building projects, while also doing a small amount of architectural design work. About 1887, he became a full-time architect. Pass also branched

Wright County Courthouse, Buffalo, 1959 (Roger Patch, Donald Erickson, John Madson, and Robert Hanson). *Photograph ca. 1960. Courtesy of Minnesota Historical Society.*

out into other business interests, including becoming president of the local Building and Loan Association and operating Mankato Lime & Stone Company, which burned lime for mortar and bricks. As a partner of Albert Schippel from the 1880s until 1902, Pass designed residences and jails, as well as commercial buildings in southern Minnesota. Late in life he was joined by Paul Rockey as a partner, and Rockey succeeded to the Pass practice after Pass's death.

Pass died in Mankato on June 9, 1931.

Notable Buildings

WITH ALBERT SCHIPPEL
Pipestone County Courthouse, Pipestone (1899)
Blue Earth County Courthouse, Mankato (1901)

Roger Patch (B. 1924)
Roger Whiting Patch was born in Wayzata, Minnesota, on December 6, 1924. He attended public schools in Wayzata, and graduated from the University of Minnesota in 1947 with his bachelor's degree in architecture. He took his master's degree from Harvard University in 1950. He worked in the office of Magney, Tusler and Setter in Minneapolis in 1944 as a draftsman, and then served in the U.S. Army for two years, returning to Magney, Tusler and Setter in 1947 as job captain. In 1950, Patch joined Loren Abbett as chief draftsman, and then returned to Magney, Tusler and Setter as a designer in 1953. Two years later, Patch, together with Donald Erickson, formed the partnership of Patch and Erickson in Wayzata. The firm moved to offices

on Wayzata Boulevard in 1957 and was incorporated in 1959 with John A. Madson and Robert D. Hanson becoming principals. The firm, which later became known as Patch Erickson Madson Watten Inc., specialized in public buildings, schools, medical, religious, and commercial structures.

Notable Buildings

PATCH AND ERICKSON
Faith-Lilac Way Evangelical Lutheran Church, 5530 42nd Avenue N., Robbinsdale (1955)
Wayzata City Hall, 600 Rice Street, Wayzata (1958)

WITH DONALD ERICKSON, JOHN MADSON, AND ROBERT HANSON
Wright County Courthouse, Buffalo (1959)
Augustana Home, 1007 E. 14th Street, Minneapolis (1960)
Anoka County Courthouse, 325 E. Main Street, Anoka (1960)
Church of the Annunciation, 509 W. 54th Street, Minneapolis (1961)
Scott County Courthouse, Shakopee (1976)

Cyril Pesek (1904–1995)
Cyril Paul Pesek was born in Minneapolis on May 30, 1904. He attended St. Thomas Academy in St. Paul, graduating in 1920, and the University of Minnesota, where he received his bachelor's degree in architecture and engineering in 1925. He worked as a designer and construction superintendent for J. C. Pendergast Company in Minneapolis for four years and, in 1929, set up his own practice. In 1931 he was joined in partnership by Glynne Shifflet, and the firm lasted until 1944, when Pesek sold the business to his partner and became vice president of engineering at Minnesota Mining & Manufacturing Company. There he oversaw the design and construction of many of the company's buildings. He remained there for the rest of his career.

Pesek died in Minneapolis on July 14, 1995.

Notable Buildings

WITH GLYNNE SHIFFLET
Church of the Visitation, Danvers (1931)
Phi Chi fraternity house, 325 Harvard Street SE, Minneapolis (1931)
Northern Pump Company, Fridley (1939–40)

Gerhard Peterson (1907–1994)
Gerhard Clifford Peterson was born on September 12, 1907, in Westby, Wisconsin. He moved to St. Paul at an unknown date and attended Mechanic Arts High School from 1922 to 1925. Following his graduation, he attended the University of Minnesota (1925–30), where he earned his bachelor's degree in architecture. He was also a student at Harvard University (1935–37) and was awarded a master's degree in architecture in 1937. Peterson worked in the offices of Toltz, King & Day (1931–35) and Ellerbe & Company (1936–38), both in St. Paul, and, after receiving his degree from Harvard, joined the firm of Tinsley, McBroom & Higgins in Des Moines, Iowa, as a draftsman and designer, from 1938 to 1940.

During World War II, Peterson worked as a draftsman with Smith, Hinchman & Grylls, Inc., of Detroit, Michigan, on the design of the Des Moines Ordnance Plant (1941–42) and then with the Hercules Powder Company of Wilmington, Delaware, to design a similar facility. After the war, he spent a year with Seth and Arthur Temple in Davenport, Iowa, before returning to Minneapolis in 1946 to enter the firm of Lang & Raugland as job captain and chief draftsman. From 1949 to 1950, he served as president of Northfield Architects in Northfield, Minnesota, and became a partner of E. Richard Cone in the firm of Cone & Peterson in 1950. They moved the company to St. Paul in 1950 and remained partners until their retirement in 1972, specializing in church design.

Peterson died in Minneapolis on May 10, 1994.

Notable Buildings
Drew Residence Hall, Field House, Power Plant, and Student Union, Hamline University, St. Paul (1936–46) (with Tinsley, McBroom & Higgins)
Cleveland Avenue Methodist Church, 225 S. Cleveland Avenue, St. Paul (1950–52) (with E. Richard Cone)

Richard Peterson (1923–2000)
Richard Allen "Bud" Peterson was born on February 26, 1923, in Hancock, Minnesota. He attended high school in Alexandria, graduating from there in 1940. He enlisted in the Army Air Corps in World War II and was assigned to the 357th Fighter Group, based in England. Peterson flew 150 missions over Europe, shooting down fifteen enemy aircraft, and was awarded the Air Medal, Silver Star, and Distinguished Flying Cross. After the war, he returned to Minnesota and continued his education at the University of Minnesota, from which he graduated with his bachelor's degree in architecture in 1949. He worked with several firms, including Maguolo & Quick and Thorshov and Cerny, before forming a highly successful partnership with Wilbur Clark Jr. and Newton Griffith in 1960. Griffith died in 1968 and the firm continued as Peterson, Clark & Associates. After leaving the partnership, Peterson formed an independent consulting practice with his son in 1983. He continued his practice until a month before he died on June 4, 2000, in Minneapolis.

Notable Buildings
Housing for the Elderly, 1707 3rd Avenue S., Minneapolis (ca. 1962) (Peterson, Clark & Griffith)
Housing for the Elderly, 1515 Park Avenue, Minneapolis (1965) (Peterson, Clark & Griffith)
Ray Mithun residence, Northome (n.d.)
Orrin Thompson residence, Fridley (n.d.)

Louis Pinault (1889–1981)
Louis Clovis Pinault was born in St. Joseph, Minnesota, on December 29, 1889. He graduated from high school in St. Cloud in 1909 and attended St. Cloud Teachers college (1909–10), the University of Minnesota (1910–11), and the University of Illinois (1911–15), from which he received a bachelor's degree in architecture. He also studied at the École des Beaux-Arts in Paris in 1919. While attending college he worked in the office of Bertrand and Chamberlin in Minneapolis during the summers of 1913 and 1914, and for Otis & Clark in Chicago in 1915. Pinault entered partnership with Frederick Mann (Mann & Pinault) in St. Cloud and Minneapolis in 1915. They closed the St. Cloud office while Pinault served in the army from 1917 to 1919. After the war, he stayed on in Paris to attend the École des Beaux-Arts and then returned

Milaca Municipal Hall, Milaca, 1936 (Louis Pinault). *Photograph 1937. Courtesy of Minnesota Historical Society.*

to resume partnership with Mann, with Pinault operating the St. Cloud office. The partnership ended in 1922, and Pinault set up his own practice in St. Cloud. Later in his career, he was joined in partnership by Peter Truszinski, who continued the firm after Pinault's retirement in 1972.

During World War II, Pinault devised the "tilt-up" method of concrete construction, in which reinforced concrete panels are poured on site and then raised or lifted upright into position to form a building wall.

Pinault moved to Seattle, Washington, after the death of his wife in 1979, and died there on February 23, 1981.

Notable Buildings
Stearns County Jail, St. Cloud (1921)
St. Boniface High School, Cold Spring (1926)
St. Joseph Grade School, St. Joseph (1926)
St. Cloud Junior High School (later Central Elementary School), St. Cloud (1930)
Woodrow Wilson Grade School, St. Cloud (1931)
Milaca Municipal Hall, Milaca (1936)
Kiehle Hall, St. Cloud State University, St. Cloud (1952)

Edmund Prondzinski (1887–1967)
Edmund J. Prondzinski was born in Minneapolis on September 20, 1887. Nothing is known of his early life and education. He spent much of his early career working with Bertrand and Chamberlin, and succeeded their practice when they left the firm. He maintained his own firm for a number of years afterward and produced a large number of building

designs, concentrating on educational facilities and apartment houses.

Prondzinski died in Minneapolis in June 1967.

Notable Buildings
School, St. Michael's Roman Catholic Church, St. Michael (1939)

Anthony Puck (1882–1922)
Anthony Puck was born in Christiana (now Oslo), Norway, on June 14, 1882. Little is known of his early life or when he came to the United States. He worked in Duluth starting about 1905, after receiving office training in John Wangenstein's firm. Puck had a short but very active career, designing numerous residences, schools, and industrial and institutional structures in Duluth and throughout northern Minnesota. At some point, he was in partnership with Ephraim Giliuson in Arnold, Minnesota, but it is not known how long this lasted. He was a member of the Duluth Boat Club and at one time rowed with its crews.

Puck died in Duluth on October 16, 1922, and is buried in Lakewood Cemetery, Minneapolis.

Notable Buildings
C. A. Eggert residence, Duluth (1905)
First Unitarian Church, Duluth (1910–11)

William Purcell (1880–1965)
William Gray Purcell was born on July 2, 1880. Early in his life he made the decision to live in Oak Park, Illinois, with his grandparents, Dr. and Mrs. William Cunningham Gray, in an environment rich in literary and cultural contacts. Purcell spent summers at the Grays' rustic fishing camp on Island Lake in northern Wisconsin, where he developed an appreciation of nature and the Native American culture and peoples around them. He entered Cornell University in 1899 and graduated in 1903 with his bachelor's degree in architecture. He returned to Chicago and met George Elmslie, who got him a job in Louis Sullivan's office. Purcell worked there for five months, then moved to San Francisco in 1904 and was employed by John Galen Howard. Before the year was out, he had moved on to Seattle, Washington, and worked in the office of Bebb and Mendel.

First Unitarian Church, Duluth, 1910–11 (Anthony Puck). *Photograph by Bob Firth.*

Merchants National Bank, Winona, 1912 (William Purcell and George Elmslie). *Photograph courtesy of Northwest Architectural Archives, University of Minnesota.*

Edna Purcell residence, Minneapolis, 1912–13 (William Purcell and George Elmslie). *Photograph courtesy of Northwest Architectural Archives, University of Minnesota.*

In January 1906 Purcell and a school friend from Cornell, George Feick, made a yearlong tour of Europe. They returned to the United States and decided to set up an architectural practice in Minneapolis in January 1907. In early 1910 they were joined by George Elmslie, and the three remained in partnership until Feick departed to rejoin his father in the contracting business in Sandusky, Ohio, in 1913. Purcell left the firm in 1917 to become director of advertising for the Alexander Brothers in Philadelphia, Pennsylvania. Two years later, the company went bankrupt and Purcell moved to Portland, Oregon, to establish the Pacific States Engineering Company. He stayed in business until the early 1930s when tuberculosis forced him to close the office and retire to southern California for treatment. He never fully regained his health and remained inactive the rest of his life.

Purcell died in Pasadena, California, on April 11, 1965.

Notable Buildings

WITH GEORGE FEICK
Stewart Memorial Presbyterian Church (now Redeemer Missionary Baptist Church), 116 E. 32nd Street, Minneapolis (1909)

WITH GEORGE ELMSLIE
Merchants National Bank, Winona (1912)
Edna Purcell residence (known as the Purcell-Cutts house), 2328 Lake Place, Minneapolis (1912–13)
Edwin Hoyt residence, Red Wing (1913)
Farmers and Merchants State Bank, Hector (1916)
Kasson Municipal building, Kasson (1917)

William Purdy (1887–1977)
William Ward Purdy was born on February 11, 1887, in Minnesota. His education and training are unknown. He worked for Walter Keith, and succeeded to his practice after the latter's retirement. Purdy also worked as architect for the real estate firm of Dickinson and Gillespie's Hennepin Housing Corporation in Minneapolis in the mid- to late 1930s. He went back into private practice at some later date, designing primarily residences and apartment buildings, and was active as late as 1973. He worked most of that time out of his home at 1500 Sheridan Avenue S. in Minneapolis.

Purdy died in Minneapolis on January 24, 1977.

Notable Buildings
Apartment house, 2932–2936 Dean Boulevard, Minneapolis (1939)

Abraham Radcliffe (1827–?)
Abraham Maby Radcliffe was born in New York City on May 11, 1827. He apparently grew up in the city and got his start in

Dakota County Courthouse, Hastings, 1896–71 (Abraham Radcliffe). *Photograph ca. 1910. Courtesy of Minnesota Historical Society.*

architecture with the firm of E. A. and R. L. Stevens in Hoboken, New Jersey, some time before 1849. He went on to work successively in Elmira, New York (1849–52), and Fort Wayne, Indiana (1852–57). In 1857, Radcliffe moved to Minnesota and opened an office in Minneapolis. The next year, he opened another in St. Paul. From 1862 to 1865 he practiced architecture in Winona, but sold his practice there to Charles Maybury and returned to St. Paul. He closed the Minneapolis office about 1868 and maintained only a St. Paul practice for the rest of his time in the area. From 1871 to 1875 he was in partnership with Leroy Buffington, and so may have kept a Minneapolis presence through that connection.

Radcliffe remained in St. Paul until 1889, when he moved to San Francisco and became a member of the firm of Randell Hunt and Company, engineers and contractors. He resided across the bay in Alameda, where he may have opened an office after leaving Randell Hunt about 1891.

Nothing is known of the rest of his life, including the date and place of his death.

Notable Buildings
Pence Opera House (later Union City Mission), Minneapolis (1867) (razed 1962)
Dakota County Courthouse, Hastings (1869–71)
Union Presbyterian Church, St. Peter (1870–71)
Boyden residence, Hudson, Wisconsin (1879)
Philip Reilly-Engelbrecht Hobe residence, 565 Dayton Avenue, St. Paul, (1881)
Engine House No. 5, (now Happy Gnome Restaurant) 498 Selby Avenue, St. Paul (1882)
Norman Kittson residence, St. Paul (1882) (razed 1905)
Judson and Mary Bishop residence, 193 N. Mackubin Street, St. Paul (1882)

Edwin Radcliffe (1851–1925)

Edwin S. Radcliffe was born on June 2, 1851, in Elmira, New York, the son of architect Abraham Radcliffe. He moved with his family to St. Paul where he attended public schools and graduated from high school in 1869. He entered the University of Minnesota that same year and graduated in 1872. Radcliffe also attended the Art Institute of New York in 1874, then returned to St. Paul and went to work as a draftsman in his father's office. He remained in the firm until his father left for San Francisco in 1889, at which time Radcliffe moved to Duluth and became a partner of Charles McMillan (1889–93). He then became a partner of Charles Willoughby until 1901, when Willoughby moved to Pittsburgh. Radcliffe practiced alone thereafter, except for a brief partnership with Vernon J. Price from 1907 to 1910. Radcliffe relocated to Superior, Wisconsin, in 1916 and practiced architecture there until his death on September 19, 1925.

Notable Buildings
Roussopoulos residence, 256 E. Prescott Street, St. Paul (1888) (possibly with Abraham Radcliffe)
Matthew Burrows residence, Duluth (1890)
Jefferson School (now Jefferson Square Apartments), Duluth (1892)

Tyrone Guthrie Theater, Minneapolis, 1961–63 (Ralph Rapson). *Photograph 1966 by Terry Garvey. Courtesy of Minnesota Historical Society.*

Ralph Rapson (1914–2008)

Ralph Rapson was born in Alma, Michigan, on September 13, 1914. He studied at Alma College (1933–35) and then at the University of Michigan, graduating with a degree in architecture in 1938. He attended Cranbrook Academy of Art in Bloomfield Hills, Michigan, for graduate work in urban and regional planning. In 1942, Rapson entered private practice in Chicago while also serving as head of the Department of Architecture at the Institute of Design under the directorship of László Moholy-Nagy. He was appointed associate professor in the School of Architecture at the Massachusetts Institute of Technology in 1946, and then opened an office in Cambridge, Massachusetts. From 1951 to 1953, Rapson worked in Europe designing American embassies in Stockholm, Copenhagen, Athens, The Hague, and Oslo (the last three were not built); a consulate and apartments in Le Havre; and embassy staff apartments in Neuilly and Boulogne, France. In 1954 he moved to the University of Minnesota to become a professor and head of the School of Architecture. Rapson remained there until his retirement in 1984, after which he resumed private practice.

He died in Minneapolis on March 29, 2008.

Notable Buildings

Prince of Peace Lutheran Church for the Deaf, St. Paul (1958) (razed 2006)

Tyrone Guthrie Theatre, Minneapolis (1961–63) (razed 2006)

Cedar-Riverside Apartments (now Riverside Plaza), Cedar Avenue between 3rd and S. 6th Streets, Minneapolis (1968–73)

St. Thomas Aquinas Church, St. Paul Park (1969)

Rarig Center, University of Minnesota, Minneapolis (1971)

Arnold Raugland (1893–1966)

Arnold I. Raugland was born in Minneapolis on December 6, 1893. He attended the University of Minnesota and received a bachelor's degree in architecture in June 1920. Between 1916 and 1922 he worked in various engineering and architects' offices in Minneapolis. During this period, too, he served in an engineering unit of the U.S. Army in France (1917–19). After the war, Raugland joined Oscar Lang in partnership in 1922, and the firm continued until his retirement in April 1966. Raugland was the firm's specialist in the design of reinforced concrete and structural steel buildings.

He died in Minneapolis on August 22, 1966.

Notable Buildings

LANG & RAUGLAND

Frank Griswold residence, 56 Russell Avenue, Minneapolis (1926)

Bethlehem Lutheran Church, 4100 Lyndale Avenue S., Minneapolis (1928)

St. Andrew's Episcopal Church, 1832 James Avenue N., Minneapolis (1928)

Greyhound Bus Depot (now First Avenue and 7th Street Entry), 701 1st Avenue N., Minneapolis (1937)

Alpha Kappa Psi fraternity house, 1116 5th Street SE, Minneapolis (1950–52)

Aldrich Avenue Presbyterian Church, 3501 Aldrich Avenue S., Minneapolis (1952)

First Presbyterian Church, Minot, North Dakota (1956)

Winona State College classroom building, Winona (1963–64)

Lang and Raugland

Oscar Lang and Arnold Raugland operated one of the most successful architectural practices in Minneapolis for many years. It began when Lang, Raugland, and Carroll Lewis formed a partnership in 1922. Lewis left the office in 1930 and Lang and Raugland continued their very successful business for several decades afterwards.

Former employees took over the practice when the last of the original partners, Raugland, left in the 1960s: George Entrikin (b. 1925), who joined the firm in 1948, subsequently became president; Orvall Domholt (1919–2004) became an employee two years later and served as treasurer; and Wilder King (1924–1999), who entered the office in 1957, served as secretary. They carried on the practice until the late 1980s, when the Wesley Temple Building, where they had their office, was slated to be demolished to make way for the new Convention Center on Grant Street.

John Rauma (1926–2005)
John Gunnar Rauma was born in Virginia, Minnesota, on January 22, 1926. He graduated from Virginia High School in 1943 and attended Virginia Junior College for half a year before entering the navy, where he trained as an aviator. While in officer training, he was stationed at Gustavus Adolphus College and spent time in the library, reading about architecture. Seeing a photograph of "Fallingwater," the famous house designed by Frank Lloyd Wright in Pennsylvania, Rauma decided to study architecture.

After World War II, Rauma received his bachelor's degree in naval science at Marquette University in Milwaukee (1946) and his bachelor's degree in architecture from the University of Minnesota (1950). He received a master's degree in architecture from the Massachusetts Institute of Technology (MIT) two years later. Rauma had begun working as a designer at Magney, Tusler and Setter in Minneapolis, in 1948, and then moved to Carl Graffunder's office in 1950, where he remained for a year. In 1951–52, he was in the prestigious firm of Pietro Belluschi in Cambridge, Massachusetts, and simultaneously in the firm of Anderson-Beckwith, also in Cambridge, while attending MIT. From 1952 to 1954, he was an instructor in the College of Architecture at the University of California, Berkeley, and, in 1954, he was back in Minneapolis as an associate designer with Thorshov and Cerny, where he spent nine years. He was an instructor at the University of Minnesota's School of Architecture beginning in 1956. In 1963, Rauma and David J. Griswold formed a partnership. Rauma retired from practice in 1994.

He died in Minneapolis on December 15, 2005.

Notable Buildings
Middlebrook Hall, University of Minnesota, Minneapolis (1967) (Griswold & Rauma)
Minneapolis HRA Housing for the Elderly, 1611 S. 6th Street, Minneapolis (1968) (with Lang, Raugland and Burnet)
Sanford Hall addition, University of Minnesota, Minneapolis (1971) (Griswold & Rauma)
Auditorium Classroom Building (Willey Hall), University of Minnesota, Minneapolis (1972) (Griswold & Rauma)
Church of St. Anthony, Superior, Wisconsin (n.d.)

James Record (1857–1944)
James Lucius Record was born in Franklin, Vermont, on April 15, 1857. He grew up in Franklin and attended schools there. In 1874, at the age of seventeen, he moved to Lake City, Minnesota, where he learned the carpentry trade. Three years later, he went to La Crosse, Wisconsin, to learn more about the building trade, and then returned to Lake City and became a contractor, also working in a threshing crew during each harvest season. In 1881, Record moved to Minneapolis and became an employee of Lewis Barnett. Four years later they formed a partnership, Barnett and Record, and specialized in designing and erecting grain elevators and warehouses. He sold his interest in the firm in 1902 and formed a partnership with Lewis and Gilbert Gillette, subsequently becoming the president of Minneapolis Steel and Machinery Company. He remained in this position until 1925. In 1929, the company merged with Minneapolis Threshing Machine Company and Moline Implement Company to form Minneapolis-Moline Plow Company.

Record became chairman of the board of this firm and remained in the position until his death.

He died in Minneapolis on March 2, 1944.

Notable Buildings

WITH LEWIS BARNETT
Cargill elevator, Duluth (1892)
Phelps-Harrington elevator, Duluth (1892)
Daisy Mill, Superior, Wisconsin (1892)
Youghioghny Coal Co. docks, West Superior, Wisconsin (1893)

Charles Reed (1857–1911)
Charles A. Reed was born in Rochester, New York, on November 16, 1857. He graduated from the Massachusetts Institute of Technology and, in 1880, moved to St. Paul and worked there for a decade, possibly as an architect with the Northern Pacific and other railroads, before forming a partnership with Allen Stem in what became a very successful practice. He was also a special lecturer in architecture at the University of Minnesota for a year (1893–94). Reed and Stem specialized in large commercial and industrial buildings, although it did produce residences and other types of structures as well.

In 1901 Reed moved to New York City to supervise construction of Grand Central Station, the commission for which the firm had received that year. An article published long after his death reported that Reed was a workaholic who died of overwork. He never married, but his sister, May, married William Wilgus (1865–1949), vice president in charge of engineering for the New York Central Railroad, and it was through this connection that Reed and Stem received the commission for Grand Central terminal. It is also interesting to note that after Reed died, the New York firm of Warren and Wetmore took complete charge of construction of the building by signing a new contract as sole architects. Stem sued Warren and Wetmore (Stem vs. Warren 227 NY 538, 1920) on behalf of Reed, and the latter's estate collected $400,000 in settlement.

Reed died in New York on November 11, 1911, just days short of his fifty-fourth birthday.

Notable Buildings

REED & STEM
Metropolitan Opera House, St. Paul (1890) (razed 1936)
Wulling Hall, University of Minnesota, Minneapolis (1892)
William J. Reed residence, 1530 Jefferson Street, Duluth (1892)
Grand Central Station, New York, New York (1901–15) (with Warren and Wetmore)
St. Paul Civic Auditorium (later, Stem Hall), St. Paul (1907) (razed 1982)
Denver Auditorium, Denver, Colorado (1908) (razed 1990)
St. Paul Hotel, 350 Market Street, St. Paul (1909)

George Ries (1860–1937)
George Joseph Ries was born in Lohr, Bavaria, on March 14, 1860. He attended public schools in that city as well as the Warzburg Architectural School, where he received professional training. He served in the First Pioneer Battalion of the First Army Corps of Bavaria and was discharged with the rank of sergeant. Ries came to the United States in 1881 and worked briefly as a coal miner in Pennsylvania. In 1882, he moved to St. Paul by way of Le Sueur and Winnipeg, Manitoba,

and entered the building business, first as a bricklayer, then a contractor. After his business failed in 1889, he moved his family to Tacoma, Washington, and then Portland, Oregon, where they lived until 1892. He returned to St. Paul and restarted his contracting business, which was more successful this time. By 1900 he was giving more time to architecture while still maintaining the building firm.

St. Paul Hotel, St. Paul, 1909 (Reed and Stem). *Photograph ca. 1911 by Charles P. Gibson. Courtesy of Minnesota Historical Society.*

Ries entered politics in 1906 by being appointed alderman of the newly created Twelfth Ward; two years later, he was elected to the same position. The Democratic Party bosses in St. Paul were sufficiently impressed with his popularity to persuade him to run for Ramsey County auditor in the fall of 1910. He won the election and served as county auditor for the next twenty-six years. He appears to have abandoned the practice of architecture about the same time as he began his political career.

Ries died in St. Paul on October 7, 1937.

Notable Buildings
St. Agnes Church, 548 Lafond Avenue, St. Paul (1897–1912)
Church of St. Mary, New Trier (1909)

Church of St. Mary, New Trier, 1909 (George Ries). *Photograph by Bob Firth.*

Robert Rietow (B. 1937)
Robert Rietow was born in Sheboygan, Wisconsin, on May 14, 1937. He received his bachelor's degree in architecture from the University of Minnesota in 1959 and then worked in the office of Thorshov and Cerny in Minneapolis from 1960 to 1964. He was with Miller, Whitehead, Dunwiddie, Inc., from 1964 to 1967, also in Minneapolis, and in 1967 he rejoined Cerny & Associates as associate and project architect. In 1971 he, along with Frederick Bentz and Milo Thompson, founded the firm of Bentz Thompson Rietow, where he serves as principal-in-charge of finance, in addition to being in charge of many major design projects.

Notable Buildings

WITH FREDERICK BENTZ AND MILO THOMPSON
Le Jeune residence, Orono, Maine (ca. 1980)
Wooddale Church, 6630 Shady Oak Road, Eden Prairie (1984–90)
Lake Harriet Band Shell, 4135 Lake Harriet Parkway W., Minneapolis (1985)
Brown Krause manor, 3600 Chicago Avenue S., Minneapolis (1996)
Beth Shalom Synagogue, Hopkins (2002)

Rhodes Robertson (1886–1974)
Rhodes Robertson was one of the most talented designers to work in Minnesota. He was born in Somerville, Massachusetts, on September 27, 1886, and received his bachelor's and master's degrees in architecture from Harvard University (1908 and 1910, respectively). He studied

abroad for two and a half years following graduation, then returned to the United States where he spent three years working in the prestigious Boston firm of Cram and Ferguson. He came to Minneapolis in the mid- or late 1910s and found employment as a draftsman and designer with Hewitt and Brown. Robertson remained with that firm until it closed in the 1930s, and then became an instructor in the School of Architecture at the University of Minnesota.

He died on June 15, 1974, in San Diego, California.

Notable Buildings
Northwestern Bell Telephone Company, 224 S. 5th Street, Minneapolis (1932)

Garth Rockcastle (B. 1951)

Garth Carl Rockcastle was born on April 4, 1951, in Rochester, New York. He received his bachelor's degree in architecture from Pennsylvania State University in 1974 and his master's degree in architecture and urban design from Cornell University in 1978. He moved to the Twin Cities in 1976 and worked for a succession of local firms until becoming a partner with Thomas Meyer and Jeffrey Scherer in 1981, in the firm now known as MS & R Ltd. The firm has become one of the most successful in the Upper Midwest and has designed residences, museums, libraries, and commercial buildings, a number of which have won design awards. Rockcastle also held a faculty position in the College of Architecture and Landscape Architecture at the University of Minnesota beginning in 1978, serving as head of the Department of Architecture from 1991 to 1997. In 2004, he was appointed dean of the School of Architecture at the University of Maryland while also maintaining his interest in MS & R.

Notable Buildings

WITH THOMAS MEYER AND JEFFREY SCHERER
Spencer residence, Long Lake (1985)
Dayton residence, Orono (1985)
St. Anthony Main—Phase IV, SE Main Street, Minneapolis (1985)
Von Blon residence, Minnetrista (1987)
Merriam Park Public Library, 1831 Marshall Avenue, St. Paul (1992)
Mill City Museum and Washburn Crosby A Mill ruins study, 704 S. 2nd Street, Minneapolis (1995–2003)
Minnesota Center for the Book Arts, 1011 Washington Avenue S., Minneapolis (1998)

Paul Rockey (1894–1979)

Paul Thomas Rockey was born on July 12, 1894, in Freeport, Illinois. He graduated from high school in Freeport in 1912 and received his bachelor's degree in architecture and structural engineering from the University of Illinois in 1917. Rockey worked as a draftsman in the firm of Grabe & Helleberg in Columbus, Nebraska, until September 1917, when he entered the armed forces during World War I. In June 1919, he returned to Grabe & Helleberg and remained with that firm until January 1921. He moved to Mankato, Minnesota, and joined George Pass & Son, Architects, as draftsman. In 1927, he became a partner (Pass & Rockey) and continued the firm after Pass's death in 1931. During World War II, he worked as a structural engineer for Giffels & Vallet in Detroit (April–August 1942) and then for Graham, Anderson, Probst & White of Chicago from August 1942 to April 1943, working at the naval ordnance plant in Grand Island, Nebraska. In the 1970s he became a partner of Walter B. Cheever (Rockey and Cheever). The firm continues active today as Cheever and Aslesen.

Rockey died in Mankato on November 3, 1979.

Notable Buildings
Citizens Telephone Company, Mankato (1926) (Pass & Rockey)
Municipal Hospital, Sleepy Eye (1941)
Mankato West High School, Mankato (1949–51)
Mankato Free Press Building, Mankato (1951)

Fritz Rohkohl (B. 1931)
Fritz Carl Rohkohl was born in Minneapolis on July 6, 1931. He received his bachelor's degree in architecture from the University of Minnesota in 1955. He worked part-time in the office of Bergstedt and Hirsch from 1953 to 1955 and, after graduation, became a full-time employee. He moved up to associate in 1968 and became a partner in 1974, adding his name to the firm (Bergstedt, Wahlberg, Bergquist and Rohkohl).

Notable Buildings
WITH MILTON BERGSTEDT, CHARLES WAHLBERG, AND LLOYD BERGQUIST
Murray High School (now Hill-Murray High School), 2625 Larpenteur Avenue E., St. Paul (1962)
Rochester YMCA, Rochester (1967)
Inver Hills Junior College, Inver Grove Heights (1970)

Alexander Rose (1875–?)
Alexander Fraser Rose was born in Creiff, Scotland, in 1875. He came to the United States with his family some time in the next decade and was naturalized as a citizen in 1887. It is not known where he was educated or when he arrived in Minnesota, but he began working as an

Commodore Hotel, St. Paul, 1921 (Alexander Rose). *Photograph ca. 1925 by Charles P. Gibson. Courtesy of Minnesota Historical Society*

architect about 1903 and was employed by Minneapolis Steel and Machinery Company as a structural engineer for about a decade starting in 1911. Around 1920 Rose was designing buildings for the Fleisher Construction Company, owned by Samuel Fleisher. Rose was also a part owner for an undetermined time. Fleisher was busy erecting apartment houses near the south edge of downtown Minneapolis. Rose designed the buildings that Fleisher was constructing and, after he left the firm and opened his own office, continued to design primarily apartment houses for Fleisher. The 1927 Minneapolis city directory notes that he had moved to Miami, Florida, probably the previous year. In 1930, possibly a victim of the Great Depression, he was employed as a gardener in Alameda, California. Nothing more is known of his life and career after that and his place and date of death are unknown.

Greve Oppenheim residence, St. Paul, 1913 (Ellerbe & Round). *Photograph ca. 1973 by Thomas J. Lutz. Courtesy of Minnesota Historical Society.*

Notable Buildings
Buckingham Apartments, 1500 La Salle Avenue, Minneapolis (1920)
Commodore Hotel, 79 Western Avenue, St. Paul (1921)
Bronzin Apartments, (now 125 Oak Grove Street) 125 Oak Grove Street, Minneapolis (1921)
The Parkway (apartments), 1501 La Salle Avenue, Minneapolis (1921–22) (addition of three floors to original Harry Jones structure)
Apartment buildings, 1812 and 1820 First Avenue S., Minneapolis (1924)

Olin Round (1867–1927)
Olin Hart Round was born in Michigan in 1867. He was educated at the Art Institute of Chicago, but information about his early life is sketchy. He worked in Le Mars, Iowa, beginning about 1893 as a partner in the firm of Round and Burkhead. He probably moved to St. Paul between 1896 and 1899 and was employed as a draftsman by Mark Fitzpatrick. Round remained in the office until 1909, when he joined Franklin Ellerbe as partner from 1910 to November 1913. Round then entered partnership with Service Wager (1914–15). Afterward, he established a private practice which he maintained, except for a brief partnership with Silas Jacobson (1917), until his death in St. Paul on August 10, 1927.

Notable Buildings
Zumbro Hotel, Rochester (1912) (Ellerbe & Round)
Greve Oppenheim residence, 509 Summit Avenue, St. Paul (1913) (Ellerbe & Round)
School, Dundas (1914) (Round & Wager)
F. D. Parker residence, White Bear Lake (1914) (Round & Wager)

High School, Independence, Wisconsin (1915)
Hastings Casket Company, Hastings (1915)
William Fitzgerald residence, Rochester (1915)
W. F. Bachrach residence, Rochester (1915)
High School, Owatonna (1917) (Round & Jacobson)

David Salmela (B. 1945)
David Daniel Salmela was born in Wadena, Minnesota, on March 28, 1945. He grew up on a farm and attended public schools in Sebeka, Minnesota. He is one of a few prominent architects never to have received a formal education in architecture. In 1965, he began working as a draftsman in the office of McKenzie, Hague and Gilles in Minneapolis, a position he held for a year. He then moved to Hibbing and was employed by A. G. McKee and then ABI Contracting, Virginia (1966–69). He joined Aguar, Jyring, Whiteman and Moser in Hibbing for a year and then went to work for Damberg, Scott, Peck and Booker in Virginia, where he stayed twenty years. In 1989, Salmela was made the head of the Mulfinger Susanka office in Duluth and a year later formed a partnership with Cheryl Fosdick. Salmela bought out Fosdick's interest in the firm and launched his own practice in 1994, which he still maintains.

Notable Buildings
Luken residence, Duluth (1990) (Salmela Fosdick)
Gooseberry Falls State Park Visitors Center, Two Harbors (1992) (Salmela Fosdick)
Lutz residence, Pike Lake, Duluth (1993) (Salmela Fosdick)

Emerson sauna, Duluth, 2002 (David Salmela). *Photograph by Peter Bastianelli-Kerze.*

Our Savior's Lutheran Church, Pilgrim's Chapel, Hibbing, 1958 (Robert Sandberg). *Photograph by Bob Firth*.

Ravenwood Studio (for photographer Jim Brandenburg), Ely (1995)
Emerson residence and sauna, Duluth (1997–2002)
Jackson Meadow residential development, Marine on St. Croix (1998)
Albrecht residence, Red Wing (1999)
Streeter residence, Greenwood (2002)
Salmela residence, Duluth (2006)

Robert Sandberg (B. 1922)
Robert Y. Sandberg was born in Rice Lake, Wisconsin, on January 10, 1922. He attended the public schools of Rice Lake, and then the University of Minnesota's School of Engineering from 1940 to 1942. In 1943 he enlisted in the Army Air Corps and served until 1946; after the war Sandberg returned to the University of Minnesota and studied for a year until he signed a professional football contract, first with the American Football League and then with the Canadian Football League. He received a bachelor's degree in architecture at the University of Manitoba in 1949 and practiced architecture in Winnipeg while playing football. In 1951, he moved to Hibbing and established a private practice, which he maintained until 1990. Sandberg continues to practice at Lake Vermillion.

Notable Buildings
Our Savior's Lutheran Church, Pilgrim's Chapel, Hibbing (1958)
Itasca Community College, Grand Rapids (1986–88) (with Val Michelson)

Glenn Saxton (1877–1958)

Glenn Lyle Saxton was born in Coldwater, Minnesota, on September 22, 1877. Nothing is known of his education and early career. He came to Minneapolis in the late 1890s and worked as a draftsman for Charles Sedgwick. Saxton went into private practice soon afterwards and became noted for publishing stock plan books and plans of residences in local newspapers for a number of years. He moved to California about 1915 and practiced there until the late 1920s. By 1930, he was a stocks and bonds salesman in Los Angeles, having forsaken the profession of architecture.

Saxton died in San Bernardino County, California, on March 13, 1958.

Notable Buildings
Residence, 2927 46th Avenue S., Minneapolis (1915)
Karcher-Sahr residence, 222 E. Prospect, Minneapolis (n.d.)
Residence, 727 E. 24th Street, Minneapolis (n.d.)

Albert Schippel (1862–1935)

Albert Schippel was born in Wisconsin in January 1862. His family, of Saxon-Prussian descent, moved to Mankato, Minnesota, the same year. Schippel began working as a carpenter and went into business with George Pass at an unknown date, forming an architectural practice known as Pass and Schippel. The partnership dissolved in 1902 and Schippel opened his own office in Mankato, designing a great many buildings in the area. About 1920 he became a partner of Ernest H. Schmidt.

Schippel died in Dallas, Texas, on January 22, 1935.

Notable Buildings
Oleander Saloon, Mankato (1901) (razed) (with George Pass)
Immanuel Lutheran School, Mankato (1903)
Bethany Lutheran College (originally German Evangelical Ladies Seminary), Mankato (1910)

Charles Sedgwick (1856–1922)

Charles Sumner Sedgwick was born in Castille, New York, on May 9, 1856. While she was still very young, the family moved to Oberlin, Ohio, where his father worked as superintendent of public schools. Sedgwick attended schools in Oberlin and then in Poughkeepsie, New York, when the family moved there. In 1872, the family moved yet again, to Binghampton, New York, and Sedgwick entered the firm of architect Isaac G. Perry as an apprentice, remaining with Perry for twelve years, working as a draftsman and foreman of the drafting room. He moved to Minneapolis in 1884 and set up his own office which he maintained the rest of his life. He designed many public buildings, residences, and churches. Sedgwick published plans for houses in a syndicated weekly newspaper column, and issued a book of house designs in 1904.

Sedgwick died in Minneapolis on March 12, 1922, of Bright's disease, from which he had suffered for several years.

Notable Buildings
Minneapolis Academy (later Minnesota College), Harvard and Delaware Streets SE, Minneapolis (1889) (razed ca. 1947)
Burton Hall, University of Minnesota, Minneapolis (1893–95)

Dayton's department store (now Macy's), Minneapolis, 1902 (Charles Sedgwick). *Photograph ca. 1916 by Charles J. Hibbard. Courtesy of Minnesota Historical Society.*

Westminster Presbyterian Church, Nicollet Avenue and 12th Street, Minneapolis (1898)

Dayton's department store (now Macy's), 700 Nicollet Avenue, Minneapolis (1902)

Oliver Presbyterian Church, 2647 Bloomington Avenue S., Minneapolis (n.d.) (partially razed 1982)

Donald Setter (1904–1990)

Donald P. Setter was born on September 8, 1904, in Cattaragus, New York. He was educated in the public schools and obtained his professional training at Cornell University, from which he graduated with his bachelor's degree in architecture in 1930. He worked as a draftsman and architect in Buffalo, New York, in the offices of E. B. Green and Sons (1924–25), and with Bryant Fleming in Ithaca, New York (1927–29), before moving to Minneapolis in 1930. He joined the firm of Hewitt and Brown, which became Hewitt, Setter & Hamlin, with the addition of Ralph Hamlin. In 1939, Setter joined Magney & Tusler, and became a partner soon afterward, remaining in the firm for the rest of his career. He was named secretary and vice president in 1959, when it was renamed Setter, Leach & Lindstrom.

Christ Chapel, Gustavus Adolphus College, St. Peter, 1961 (Setter, Leach & Lindstrom). *Photograph 1973. Courtesy of Minnesota Historical Society.*

Setter retired in 1964 and moved to Silverdale, Washington, where he died on July 29, 1990.

Notable Buildings

MAGNEY, TUSLER & SETTER
Sumner Field Housing Project, Minneapolis (1938) (razed 2002)
Walker Art Center alterations, Minneapolis (ca. 1947) (razed 1970)
Ford Hall, University of Minnesota, Minneapolis (1949)
Peik Hall, University of Minnesota, Minneapolis (1954)
Faribault High School, Faribault (1958)

SETTER, LEACH AND LINDSTROM
Christ Chapel, Gustavus Adolphus College, St. Peter (1961)

Setter, Leach, and Lindstrom

As with so many other firms, Setter, Leach and Lindstrom began life under an entirely different name.

In 1908, a young architect and engineer named Gottfried Magney arrived in Minneapolis and sought employment in the prestigious firm of Edwin Hewitt. Magney had already been working as a draftsman for three years in Seattle and San Francisco. Hewitt hired him, but he stayed there just four years before leaving to form a partnership with Cecil Chapman. Three years later Chapman departed and Magney was joined by Wilbur Tusler. The resulting firm was to become one of the best known and most successful in Minneapolis.

Magney and Tusler flourished in the 1920s and even in the 1930s, when other architects struggled to survive the Great Depression. Near the end of the decade, they hired Donald Setter, who had been one of the last associates of Edwin Hewitt. Setter became a partner shortly afterward and his name joined the other two men as Magney, Tusler and Setter.

With the retirement of Magney in 1954 and Tusler in 1961, and with the addition of Stowell Leach and John Lindstrom as partners in the 1950s, the firm was renamed Setter, Leach and Lindstrom, under which it operated for almost four decades until its merger with Leo A. Daly in the 1990s.

Monroe Sheire (1834–1887)

Monroe Scheire was born in Lexington, New York, on May 11, 1834. He was the son of a building contractor who moved to Detroit the following year. Young Sheire was self-educated, studying architecture in various offices in Detroit, and then joined his father in the building business. In 1860, he moved to St. Paul and in 1862 became a partner of Charles Leonard in an architecture and construction company. In 1865 Sheire's older brother, Romaine Sheire, joined the firm. Sheire was the designer and the others were the builders. Leonard left the company about 1874 and the two brothers continued on with the business.

Sheire died in White Bear Lake, Minnesota, on July 23, 1887.

Notable Buildings

WITH CHARLES LEONARD AND ROMAINE SHEIRE

Plymouth Congregational Church, Faribault (1867)
Alexander Ramsey residence, 265 Exchange Street, St. Paul (1868–72)
Church of St. Joseph, St. Joseph (1871)
First Baptist Church, 499 Wacouta Street, St. Paul (1872–74) (with W. W. Boyington)

WITH ROMAINE SHEIRE

Anthony Yoerg residence, 215 W. Isabel Street, St. Paul (1875)

Romaine Sheire (1833–1905)

Romaine Sheire was born in Lexington, New York, in 1833. He moved to Detroit with his family about 1835 and during

Alexander Ramsey residence, St. Paul, 1868–72 (Monroe Sheire, Charles Leonard, and Romaine Sheire). *Photograph 1962 by Eugene Debs Becker. Courtesy of Minnesota Historical Society.*

the Civil War served in Company F, 1st Regiment of Michigan Engineers and Mechanics, organized in Detroit. He relocated to St. Paul in October 1865, where his brother Monroe was already living. Besides becoming a partner with his brother in an architecture and building company in 1865 he was active in the Odd Fellows, serving as "Grand Patriarch" in the early 1880s.

Sheire died in St. Paul on September 11, 1905.

Notable Buildings

WITH MONROE SHEIRE AND CHARLES LEONARD
Plymouth Congregational Church, Faribault (1867)

Church of the Visitation, Danvers, 1931 (Glynne Shifflet). *Photograph by Bob Firth.*

Alexander Ramsey residence, 265 Exchange Street, St. Paul (1868–72)
Church of St. Joseph, St. Joseph (1871)
First Baptist Church, 499 Wacouta Street, St. Paul (1872–74) (with W. W. Boyington)
Anthony Yoerg residence, 215 W. Isabel Street, St. Paul (1875) (with Monroe Scheire)

Glynne Shifflet (1907–1971)
Glynne William Shifflet was born in Winfred, South Dakota, on March 17, 1907. He was educated in the public schools of Aberdeen, South Dakota, and graduated from the University of Minnesota with a bachelor's degree in architecture in 1929. He attended the École des Beaux-Arts in Paris, for two months in 1930. He returned to the United States to work as a designer and draftsman for Cass Gilbert in New York and Cyril Pesek in Minneapolis. In 1931, Pesek and Shifflet formed a partnership that lasted until 1942, when Pesek joined Minnesota Mining and Manufacturing Company. Shortly after World War II, Kenneth A. W. Backstrom entered the firm as a partner, followed in the next several years by Marlin Hutchison and Arthur Dickey. The firm, known as Shifflet, Backstrom, Hutchison and Dickey, flourished in the 1950s and 1960s.

Shifflet died on May 23, 1971, in Minneapolis.

Notable Buildings

PESEK & SHIFFLET
Church of the Visitation, Danvers (1931)
Phi Chi fraternity house, 325 Harvard Street SE, Minneapolis (1931)
Northern Pump Company, Fridley (1939–40)

Hamline University Methodist Church, St. Paul, 1928 (Slifer & Abrahamson). *Photograph ca. 1930. Courtesy of Minnesota Historical Society.*

Frederick Slifer (1885–1948)
Frederick Abner Slifer was born in St. Paul on May 9, 1885. He attended schools in the city and studied architecture in the Atelier Masqueray under Emmanuel Masqueray. He also worked for Masqueray as a draftsman, as well as in the offices of Thomas Holyoke and Cass Gilbert. Following Masqueray's death in 1917, Slifer formed a partnership with two other draftsmen, Frank Abrahamson and Edwin Lundie, to finish the work then underway in the office. In 1919, the partnership broke up; Slifer and Abrahamson formed a practice and Lundie went into business on his own. Slifer and Abrahamson were joined by E. Richard Cone in 1936, and Abrahamson departed soon after Cone joined. Slifer & Cone specialized in church design throughout the Upper Midwest.

Slifer died on November 19, 1948, in St. Paul. The firm continued as Cone & Peterson until 1972.

Notable Buildings

SLIFER & ABRAHAMSON
Evangelical Lutheran Church of the Redeemer, 285 N. Dale Street, St. Paul (1922)
St. Casimir School, 930 Geranium Avenue E., St. Paul (1923)
Mount Olive Lutheran Church, 3045 Chicago Avenue S., Minneapolis (1925)
Hamline University Methodist Church, 1514 Englewood Avenue, St. Paul (1928)

Saul Smiley (B. 1918)
Saul Charles Smiley was born on February 5, 1918, in Minneapolis. He attended South High School for half a year and then transferred to North High School, where he graduated in 1935. He entered the University of Minnesota and studied there for six years, graduating in 1942 with a bachelor's degree in architecture. From 1940 to 1942 Smiley worked as a draftsman with Perry Crosier in Minneapolis and, after World War II, joined McEnary and Krafft as a junior draftsman in 1946. The following year he was employed by Irving Coryell as chief draftsman and, in 1949, left that office to work for George Becker. He formed his own practice about 1950, which merged with Liebenberg, Kaplan and Glotter in 1973 to form Liebenberg Smiley Glotter and Associates. Smiley specialized in the design of medical facilities, especially hospitals. The firm continues as Smiley Glotter and Nyberg Architects.

Notable Buildings
Eveleth Fitzgerald Hospital, Eveleth (1958–59)
Franklin Towers, 4th Avenue S. and Franklin Avenue, Minneapolis (1964–65)
Unity Hospital, 550 Osborne Road NE, Fridley (1965–66)

Claude Smith (1889–1967)
Claude Herbert Smith was born in Strathray, Ontario, on March 28, 1889. He was educated in the public schools of London, Ontario, and studied architecture in London and Toronto. He moved to Duluth in 1907 and worked in the office of Geman and Lignell until 1917. He then joined William Bray and became a partner in 1923. Smith opened his own practice in 1925, when Bray retired, and closed his office when he himself retired in 1957.

Smith died in Duluth on January 23, 1967.

Notable Buildings
Lakewood Pumping Station and boiler house remodeling, Duluth (1932)
Civic Center, Duluth (1936) (codesigned landscaping with Arthur Nichols)
Itasca County Courthouse, Grand Rapids (1940)

Julie Snow (B. CA. 1950)
Julie VandenBerg Snow was born in Grand Rapids, Michigan. She earned a bachelor's degree in architecture from the University of Colorado in 1971 and then moved to Minneapolis where she eventually joined Hammel Green and Abrahamson (HGA) in 1974. Snow left that firm in 1988 to work for Phillips Plastics Corporation, a former client at HGA. Two years later, she entered partnership with Vincent James. The firm dissolved in 1995 and Snow established her own practice, Julie Snow Architects. Her designs have won numerous awards and received national recognition.

Notable Buildings
Minnesota Transportation Museum, Jackson Street and Pennsylvania Avenue, St. Paul (1993) (James/Snow Architects)
Minnesota Children's Museum, 10 W. 7th Street, St. Paul (1995) (with Vincent James and Architectural Alliance)
Origen Center, Phillips Plastics Corporation, Menomonie, Wisconsin (1995–96)
Fifth Precinct Police Station, Minneapolis (1998)

Fifth Precinct Police Station, Minneapolis, 1998 (Julie Snow). *Photograph 1999. Copyright Don Wong Photography. Courtesy of Julie Snow Architects, Inc.*

Jerstad Center, Evangelical Lutheran Good Samaritan Society, Sioux Falls, South Dakota (1999)
Koehler residence, New Brunswick, Canada (2000)
Humboldt Lofts, 715 S. 2nd Street, Minneapolis (2004)
The Museum of Russian Art (formerly Mayflower Congregational Church), 5500 Stevens Avenue S., Minneapolis (2005)

Kirby Snyder (1881–1967)
Kirby Theron Snyder was born on April 19, 1881, in Elmwood, Illinois. He attended Abingdon Normal College, in Abingdon, Illinois, for three years and Knox College in Galesburg, Illinois, for one year. He worked in the office of J. J. Hotz in Iowa City, Iowa, for two years and came to Minneapolis in 1907. He practiced there for fifteen years, and then moved to Sawtelle and Los Angeles, California, in 1923 and 1927, respectively.

Snyder died in Twentynine Palms, California, on July 31, 1967.

Notable Buildings
Louisburg School, Louisburg (1911)
Wadena Fire and City Hall, Wadena (1912)
German Evangelical Lutheran Church, Paynesville (1913)
Kirby Snyder residence, 4101 Lyndale Avenue S., Minneapolis (1915)

Vinje Lutheran Church, Willmar, 1962–64 (Sovik, Mathre & Madson). Photograph by Bob Firth.

Edward Sovik Jr. (B. 1918)
Edward Sovik Jr. was born in 1918 in Honan Province, China, to missionary parents. He, his twin brother Arne, and an older sister were educated in the mission boarding school until warfare forced the school to move to Kiangsi Province in southern China. The family returned to the United States shortly thereafter and the three children enrolled at St. Olaf College in Northfield, where Edward and Arne graduated in 1939. Sovik studied art at St. Olaf and chose to pursue painting at the Art Students League in New York City. After a year, he left and entered Luther Theological Seminary in St. Paul, intending to become a missionary in China. However, with the entry of the United States in World War II, he enlisted in the Marine Corps and became a pilot.

After the war, Sovik attended Yale University's School of Architecture and, while there, became interested in church design. He felt that religion was "entrenched in the past" while architectural styles were moving ahead in new directions. "By the time I was ready to start working myself," he recalled, "I had decided that any church buildings I did would have to be contemporary in style." Sovik graduated with a bachelor's degree from Yale in 1949 and returned to Northfield to open an office. He went on to become a partner of Sewell J. Mathre and Norman Madson in 1953, and later with Clinton Sathrum and Robert Quanbeck. The firm is known today as SMSQ Architects.

Notable Buildings

SOVIK, MATHRE & MADSON
Lutheran Social Services Building, 2414 Park Avenue, Minneapolis (1957)
Trinity Lutheran Church, Brainerd (1957)
Calvary Lutheran Church, 6817 Antrim Road, Edina (1959)
Vinje Lutheran Church, Willmar (1962–64)
Lutsen Sea Villas, Lutsen (1968)
St. Leo's Catholic Church, Pipestone (1969)

James Stageberg (B. 1925)

James Edgar Stageberg was born in Dawson, Minnesota, on April 29, 1925. He received his bachelor's degree in architecture from the University of Minnesota in 1952 and his master's degree from Harvard University in 1954. He worked as a draftsman with Saul Smiley in Minneapolis from 1948 to 1949 and in the same capacity with Armstrong and Schlichting from 1951 to 1952. Stageberg was employed as a draftsman by Carl Koch in Cambridge, Massachusetts, while attending Harvard (1953–54) and returned to Minneapolis to enter the firm of Magney, Tusler, Setter and Lindstrom in 1954. He formed a partnership with Thomas Hodne in 1968, which lasted until 1982. The firm became Stageberg Beyer and Sachs in subsequent years and closed its doors in 2006. Stageberg retired in 2000.

Notable Buildings

Edina Evangelical Free Church, 5015 70th Street W., Edina (1966)

HODNE/STAGEBERG PARTNERS

Mary Mother of the Church, 3333 E. Cliff Road, Burnsville (1969)

Hennepin County Library, Southdale Branch, 7001 York Avenue S., Edina (1974)

1199 Place, New York, New York (1974)

Urban American Indian Center (now Minneapolis American Indian Center), 1530 Franklin Avenue E., Minneapolis (1974–75)

McNeal Hall (addition and alterations), University of Minnesota, St. Paul (1975)

Elmer L. Andersen Library, University of Minnesota, Minneapolis, 1999 (Hodne/Stageberg Partners). *Photograph courtesy of Northwest Architectural Archives, University of Minnesota.*

Stageberg residence, 4820 Penn Avenue S., Minneapolis (1981)

STAGEBERG BEYER SACHS
Elmer L. Andersen Library, University of Minnesota, Minneapolis (1999)

Edward Stebbins (1854–1934)
Edward Somerby Stebbins was born on February 9, 1854, in Boston. He resided in the city until 1868, when he moved to Troy, New York, and then, two years later, to Saratoga, New York. From his arrival in 1870 until 1877, he worked with architect E. D. Harris, part of the time on the Grand Union Hotel, a very large resort hotel under construction in Saratoga. In 1874, Stebbins had the entire supervision of the work. During this time he also studied architecture at the Massachusetts Institute of Technology (MIT), and in France, and worked with McKim, Mead & White in New York City, but it is unclear how much time or exactly when he was with the latter firm. It is likely that this all took place between 1874 and 1877.

In 1877, Stebbins left New York and moved to Minneapolis, where he spent the rest of his life. He established his own practice and specialized in schools, churches, and public buildings. He was the first architect in the city to have received collegiate architectural education. Stebbins had a brief partnership with George R. Mann (1878–79), a former classmate at MIT, and from 1880 until 1914

Gethsemane Episcopal Church, Minneapolis, 1883 (Edward Stebbins). *Photograph ca. 1905 by Sweet. Courtesy of Minnesota Historical Society.*

University Club, St. Paul, 1912 (Reed & Stem). Photograph ca. 1912. Courtesy of Minnesota Historical Society.

he practiced alone. In the latter year, he entered partnership with Robert Haxby, and then with Cyrus Bissell in 1920.

Stebbins was a charter member of the Architectural Association of Minnesota (1881) and served as president of the Minnesota Chapter of the American Institute of Architects. He died in Minneapolis on March 3, 1934.

Notable Buildings
Edward Stebbins residence, 320 Oak Grove Street (moved in 1982 to 2404 Stevens Avenue S.), Minneapolis (1879)
Gethsemane Episcopal Church, 905 4th Avenue S., Minneapolis (1883)
Holy Rosary Catholic Church, 18th Avenue S. and E. 24th Street, Minneapolis (1887)
D. B. Lyons residence, 419 Oak Grove Street, Minneapolis (1892)
Sidney Pratt School (now Pratt Community Center), 66 Malcolm Avenue SE, Minneapolis (1898–99)
West High School, Hennepin Avenue and 28th Street, Minneapolis (1906–07) (razed 1984)

Allen Stem (1856–1931)
Allen Hartzell Stem was born in Van Wert, Ohio, on January 28, 1856. While still in his youth, Stem moved with his family to Indianapolis, where he studied architecture at the Indianapolis Art School, and started his career with his father in 1876. In 1884 he relocated to St. Paul, and two years later became a partner of Edgar Hodgson (son of Isaac Hodgson Sr.). This partnership lasted until 1890, when Stem joined Charles Reed in what was to become a highly successful and lucrative practice. The firm became nationally known when, in 1901, they won the commission for Grand Central Station in New York City.

Reed died in 1911 and Stem took on two new partners, Alfred Fellheimer in the New York office, and Roy Haslund in the St. Paul office. Stem retired in 1920, and the firms continued on. Haslund remained in business until 1955. Fellheimer & Wagner, as the New York office came to be called, is still in business today as Wank Adams Slavin Associates.

Stem died in St. Paul on May 19, 1931.

Notable Buildings

REED & STEM

Palazzo Apartments (later Colonnade Apartments), 10th and St. Peter Streets, St. Paul (1890)

William Hamm residence, 668 Greenbrier Street, St. Paul (1892)

Michigan City Public Library (now John G. Blank Center for the Arts), Michigan City, Indiana (1897)

St. Paul Hotel, 350 Market Street, St. Paul (1909)

University Club, 420 Summit Avenue, St. Paul (1912)

WITH ROY HASLUND

St. Paul Athletic Club, 340 Cedar Street, St. Paul (1917)

Allen Stem residence, Dellwood (ca. 1920)

St. Paul Casket Co., 1222 University Avenue N., St. Paul (1922)

J. Walter Stevens (1856–1937)

John Walter Stevens was born on June 13, 1856, in Wakefield, or South Reading, Massachusetts. His early life and education are cloaked in mystery, but he first appeared in St. Paul in 1879. As far as can be determined, he never had a partner during his career, and his office was a training ground for many younger architects. Among the latter was Harvey Ellis.

Stevens was very active in the profession and belonged to the Architectural Association of Minnesota and the Minneapolis Chapter of the American Institute of Architects, serving as president of the latter in 1906. He was also secretary and member of the editorial board of *Western Architect* magazine from 1902 to 1904. His thorough respect and adherence to professional ethics was demonstrated in an 1885 letter he sent to the Architectural Association of Minnesota in which he tendered his resignation due to unprofessional conduct among some of his colleagues in St. Paul. Among the charges Stevens leveled at his colleagues was the acceptance of commissions below the standard percentage rate and doing work at no cost in return for free advertising. The association asked that he remain in the group and head an investigation of his charges, but it is unknown if he did so.

Stevens practiced until his retirement in 1935. He died on April 26, 1937, reported to be the oldest architect in both age and years of service in St. Paul at the time of his death.

Notable Buildings

A. B. Stickney residence, 288 Summit Avenue (1884) (razed 1930)

Noyes Brothers & Cutler Co. building (now Park Square Court), 6th and Sibley Streets, St. Paul (1886)

Noyes Brothers & Cutler Co. building (now Park Square Court), St. Paul, 1886 (J. Walter Stevens). *Photograph ca. 1892 by Truman Ward Ingersoll. Courtesy of Minnesota Historical Society.*

Pattee Hall, University of Minnesota, Minneapolis (1889)

Germania Bank Building (now St. Paul Building), 6 W. 5th Street, St. Paul (1890)

Charles Stinson (B. 1951)

Charles Robert Stinson was born in Minneapolis on October 2, 1951. He grew up in Red Wing, Minnesota, and received his bachelor's degree in architecture at the University of Minnesota in 1975.

Stinson worked with the firm of Orlin Fjelstad & Associates in Northfield, Minnesota, from 1976 to 1978 and then with Rauenhorst (now Opus) Corporation, Bloomington, Minnesota, from 1978 to 1980. He opened a private practice at Jensen Beach, Florida, in 1980 and six years later moved his firm to Deephaven, Minnesota. He was the recipient of the Architect of Distinction award from the American Institute of Architects in March 2005.

Notable Buildings

Charles Stinson and Carol Eastlund residence, 4733 Eastwood Road, Minnetonka (1994)

Erik and Marsha Larson residence, 14730 Stone Road, Minnetonka (2003)

Fred and Gloria Sewell residence, 16 Park Lane, Minneapolis (2004)

North American State Bank, 2800 First Street S., Willmar (2007)

Peter and Mona Vrijsen residence, 2545 Huntington Avenue S., St. Louis Park (2009)

Sidney Stolte (1905–1978)

Sidney Lloyd Stolte was born in Buffalo Lake, Minnesota, on February 28, 1905. He graduated from South High School in Minneapolis in December 1922 and, although he was offered a scholarship to study at Carleton College in Northfield, declined it, and instead entered the University of Minnesota where he earned a bachelor's degree in architectural engineering in 1927. He worked as a draftsman and estimator at the John Clark Granite Company in Rockville, Minnesota, while attending the university (1923–27) and then, following graduation, entered the firm of Long and Thorshov in Minneapolis as a designer, detailer, draftsman, and construction supervisor. From 1930 to 1931 he was employed as a designer, draftsman and estimator at A. Moorman & Company, St Paul, then moved to Magney & Tusler in Minneapolis from 1931 to 1932.

Stolte returned to John Clark Granite Company from 1933 to 1934, and left that firm to join the State Emergency Relief Administration in St. Paul as a construction engineer (1934–35) and the Works Projects Administration in St. Paul as director of the Division of Operations (1935–39). From 1939 to 1943 he was state administrator in the WPA in St. Paul. Stolte left government relief agencies in 1943 and became a partner in the architectural firm of P. C. Bettenburg and Company in St. Paul. He remained in the firm for the remainder of his career.

Stolte died in Minneapolis on October 10, 1978.

Notable Buildings

BETTENBURG TOWNSEND STOLTE & COMB

City Hall, Anoka (1954)

Northwestern Hospital, Thief River Falls (ca. 1958)

Sheridan School, 525 N. White Bear Avenue, St. Paul (1960)

Edgewater Baptist Church, 5501 Chicago Avenue S., Minneapolis (1961)

Carl Stravs (1880–1966)
Carl B. Stravs was born on September 29, 1880, in Yugoslavia. No information has been found concerning his early life and education. He came to Minneapolis in the early 1900s and practiced in Minneapolis for many years, designing mostly residences and commercial buildings. He was in partnership with John Jager from 1905 to 1909, but otherwise spent his career in private practice until his retirement in 1959.

Stravs died in Twin Falls, Idaho, in October 1966.

Notable Buildings
Robert Giles residence, 4106 Vincent Avenue S., Minneapolis (1908) (with Jager)
Phi Gamma Delta fraternity house, 1129 University Avenue SE, Minneapolis (1910–11)
Apartment house, 4418 W. Lake Harriet Parkway, Minneapolis (1922)
Emil Geist residence, 2904 Seabury Avenue, Minneapolis (ca. 1923)

Carl Struck (1842–1912)
Carl Frederick Struck was born in Christiana (now Oslo), Norway, on January 27, 1842. He studied architecture in Christiana and Copenhagen before immigrating to the United States in 1865. He settled first in Marquette, Michigan, where he lived for three years, then moved to La Crosse, Wisconsin, and

Denfeld High School, Duluth, 1925–26 (William Sullivan and Abraham Holstead). *Photograph courtesy of Minnesota Historical Society.*

resided there for five years. Struck came to Minneapolis in 1881 and remained there until 1905, when he relocated to Spokane, Washington. For part of the time in Spokane, he was an associate of Albert Held.

Struck specialized in fraternal halls and churches for Scandinavian groups. He is also credited with courthouses and commercial buildings throughout the Upper Midwest. He was reputed to have had an excellent tenor voice and was a member of a male chorus. His wife was the daughter of Marcus Thrane, Norway's first labor leader.

Struck died in Spokane, Washington, on March 30, 1912.

Notable Buildings
Dania Hall, Minneapolis (1886) (burned 2000)
Normanna Hall, Minneapolis (1888–89) (razed ca. 1965)
Pracna building, 117 SE Main Street, Minneapolis (1890)

Dania Hall, Minneapolis, 1886 (Carl Struck). *Photograph ca. 1903. Courtesy of Minnesota Historical Society.*

William Sullivan (1884–1942)
William Jeremiah Sullivan was born on July 1, 1884, in Mankato, Minnesota. His father was in the contracting business, which no doubt influenced young Sullivan to enter the architecture profession. He was educated in the public schools of Mankato and attended the University of Illinois for three years and Cornell University for one year, studying architecture. He worked first in Chicago as a draftsman for an unknown firm and then moved to Duluth where he opened an office in 1910. Two years later, he was joined in partnership by Abraham Holstead, and the firm of Holstead and Sullivan became one of the most successful in the city. The partnership lasted at least through the 1920s and Sullivan later went into business with Henning N. Orrfalt. He retired in 1936 and moved to Phoenix, Arizona, and the firm continued as Sullivan, Orrfalt, and Burrell for a number of years.

Sullivan died in Phoenix on December 7, 1942.

Notable Buildings
WITH ABRAHAM HOLSTEAD
St. Louis County Jail, Duluth (1923)
Denfeld High School, Duluth (1925–26)
Naniboujou Club, Grand Marais (1928–29)
Village Hall, Grand Rapids (1928–29)

Herbert Sullwold (1883–1969)

Herbert A. Sullwold was born in Minnesota on August 24, 1883. He was educated at the Massachusetts Institute of Technology, graduating in 1907. His early work experience is unknown. He began practicing in St. Paul about 1912 and, at one time, probably only briefly, worked for Emmanuel Masqueray. It is not known when he opened his own office, but he appears to have maintained a private practice for most of his life. Sullwold moved to Los Angeles, California, between 1920 and 1930 and maintained a firm there for a number of years.

He died in Palos Verdes Estates, California, on November 25, 1969.

Notable Buildings
J. L. Sullwold residence, 1773 Summit Avenue, St. Paul (1910)
Residence, 1640 Portland Avenue, St. Paul (1912)
Chris Hanson Jr. residence, 1695 Summit Avenue, St. Paul (1920)
Our Lady of Victory Chapel, College of St. Catherine, St. Paul (1924)

Engebret Sund (1879–1938)

Very little is known of the life and career of Engebret H. Sund. He was born in Norway on December 19, 1879, but nothing is known of his education and career or when he came to the United States. He practiced in Minneapolis for many years, forming a partnership with Arthur Dunham in the 1910s, which lasted until the latter's departure in the early 1930s. It is not known if Sund continued in practice afterward.

He died in Minneapolis on May 30, 1938.

Our Lady of Victory Chapel, College of St. Catherine, St. Paul, 1924 (Herbert Sullwold). *Photograph 1954 by Norton & Peel. Courtesy of Minnesota Historical Society.*

Notable Buildings

WITH ARTHUR DUNHAM
Mineral Springs Sanatorium, Cannon Falls (1915–29) (razed 1991)
Glen Lake Sanatorium Nurses Home, Chaska (1922)
Glen Lake Children's Camp, Eden Prairie (1925)
Wooddale School, Edina (1926)
Central Lutheran Church, 1300 4th Avenue S., Minneapolis (1926–28)

Sarah Susanka (B. 1957)
Sarah Hills Susanka was born on March 21, 1957, in Bromley, Kent, England. She received a bachelor's degree in architecture from the University of Oregon and was awarded a master's degree from the University of Minnesota in 1983. That same year, she formed a partnership with Dale Mulfinger. Michaela Mahady joined as a partner in 1987. In 1999, Susanka left and founded Susanka Studios in St. Paul. She wrote several bestselling books, including *The Not So Big House* (1998) and *Home by Design* (2004), and lectured on energy efficiency through a grant from the U.S. Department of Energy. Susanka currently resides in North Carolina.

Notable Buildings

WITH DALE MULFINGER AND MICHAELA MAHADY
Thiry residence, Eagan (1987)
Gleason Lake Townhouses, Minnetonka (1987)

James Taylor (1857–1929)
James Knox Taylor was born in Knoxville, Illinois, on September 11, 1857. He moved with his parents to St. Paul in 1861 and was educated in the public schools. After graduating from high school, Taylor obtained an apprenticeship in the office of Edward Bassford. He attended the Massachusetts Institute of Technology (MIT), graduating in 1879, and was a classmate of Cass Gilbert and Clarence Johnston.

Taylor returned to St. Paul after graduation and, after working for a short time in Abraham Radcliffe's office, opened his own practice in 1882. In about 1885 he formed a partnership with Gilbert, with whom he practiced until 1892. He then moved to Philadelphia to become a partner of Amos J. Boyden. Two years later, he joined Peabody & Stearns of Boston as head of their New York office and, in 1897, was appointed Supervising Architect of the Treasury in Washington, D.C., a position he held until 1912. Taylor then became head of the Department of Architecture at MIT for two years, followed by a fairly peripatetic life in which he lived at various times in Philadelphia; Northampton, Massachusetts; Yonkers, New York; and Tampa, Florida, the latter becoming his home in 1923.

He died in Tampa on August 27, 1929.

Notable Buildings
Frederick Jackson House, 467 Ashland Avenue, St. Paul (1882)
Everett Bailey House, 459 Holly Avenue, St. Paul (1885)

WITH CASS GILBERT
David McCourt residence, 161 Cambridge Street, St. Paul (1887)
Endicott Building, 4th Street between Jackson and Robert Streets, St. Paul (1889)
Residence at "Acorn Point," Manitou Island, White Bear Lake (1891)

Governor Lind residence, New Ulm, 1887 (Frank Thayer). *Photograph 1974 by Lynne Van Brocklin. Courtesy of Minnesota Historical Society.*

Frank Thayer (CA. 1853–1946?)
The *Mankato Free Press* reported in 1895 that Frank Thayer was born in New York State and, after receiving a public school education, began learning the carpenter's trade at the age of fourteen, presumably in his home state, and that he came to Minnesota about 1875. The newspaper reported that after Thayer arrived in Minnesota "as a contractor and builder [he] erected many public and private buildings in the southern part of the state," but did not say where his business was located. After moving to Mankato in 1885, Thayer became exclusively an architect and also "accumulated a large amount of property in various places," including a residence on Prospect Heights. It is not known how long he practiced in Mankato. He entered partnership with Olof Hanson in 1901 and the next year they moved to Seattle, Washington, to be closer to Juneau, Alaska, because they had won the competition to build the courthouse and jail there. The partnership broke up about 1904 and Thayer continued to practice in Seattle for a number of years afterward.

His place and date of death are uncertain, but he may have died in Snohomish, Washington, in 1946.

Notable Buildings
Governor Lind residence, New Ulm (1887)
Mankato Savings Bank, Mankato (ca. 1894)
F. Thayer's building, Mankato (ca. 1895)
Odd Fellows Hall, Mankato (ca. 1897)
J. H. Lang residence, Mankato (n.d.)

Milo Thompson (B. 1935)

Milo Thompson was born in Minneapolis on May 28, 1935. He received a bachelor's degree in liberal arts at the University of Minnesota in 1957 and a bachelor's degree in architecture in 1962 from the same institution. He attended Harvard University and was awarded a master's degree in architecture in 1963. Two years later Thompson received the Rome Prize, which made it possible for him to study at the American Academy of Rome. He returned to Minneapolis and was employed as a draftsman in the office of Thorshov and Cerny. He then worked for Carl Koch in Cambridge, Massachusetts, as James Stageberg had about fifteen years earlier, then joined Brown, Dallas Associates in Rome. Thompson came back to Minneapolis to become vice president and chief of design for Cerny & Associates before forming a partnership with fellow employees Frederick Bentz and Robert Rietow in 1971. He continues to be active in his firm.

Thompson is credited with the design of two of the early skyway bridges, which won him an AIA Honor Award in 1969. Thompson retired in the 1990s from a professorship at the College of Architecture at the University of Minnesota, where he taught for more than thirty years.

Wooddale Church, Eden Prairie, 1984-90 (Bentz Thompson Rietow). *Photograph by Bob Firth.*

Notable Buildings

BENTZ THOMPSON RIETOW
Le Jeune residence, Orono, Maine (ca. 1980)
Wooddale Church, 6630 Shady Oak Road, Eden Prairie (1984-90)
Lake Harriet Band Shell, 4135 Lake Harriet Parkway W., Minneapolis (1985)
Brown Krause manor, 3600 Chicago Avenue S., Minneapolis (1996)
Beth Shalom Synagogue, Hopkins (2002)

Martin Thori (1864-1905)

Martin B. Thori's early life and career are mostly unknown. He was born in Norway in September 1864, and the family came to Minnesota about three years later. He settled in St. Paul about 1885 and was a partner of Didrik Omeyer there by 1888. After the partnership ended around 1900, Thori went into business with William Alban, and the firm ended with his death from tuberculosis in St. Paul on February 8, 1905.

Notable Buildings

WITH DIDRIK OMEYER
Thomas Swem residence, 775-777 W. Fairmount Avenue, St. Paul (1890)
Union Opera House, Leroy (ca. 1895)
E. J. Webber residence, Fergus Falls (1896)

WITH WILLIAM ALBAN
Ada City Hall, Ada (1903–04)
Cottonwood County Courthouse, Windom (1904)

Willard Thorsen (1924–1998)
Willard Lien Thorsen was born in Mason City, Iowa, on March 10, 1924. He graduated from the Mason City high school in 1942 and attended Mason City Junior College for a year before entering the U.S. Army Air Force meteorology program, training at the University of Chicago for a year and a half during World War II. After the war, he returned to Minnesota and entered the University of Minnesota, where he earned a bachelor's degree in architecture in 1949. He went to work as a draftsman at Thorshov and Cerny in Minneapois and remained there for most of the rest of his career. In 1960, he and Roy Thorshov formed a partnership after Thorshov and Cerny was dissolved; the firm remained active until 1987 when it was sold to Hammel, Green & Abrahamson. The firm specialized in the design of shopping centers.

Thorsen died in Moose Lake, Minnesota, on March 23, 1998.

Walker Art Center, Minneapolis, 1923 (Olaf Thorshov, Lowell Lamoreaux, and Louis Long). *Photograph ca. 1925 by Charles P. Gibson. Courtesy of Minnesota Historical Society.*

Notable Buildings
Apache Plaza Shopping Center, 37th Avenue NE and Silver Lake Road, St. Anthony (1959–61) (Thorshov & Cerny)

THORSEN & THORSHOV
Sons of Norway, 1455 W. Lake Street, Minneapolis (1961)
Har-Mar Mall, 2100 Snelling Avenue, Roseville (1962–63)
Northtown Shopping Center, 398 Northtown Drive, Blaine (1970–72)
Ebenezer Tower Apartments, 2533 Portland Avenue S., Minneapolis (1971)

Olaf Thorshov (1883–1928)
Olaf Thorshov was born near Oslo, Norway, on January 16, 1883. He came to the United States and to Minnesota at the age of eighteen. He worked briefly in a sash and door factory in Stillwater, Minnesota, and then moved to St. Cloud for a year before coming to Minneapolis in 1906. He attended the University of Minnesota and graduated with a Bachelor of Science degree in architecture in 1921. Thorshov worked for Long, Lamoreaux & Long in Minneapolis before becoming a partner in 1920. After Louis Long and Lowell Lamoreaux died in the early 1920s, the firm was renamed Long & Thorshov.

Thorshov died in Minneapolis on June 16, 1928.

Notable Buildings

WITH LOWELL LAMOREAUX AND LOUIS LONG
Olaf Thorshov House, 208 Cecil Street SE, Minneapolis (1912)
Dayton's department store addition (now Macy's), 8th Street and Nicollet Mall, Minneapolis (1916–29)
Walker Art Center, Hennepin Avenue and Vineland Place, Minneapolis (1923) (razed 1970)

Roy Thorshov (1905–1992)
Roy Norman Thorshov was born in Minneapolis on March 13, 1905. He graduated from the University of Minnesota in 1928 with his bachelor's degree in architecture and joined his father's firm just before the latter's death. Thorshov became a full partner in Long & Thorshov and, in 1942, was joined by Robert Cerny. The firm, renamed Thorshov & Cerny, became very successful. It was dissolved in 1960, and Thorshov went into partnership with Willard Thorsen.

Thorshov died in Minneapolis on March 13, 1992.

Notable Buildings
Hastings State Hospital, Hastings (1960)

James Tillitt (1926–2004)
James C. Tillitt was born in Foley, Minnesota, on June 26, 1926. He earned a bachelor's degree in architectural engineering from the University of Illinois and a master's degree in civil engineering from the University of Minnesota. He worked twelve years as a professional engineer in various firms until he joined Walter Wheeler in Minneapolis in 1960. Wheeler died in 1974 and Tillitt continued the firm, which became Tillitt & Associates in 1980. He retired about 1996.

Tillitt died in Littleton, Colorado, on April 10, 2004.

Notable Buildings

Lamplighter Square Shopping Center, Crystal (1968) (with Gerrish Associates Inc.)

Arrowhead Resort, Alexandria (1968) (with BWBR)

Anheuser-Busch Inc. Malt Plant, storage silos, and warehouse, Moorhead (1975) (with Foley Brothers)

U.S. Customs and Immigration Building, International Falls (1975)

Barge unloading facility, U.S. Salt, Inc., Burnsville (1988)

Max Toltz (1857–1932)

Maximilian R. Toltz was born on September 2, 1857, in Koeslin, Germany. He studied at the Royal Academy of Science and Engineering in Berlin, where he received a degree in civil engineering in 1877. He served in the German army after graduation, rising to the rank of second lieutenant.

After his military service, Toltz worked as a civil engineer. In the course of this work, his firm was engaged to build a road where, as they were making a cut

Robert Street Bridge, St. Paul, 1926 (Toltz, King & Day). *Photograph courtesy of Northwest Architectural Archives, University of Minnesota.*

From Toltz, King and Day to TKDA

One of the most important architecture and engineering firms in Minnesota got its start in 1910 when Max Toltz left his job as chief engineer for the Great Northern Railway to found his own firm, Toltz Engineering Company. He was quickly joined by Wesley King and then, in 1918, by Beaver Wade Day. The firm, known then as Toltz, King and Day, grew into a major company, well-known not only in Minnesota but also across the nation.

Day died in 1931 and Toltz the year after, but King maintained the company name until 1956, when Arndt Duvall and Gerald Anderson, longtime employees, became partners. The company was renamed Toltz, King, Duvall and Anderson (TKDA). King died in 1959 and Duvall assumed the presidency. The firm operates today as TKDA.

---

through a hill, they encountered solid rock instead of gravel and defaulted on the contract. The government viewed the default as a criminal act, possibly verging on neglect on the part of Toltz's company. He fled Germany "in the dark of night," so it is said, and barely escaped into Switzerland ahead of the police.

Toltz immigrated to Montreal, Canada, about 1880 and soon found work in St. Paul as a draftsman with the St. Paul, Minneapolis, and Manitoba Railroad. He rose through the ranks to the position of assistant engineer but left the company after a dispute with James J. Hill, the company's owner. Toltz returned to Montreal in 1904 and briefly joined the Canadian Pacific Railroad before being asked by Louis Hill, successor to James J. Hill, to come back to work for the Great Northern Railway a year later. Toltz moved to St. Paul in 1905 and took on the task of engineering the electrification of the Cascade Tunnel in Montana. He was sent to Switzerland for six months to study tunnel electrification and returned to St. Paul to become chief engineer for the railroad.

About 1909, while still employed at the Great Northern Railway, Toltz formed the Superheating and Engineering Company in downtown St. Paul, which was renamed the Toltz Engineering Company the following year. His associate in the firm was Wesley King, and when Toltz left the railroad in 1910 to devote his time exclusively to his own business, King became a partner. During World War I he was assigned to Fort McHenry, near Baltimore, to build barracks and a hospital. He returned to St. Paul after the war and was joined in partnership by Beaver Wade Day in 1918 and the firm became Toltz, King and Day. The company grew into one of the largest and most successful in the Twin Cities, designing and constructing many bridges, power plants, and commercial buildings of all types. In 1956 the company was renamed Toltz, King, Duvall and Anderson (TKDA) and continues to be a highly successful architecture and engineering firm today.

Toltz died in St. Paul on January 11, 1932.

Notable Buildings
West Publishing Company (now Ramsey County Government Center West), 50 Kellogg Boulevard, St. Paul (1910–11) (with Reed & Stem, architects)
Sanitary Foods Manufacturing Company (now Griggs Midway building), 1821 University Avenue, St. Paul (1912) (Toltz Engineering Company)

TOLTZ, KING AND DAY
Hamm Building, 408 St. Peter Street, St. Paul (1919)
St. Paul Gas Light Company Service Building (now Xcel Energy), 825 Rice Street, St. Paul (1924)
Robert Street Bridge, St. Paul (1926)

Oliver Traphagen (1854–1932)
Oliver Green Traphagen was born in Tarrytown, New York, on September 3, 1854. He and his family moved to St. Paul about 1870 and he became an apprentice to architect George Wirth. He relocated to Duluth in 1882 and worked as a carpenter and architect during the 1880s. In 1890 he became a partner of Francis Fitzpatrick.

This very successful partnership lasted until 1896, when Fitzpatrick moved to Washington, D.C. Traphagen remained in Duluth for two more years, then moved to Honolulu, Hawaii, because of the ill health of one of his daughters. He set up a practice and designed the Moana Beach Club (1901), the first tourist hotel on Waikiki Beach. He maintained his practice there until 1907, when he moved to Alameda, California. Traphagen worked as an architect in Alameda until his retirement in 1925.

Traphagen died in Alameda on October 21, 1932.

Notable Buildings
Wirth Building, 13 W. Superior Street, Duluth (1886)
Fire House No. 1, First Avenue E. and Third Street, Duluth (1889)

WITH FRANCIS FITZPATRICK
Fitger's Brewing Company (now hotel), Duluth (1890)
Chester Terrace, 1210–1232 E. First Street, Duluth (1890)
First Presbyterian Church, Duluth (1891)

Fitger's Brewing Company (now Fitger's Inn), Duluth, 1890 (Oliver Traphagen and Francis Fitzpatrick). *Photograph ca. 1925. Courtesy of Minnesota Historical Society.*

Oliver Traphagen residence, 1509–1511 E. Superior Street, Duluth (1892)
Torrey Building, Duluth (1892)
Lyceum Theater, Duluth (1893) (razed 1966)

Fred Traynor (1911–1996)

Fred Vincent Traynor was born on December 22, 1911, in Devils Lake, North Dakota. He graduated from high school there and attended the University of North Dakota in Grand Forks for two years. He then transferred to the University of Illinois, where he received his bachelor's degree in architecture in 1935. Traynor moved to St. Cloud, Minnesota, and was employed in Nairne Fisher's firm from 1935 to 1938. He worked in the offices of Pesek and Shifflet, Minneapolis, from 1938 to about 1942, and for Frank W. Jackson, St. Cloud, in the same years. He served in the U.S. Navy during World War II, after which he returned in 1946 to his employment with Frank Jackson. In 1949, Traynor formed a very successful partnership with Raymond Hermanson and they were joined by Gilbert Hahn in the 1960s.

Traynor retired from practice in 1986 and died in St. Cloud on April 5, 1996.

Notable Buildings

WITH RAYMOND HERMANSON
St. Anastasias Elementary School, Hutchinson (1957)
Halenbeck Hall, St. Cloud State University, St. Cloud (1965)
Warner Palestra, St. John's University, Collegeville (1973–75) (Traynor, Hermanson & Hahn)

Peter Truszinski (1918–1979)

Peter Truszinski was born in St. Cloud, Minnesota, on November 1, 1918. His education and training are unknown. He served in the navy in World War II, and worked in Louis Pinault's firm in St. Cloud for many years, becoming a partner at an unknown date. Truszinski became the owner of the practice when Pinault retired in 1972, and was the in-house architect for the Jim Miller Construction Company for four years. Truszinski also maintained a private practice for a time.

He died in St. Cloud on October 2, 1979.

Notable Buildings
No buildings attributable to Truszinski have been found.

Claude Turner (1869–1955)

Claude Allen Porter Turner was born in Lincoln, Rhode Island, on July 4, 1869. He was educated at the school of engineering at Lehigh University, Bethlehem, Pennsylvania, graduating in 1890. He worked for numerous companies in the following decade, including the New York & New England Railroad, Edgmore Bridge Company (Philadelphia), Columbus (Ohio) Bridge Company, Pittsburgh Bridge Company, and Pottsville (Pennsylvania) Iron and Steel Company, before coming to Minneapolis in 1897, where he spent the remainder of his career. Turner was employed as an engineer with the Gillette Herzog Company and American Bridge Company until 1901, when he formed his own firm. In 1908, he received a patent for a reinforced concrete support system called the "mushroom cap" column system, which he used in many later buildings. He went on to be granted

Soo Line Railroad bridge, Washington County, 1910–11 (Claude Turner). *Photograph 1976 by Liza Nagle. Courtesy of Minnesota Historical Society.*

more than thirty patents for reinforcement and reinforced concrete.

Turner retired to Columbus, Ohio, in the 1930s and died there on January 10, 1955.

Notable Buildings
Milwaukee Railroad bridge, Mississippi River between Franklin Avenue and Lake Street, Minneapols (1902)
C. A. Bovey Building, Minneapolis (1906) (razed 1975)
Aerial Lift Bridge, Duluth (1906)
Wisconsin Central Freight Station, Bridge Square, Hennepin Avenue, Minneapolis (1907) (razed ca. 1995)
Minnesota State Prison, Stillwater (1908)
Soo Line Railroad bridge, Washington County (1910–11)

Wilbur Tusler (1890–1985)
Wilbur H. Tusler was born in Miles City, Montana, on August 26, 1890. He moved with his family to St. Paul at the age of two. He studied architecture at the University of Minnesota, and then transferred to the University of Pennsylvania, where he received his bachelor's degree in 1914. In 1917, he returned to Minneapolis and entered partnership with Gottlieb Magney and remained in the firm until his retirement in 1961. The firm of Magney & Tusler became one of the most successful in Minnesota. It became known as Setter, Leach & Lindstrom as new partners were added, and exists today as Leo A. Daly.

Tusler died in Fort Myers, Florida, on August 14, 1985.

Young Quinlan store, Minneapolis, 1928 (Wilbur Tusler and Gottlieb Magney). *Photograph by Hibbard Studio. Courtesy of Minnesota Historical Society.*

Notable Buildings

WITH GOTTLIEB MAGNEY

Mrs. Wilbur Tusler residence, 2444 W. 24th Street, Minneapolis (1928)

Young Quinlan store, 901 Nicollet Mall, Minneapolis (1928)

Foshay Tower, 9th Street and 2nd Avenue S., Minneapolis (1929)

Swedish Hospital, S. 9th Street near 11th Avenue S., Minneapolis (1929)

Ford Hall, University of Minnesota, Minneapolis (1949) (with Magney and Donald Setter)

William Tyrie (1874–1943)

William Wallace Tyrie was born in New Hampshire in May 1874, the son of a clergyman. He worked in Lawrence, Massachusetts, as a draftsman in 1891–92 and graduated from Pratt Institute in Brooklyn, New York, in 1896 with a degree in architecture. He took postgraduate work in design, possibly at the same school. In 1897 Tyrie began practicing architecture in Ogdensburg, New York, with George Chapman. After the partnership broke up, Tyrie spent nine years with firms in New England and New York, including Van Vleck & Goldsmith and Lord & Hewlett in New York City, serving as head draftsman in the latter's office. He briefly ran his own practice in New York in 1908, then moved to Minneapolis at the invitation of George Chapman, and helped establish the firm of Bell, Tyrie, and Chapman. The firm specialized in public buildings, mainly courthouses and schools, in the Upper Midwest.

In 1913 Charles Bell left the partnership, and Tyrie and Chapman continued their company for a number of years. Tyrie was known as a man possessing "the highest ethics and honesty of purpose," according to one account. In May 1929 he became an associate of the firm of Long and Thorshov, where he stayed until 1942.

Tyrie died in Eau Claire, Wisconsin, on March 19, 1943.

Notable Buildings

WITH GEORGE CHAPMAN
Alexander Baker School, International Falls (1914)

Jay Tyson (1926–2004)
Jay Walter Tyson was born in High Point, North Carolina, on March 17, 1926. He attended public schools there and graduated from high school in 1943. After serving for two years in the U.S. Navy, he returned to his home state and entered North Carolina Agricultural and Technical College in Greensboro, from which he graduated in 1950 with a bachelor's degree in architecture. He received a master's degree in architectural engineering from the University of Illinois in 1952 and moved to Minneapolis the following year, after serving as an instructor at his alma mater in Greensboro. He worked as a draftsman in the firm of Armstrong and Schlichting in Minneapolis, and later joined Hendricks Architects, followed by employment with Ellerbe Architects, and then became a partner of Frank Kerr for several years in the 1970s. In 1977 he established his own practice which he maintained until his retirement about twenty years later.

Tyson died in Upper Marlboro, Maryland, on May 13, 2004.

Notable Buildings
Century Plaza Building remodeling (formerly Minneapolis Vocational High School), 330 S. 12th Street, Minneapolis (1985)

Emil Ulrici (1857–1903)
Information about the life and career of Emil W. Ulrici is sparce. He was born in St. Louis, Missouri, on June 14, 1857, but nothing is known of his education and training, although it is thought he studied architecture in Europe. He appears in Milwaukee in 1880 working as an architect, and sometime prior to 1884 moved to St. Paul, where he maintained a practice for a few years, at least part of the time in partnership with Denslow Millard (ca.1886–90). Ulrici left the area in 1890 and practiced in Duluth for a time before returning to St. Louis, where he died on November 20, 1903.

Notable Buildings
Adolph Munch residence, 653 E. 5th Street, St. Paul (1884)
Smith-Davidson-Scheffer residence (alterations), 908 Mound Street, St. Paul (1886) (with Denslow Millard)
George Benz residence, St. Paul (1888) (razed 1948)

Albert Van Dyck (CA. 1867–1941)
Albert Reed Van Dyck was born in Wisconsin about 1867. Nothing is known of his education and work experience until he appeared in Minneapolis around 1908 as an associate of Harry Jones. He set up a private practice in 1911, which he

maintained the rest of his life, except for a brief partnership with Luther Twichell in 1916. Van Dyck specialized in residences and seems not to have had a very large office or output.

He died in Minneapolis on May 23, 1941.

Notable Buildings
E. E. Atkinson residence, 1901 Logan Avenue S., Minneapolis (1914)
S. G. Palmer residence, 2254 W. Lake of the Isles Parkway, Minneapolis (1917)
B. F. Gradwohl residence, 2621 Newton Avenue S., Minneapolis (1918)
M. C. Madison residence, 4637 Lake Harriet Parkway, Minneapolis (1923)
Fred Hopkin residence, 2250 W. Lake of the Isles Parkway, Minneapolis (1926)
George Stricker residence, 2240 W. Lake of the Isles Parkway, Minneapolis (1926)
Henry A. Bullis residence, 2116 W. Lake of the Isles Parkway, Minneapolis (1930)

Marquette National Bank, Minneapolis, 1925 (Joseph Vanderbilt and Carl Gage). *Photograph 1926 by Hibbard Studio. Courtesy of Minnesota Historical Society.*

Joseph Vanderbilt (1878–1966)
Joseph Victor Vanderbilt was born in New York City on October 22, 1878, and attended public schools there and in Rochester, New York. He received his high school preparatory education at Englewood Military Academy, and attended the Society of Beaux Arts Architects in New York for four years. During that time, Vanderbilt was a student in the ateliers of Emmanuel Masqueray and Claude Bragdon.

After completing his architectural training, Vanderbilt worked successively for C. H. Haswell, a civil and structural engineer in New York (1895–97); E. L. Young, architect, New York (1897–99); the Buffalo, Rochester and Pacific Railroad (1899–1902); Breeze and Ferguson, architects, Norfolk, Virginia (1902–05); and as the supervising architect of the Treasury, Washington, D.C. (1905–10). In 1910, he moved to Minneapolis and became head of the design staff in the office of Hewitt and Brown (1910–24) before entering a brief partnership with Carl Gage in 1925. In 1929, Vanderbilt formed a partnership with Carl Bard that existed for nearly twenty years, ending in 1948 when Bard retired and left town. Vanderbilt operated a private practice until his retirement in 1962.

He died in Minneapolis on February 13, 1966.

Notable Buildings

WITH CARL GAGE
Marquette National Bank, 517 Marquette Avenue, Minneapolis (1925) (only the façade remains)

WITH CARL BARD
Linden Hills Branch Library, 43rd Street and Vincent Avenue S., Minneapolis (1930)
Mayflower Congregational Church (now The Museum of Russian Art), 5500 Stevens Avenue S., Minneapolis (1935)
Hazel Park Congregational Church, 1831 Minnehaha Avenue E., St. Paul (1946–47)
Archbishop Dowling School, 40th Street and Thomas Avenue S., Minneapolis (1949)

Service Wager (1881–?)
The facts of Service Arthur Wager's life are few indeed. His birth date was June 24, 1881, but his birthplace is unknown. It is not known exactly when he came to St. Paul, where he spent several years. He formed a partnership for less than a year with Olin Round in 1914, and set up a private practice in August of the same year, which continued for about a year. Apparently he discovered that architecture was not for him and he began hopping around from job to job, trying out different careers as a travel agent, hardware salesman, and finally, partner in the Law-Wager real estate agency. Wager disappeared from St. Paul in 1927 and his whereabouts after that remain a mystery.

Notable Buildings
School, Dundas (1914) (with Olin Round)
Grade school, Anoka (1915)
Armory, Northfield (1915)
J. G. Phillips residence, Northfield (1915)

Charles Wahlberg (B. 1923)
Charles Douglas "Chuck" Wahlberg was born in Oberon, North Dakota, on April 6, 1923. He graduated from high school in Butte, Montana, in 1940 and earned his bachelor's degree in architecture at the University of Minnesota in 1949. He began working as a draftsman in the firm of J. C. Link and Company in Butte in September of that year, and returned to the Twin Cities the following spring to enter the office of Ingemann, Bergstedt and Cavin in St. Paul. He was then employed by Magney, Tusler, Setter and Lindstrom for three years before returning to Ingemann and Bergstedt. When that partnership ended, Wahlberg briefly joined Brooks Cavin's practice and then returned to Bergstedt and Hirsch in 1954, where he remained for the rest of his career. He became a partner and president (1974–80) in Bergstedt, Wahlberg, Bergquist and Rohkohl (BWBR). Wahlberg retired in 1985.

Notable Buildings

WITH MILTON BERGSTEDT, LLOYD BERGQUIST, CLARK WOLD AND LLOYD BERGQUIST
Valley National Bank, Eagan (1963)
Village of Burnsville Maintenance Building, Burnsville (1969)
Inver Hills Community College, Inver Grove Heights (ca. 1971)
St. Stephen Lutheran Church, Bloomington (ca. 1972)

John Wangenstein (1858–1942)
John Johnen Wangenstein was born in Valdres, Norway, in 1858. He studied architecture in Trondheim, Norway, and then immigrated to the United States and arrived in St. Paul about 1878. He worked

DeWitt-Seitz building, Duluth, 1911 (John Wangenstein). *Photograph by Hugh McKenzie. Courtesy of Northeast Minnesota Historical Center, Duluth.*

as an architect in the city for five years, then moved to Duluth in 1883 and set up a private practice, associating with Olaf Roen and Ernest Baillie at various times. His firm became one of the most successful in the growing port town, designing residences, apartment buildings, and commercial and institutional structures. Starting in 1913, Wangenstein served as the local architect for the St. Louis County Courthouse project, in association with Daniel H. Burnham of Chicago. He was also a partner of Ephraim Giliuson, but it not known how long this partnership lasted.

Wangenstein died on July 24, 1942, in Duluth.

Notable Buildings
Ingalls Flats, 216 E. 4th Street, Duluth (1891) (with Olaf Roen)
Chales Elston residence, 1609 E. Superior Street, Duluth (1893) (with Ernest Baillie)
Providence building, 332 W. Superior Street, Duluth (1894) (with Ernest Baillie)
Masonic Temple, 4 W. 2nd Street, Duluth (1905)
DeWitt-Seitz building, 327 Lake Avenue S., Duluth (1911)

Wesley Wells (1901–1981)
Wesley G. Wells was born on February 5, 1901, in Minnesota. He was educated in both architecture and engineering, probably at the University of Minnesota, and spent most of his career in the state. In 1922, he began working for the Department of Public Works of the city of St. Paul, and the following year was employed by the Northern Pacific Railroad, both jobs being held while he finished college. From 1924 to 1926, Wells worked on the construction of the St. Paul Union Depot and, when that project ended, went into private practice, which he maintained, off and on, until 1928. He

Joseph Wolf Brewing Company (now condominiums and retail), Stillwater, 1933–34 (Wesley Wells). *Photograph by John Runk. Courtesy of Minnesota Historical Society.*

returned to railroad employment briefly that year and then became a professor of Engineering Drawing and Descriptive Geometry at the College of St. Thomas in St. Paul while maintaining a private practice (1928–30).

With the onset of the Depression, Wells took various jobs with the state of Minnesota for the next two years, and resumed private practice when funding ended. In 1933, following the repeal of Prohibition, he was commissioned by several local breweries to design new facilities. The completion of these projects early in 1934 forced him back to state employment under the Civil Works Administration (CWA) programs, and then he joined the National Parks Service to design buildings and grounds at Itasca State Park and Cottonwood State Park. In 1936, Wells was promoted to Assistant Engineer, Region II, headquartered in St. Paul, in charge of preparing plans and supervising building projects at twenty-six state parks in Minnesota and Iowa. He remained employed in either state park jobs or those under the Public Works Administration until 1940, when he resumed private practice.

His private practice was short-lived, however, for in 1940 he rejoined the Great Northern Railway, for whom he had worked in 1928 as a draftsman and designer. With the outbreak of World War II, Wells was hired by the Army Corps of Engineers to work on ordnance plant construction in Kansas. After the war, he returned to St. Paul and was associated with the firm of Kindy C. Wright, helping to design and construct the Agricultural-Horticultural Building and the Hippodrome at the Minnesota State Fair (1945 and 1947, respectively).

Wells died in St. Paul on May 1, 1981.

Notable Buildings
Joseph Wolf Brewing Company (now condominium and retail), Stillwater (1933–34)
Schutz and Hilgers Brewing Company (now apartments), Jordan (1933–36)

Samuel Wentworth (1890–1962)
Samuel Clinton Wentworth was born on April 17, 1890, in Evanston, Illinois. He attended high school in Pittsburgh, Pennsylvania, for two years and Carnegie Technical Institute in the same city for three years, but did not graduate from either. From 1911 to 1925 he was employed successively with D. H. Burnham and Company, Marshall and Fox, and Weary and Alford in Chicago as a draftsman. In 1926, he moved to Minneapolis and entered the office of Larson and McLaren where he worked until 1931. During the Depression, Wentworth was employed by the federal government in one of its relief agencies. In 1937, he went into private practice, which he maintained for the remainder of his career. He moved to Birmingham, Michigan, in 1954 where he practiced until 1959 and then retired and moved to Florida.

Wentworth died in Clearwater, Florida, in April 1962.

Notable Buildings
No buildings attributable to Wentworth have been found.

Hans Wessel (1906–1969)
Hans J. Wessel was born in Malmo, Sweden, on July 5, 1906. He moved to the United States as a child and graduated from South High School in Minneapolis in 1925. He attended the University of Minnesota and received a bachelor's degree in architecture in 1930. He began working as a draftsman in local architecture offices and then formed a partnership in Richfield, Minnesota, with James Brunet in 1931. In 1934 they were joined by Marvin Kline, who continued in the practice while serving as mayor of Minneapolis (1941–44). Wessel also served for a time up to 1942 as an executive in the Reconditioning Department of the Home Owner's Loan Corporation. The partnership broke up in the late 1940s and Wessel continued in private practice in Richfield until the early 1950s, when he joined Minnesota Mining and Manufacturing Company as an executive engineer. Brunet moved to Santa Fe, New Mexico, in the 1960s and maintained a practice there for many years.

Wessel died in Washington County, Minnesota, on July 9, 1969.

Notable Buildings
Wessel residence, 5446 3rd Avenue S., Minneapolis (1932)
Flame Bar and Café, 1521 Nicollet Avenue, Minneapolis (1938) (razed 1978) (with Marvin Kline)

O. K. Westphal (1868–1935)
Otto Kurps Westphal was born on April 11, 1868, in Heydekrug, Germany. He came to the United States at age fifteen, but it is not known where his family first settled. Westphal was employed as a carpenter in Minneapolis by 1895 and studied architecture through a correspondence course

in 1907. He established what became a prolific private practice the following year and maintained an office in Minneapolis for the remainder of his career. For a short time around 1910 he was a partner of Edgar Hodgson. He is credited with an innovative restaurant design that was adopted throughout the nation, and also prepared tables for calculating stress in concrete and reinforcing steel.

Westphal died in Mineapolis on October 6, 1935.

Notable Buildings
Agate Theater, 2221–2225 E. Franklin Avenue, Minneapolis (1915)
Stores, flats, and offices, 810–822 W. Lake Street, Minneapolis (1917)
Priebe residence, 1616 James Avenue N., Minneapolis (1925)
Alhambra Theater, 3215 Penn Avenue N., Minneapolis (1927) (razed 1961)

John Wheeler (1871–1958)

John H. Wheeler was born in St. Paul on September 16, 1871. His father was born in Waterford, Ireland, and immigrated to California and then moved to St. Paul, where he established a contracting business with his brother, Thomas. Young Wheeler was educated in the public schools and then attended the College of St. Thomas for two years. After leaving college, he spent fourteen years in various architects' offices, including seven years in the office of Clarence Johnston. In 1901–02, Wheeler was in charge of the Building Inspection Department of the city of St. Paul and, in 1902, opened a private practice that he maintained for the rest of his life. He specialized in designing structures for the Catholic archdiocese. His mother, Joanna Howard Wheeler, was a cousin of Archbishop John Ireland and the latter was a frequent visitor at the Wheeler home.

Wheeler died in St. Paul on December 9, 1958.

Church of the Annunciation, Hazelwood, 1913 (John Wheeler). *Photograph by Bob Firth.*

Notable Buildings
Church of the Annunciation, Hazelwood (1913)
St. Mary's Hospital (now University of Minnesota Medical Center, Fairview, Riverside Campus), 24th Avenue S. and 6th Street, Minneapolis (1916–17)
St. Columba School, Lafond and Hamline Avenues, St. Paul (1922)
O'Halloran & Murphy funeral home, 215 W. 6th Street, St. Paul (1928)

Walter Wheeler (1883–1974)

Walter Hall Wheeler was born in Potsdam, New York, on April 15, 1883. He graduated from the University of Minnesota in 1906 with a degree in civil engineering, specializing in mining engineering. He shifted to structural engineering at a later date. He worked out of state until 1908, then returned to Minneapolis and joined his father, Charles, in a real estate, building, and investment company. In 1912, Wheeler opened his own practice, working alone until 1968 when he joined James Tillitt, who had been his employee since 1960, as a partner. Wheeler retired in that same year and Tillitt continued the practice as Tillitt and Associates. During his career, Wheeler was involved in the design of nearly nine hundred structures, including grain elevators, power plants, bridges, factories, and commercial and institutional buildings. He patented a type of reinforced concrete construction called the "smooth ceiling system," which was used in numerous buildings thereafter.

Wheeler died in Mineapolis on March 18, 1974.

Notable Buildings
Mendota Bridge, Mendota Heights (1923)

Cream of Wheat building (now CW Lofts), Minneapolis, 1927 (Walter Wheeler). *Photograph ca. 1928 by Charles P. Gibson. Courtesy of Minnesota Historical Society.*

Cream of Wheat building (now CW Lofts), 730 Stinson Boulevard NE, Minneapolis (1927)
Phyllis Wheatley House, 919 Fremont Avenue N., Minneapolis (1927–31) (razed 1965)
Lehigh Briqueting Company, Lehigh, North Dakota (1927–40)
Comstock Hall, University of Minnesota, Minneapolis (1939) (with Clarence Johnston Jr.)

Richard Whiteman (B. 1925)

Richard Frank Whiteman was born on March 24, 1925, in Mankato, Minnesota. He was educated in the public schools of Austin and received a bachelor's degree in architecture from the University of Minnesota in 1945. He earned a master's degree in architecture at Harvard University three years later. Whiteman worked briefly for Ellerbe and Company in St. Paul in 1946, and for William Riseman Associates and Bogner and Richman in Cambridge, Massachusetts (1947). He

Handicraft Guild House, Minneapolis, 1908 (William C. Whitney). *Photograph ca. 1909 by Shepard. Courtesy of Minnesota Historical Society.*

returned to Minneapolis and entered the office of Thorshov and Cerny in 1948, then left in 1952 to join Eino Jyring's firm in Hibbing. Three years later Whiteman became a partner and remained in the firm until 1972, when he moved to Duluth and joined Melander, Fugelso, Porter & Simich. Later, he established his own practice, which he operated for a number of years.

Notable Buildings
United Methodist Church, Thief River Falls (1969) (with Eino Jyring)
Tourist Information Center, Grand Portage (ca. 1985)
Old Central High School renovation, Duluth (2000–01)

William C. Whitney (1851–1945)
William Channing Whitney was born on April 11, 1851, in Worcester County, Massachusetts. He was educated at Lawrence Academy in Groton, Connecticut, and at the Massachusetts Institute of Technology. He graduated from the Massachusetts Agricultural College in 1872 with his bachelor's degree in architecture, and began working with Carl Fehmer in the firm of Emerson and Fehmer in Boston. After five years, Whitney moved to Minneapolis and entered partnership with James C. Record in 1879. The firm broke up in 1885 and Whitney opened a private practice, which lasted for the rest of his career. His firm concentrated on designs for large and prestigious residences and was a training ground for many young architects of the next generation.

Whitney retired in 1933 and died in Minneapolis on August 23, 1945.

Notable Buildings
H. Alden Smith residence (now Wells Family College Center), 1405 Harmon Place, Minneapolis (1887)
Rufus Rand residence, 1526 Harmon Place, Minneapolis (1891) (razed 1975)
Minnesota Building, World's Columbian Exposition, Chicago, Illinois (1893) (razed ca. 1894)
William Dunwoody residence, 107 Groveland Terrace (1905) (razed 1967)
E. L. Carpenter residence, 314 Clifton Avenue, Minneapolis (1906)
Handicraft Guild House, 89 S. 10th Street, Minneapolis (1908)
H. H. Irvine residence (now Governor's mansion), 1006 Summit Avenue, St. Paul (1910–12)

Clarence Wigington (1883–1967)
Clarence Wesley Wigington was born in Lawrence, Kansas, on April 21, 1883. He set out in life with the intention to study

dentistry but was persuaded by his love of art to study architecture instead. He was educated in the T. Lawrence Wallace Studio, Omaha, Nebraska, for three years and spent one year in the studios of Alfred Tuergeni in Omaha and Chicago.

Wigington joined the office of architect Thomas Kimball in Omaha as an office boy and rose to become an apprentice draftsman for six years. He then moved to the Gordon Van Tine Company in Davenport, Iowa, staying no more than two years.

In 1915 Wigington took the civil service examination for employment with the city of St. Paul and scored higher than any other applicant. He began employment in the city architect's office in 1915 and remained there until 1949. It is interesting to note that the city architect's office had two African American employees—Wigington and William Godette—during this time, a circumstance that may have been unique for that period. After his retirement in 1949, Wigington opened an office in Los Angeles, California, and then returned to St. Paul before moving to Kansas City, Missouri, to live with his daughter.

He died in Kansas City on July 7, 1967.

Notable Buildings
Zion Baptist Church, Omaha, Nebraska (1910–14)
Homecroft Elementary School, 1845 Sheridan Avenue, St. Paul (1918) (with William Godette)
Wilson Junior High School, 631 N. Albert Street, St. Paul (1924) (with William Godette)

Highland Park water tower, Snelling Avenue and Ford Parkway, St. Paul (1928) (with William Godette)
Keller Golf Course clubhouse, 2166 Maplewood Drive, St. Paul (1929) (with William Godette)
Ice palaces, St. Paul Winter Carnival, St. Paul (1936, 1939, 1940, 1942) (razed same years) (with William Godette)
Holman Field Administration Building, Holman Field, St. Paul (1938–41) (with William Godette)
Harriet Park Pavilion, Harriet Island, St. Paul (1939–40) (with William Godette)
James Griffin residence, 1592 Western Avenue, St. Paul (1957)

Highland Park water tower, St. Paul, 1928 (Clarence Wigington and William Godette). *Photograph ca. 1940 by Donaldson Photo Company. Courtesy of Minnesota Historical Society.*

William Willcox (1832–1929)

William H. Willcox was born in Brooklyn, New York, on May 26, 1832. He grew up in Brooklyn and was trained in various architects' offices. He practiced architecture in New York from 1853 to 1860 and, during the Civil War, drew maps for the Union Army. After the war, he moved to Chicago where he worked briefly for Dankmar Adler (1871) and then maintained his own practice from 1872 to 1879, including a partnership (1875–77, Willcox and Miller). Willcox moved to Nebraska to design the State Capitol (1879–81) and then to St. Paul, where he practiced from 1882 to 1891. In 1883 he was a partner of Charles Smith, and from 1885 to 1890 he was a partner of Clarence Johnston and their firm produced many prominent buildings.

In 1891, Willcox relocated to Seattle, Washington, and joined William E. Boone in the firm of Boone and Willcox (1891–93), then practiced alone for two years. He moved to Los Angeles in 1895 and to San Francisco about 1900. He left architecture in 1906 or 1907 to become a surveyor and in 1912 probably retired, as he was then eighty years old. His whereabouts afterwards are unknown until 1925 when he moved into the Veterans' Home in Yountville, California.

Willcox died in Yountville on February 1, 1929.

Notable Buildings
Old Main, Macalester College, St. Paul (1883)

WITH CLARENCE JOHNSTON
Amherst Wilder residence, 226 Summit Avenue, St. Paul (1886–87) (razed 1959)
Laurel Terrace, 294–296 Laurel Avenue, St. Paul (1887–88)

Laurel Terrace, St. Paul, 1887–88 (William Willcox and Clarence Johnston). *Photograph courtesy of Minnesota Historical Society.*

Summit Terrace, 587–601 Summit Avenue, St. Paul (1889)

George Wirth (1852–?)
George Wirth was born in Bavaria in 1852 and came to the United States in 1869. He settled first in Utica, New York, then moved to Chicago in 1875, where he may have worked for architects as an apprentice or draftsman. In 1876 he returned briefly to Utica and then studied architecture at Cornell University in Ithaca. A year later he was in Minneapolis, working both there and in Anoka. He returned to Germany and France to study architecture and came back to St. Paul in 1879, opening an office the following spring. From 1884 to 1886 Wirth was in Duluth in partnership with Oliver Traphagen before moving back to St. Paul and joining Abraham Haas in business for a year or so at the end of the 1880s. He then left the city and efforts to trace his whereabouts after 1890 have failed. Wirth's son was practicing architecture in St. Paul in 1920.

Notable Buildings
Masonic Block, Hastings (1881)
Auerbach-Ordway residence, 400 Summit Avenue, St. Paul (1882)
Henry Smyth residence, 466 Portland Avenue, St. Paul (1883)
Grand Opera House, Duluth (1883) (razed 1889)
A. H. Rodgers residence, 487–489 Ashland Avenue, St. Paul (1884)
W. W. Bishop House, 513 Summit Avenue, St. Paul (1887)

Werner Wittkamp (1903–1973)
Werner Wittkamp is virtually unknown and unappreciated today, but his work left a lasting mark on Twin Cities architectural history. He was born in Germany on December 8, 1903, and came to the United States in 1923 after studying theater design under Pavel Tschelitschev (1898–1957).

Wittkamp was employed by the great Broadway showman Flo Ziegfeld who put him to work creating sets for his stage revues. Wittkamp then left to work for Percy Strauss, president of Macy's, to design show windows for the famous New York department store. Wittkamp was drawn to Hollywood, California, at the invitation of a movie director he had known in Germany, F. W. Murnau, who signed him to a four-year contract as art director for Fox Studios. He designed sets and lighting for several pictures, including Janet Gaynor's first film, *Sunrise*, in 1926. He also designed an Art Deco stationery shop, Chryson's, in Los Angeles (1929). He moved to St. Paul where he designed a Streamline Moderne building for Cinderella Cosmetics at 2218 University Avenue.

After Prohibition ended in early 1933, Wittkamp became popular as a designer of cocktail lounges for the Curtis and Lowry Hotels in Minneapolis and St. Paul, respectively, and, most famously, the Art Deco bar in the Commodore Hotel in St. Paul. He also designed other restaurants, bars, and even funeral homes, trying to work ideas from the stage sets into them to make them more attractive, imaginative, and aesthetically soothing. A stroke partially disabled Wittkamp in 1961, but he continued working for some years afterward.

He died in Minneapolis in December 1973.

Osborn Building (now Ecolab), St. Paul, 1968 (The Wold Association). Photograph 1975 by Plattner. Courtesy of Minnesota Historical Society.

Notable Buildings
Bar and lounge, Curtis Hotel, 3rd Avenue S. and 10th Street, Minneapolis (ca. 1933) (razed 1984)
Bar, Commodore Hotel, 79 Western Avenue N., St. Paul (1934)
Lexington Restaurant (interior), Grand and Lexington Avenues, St. Paul (1938, 1953, 1969)
Wilwerscheid funeral home, 1167 Grand Avenue, St. Paul (1942)
Tip Top Tap (now Town House), 1415 University Avenue, St. Paul (1946)

Clark Wold (1926–1995)
Clark D. Wold was born in Aitkin, Minnesota, on August 20, 1926. Following high school he enlisted in the Army Air Corps in 1945. He returned to his home state after the war and entered the University of Minnesota, from which he graduated with his bachelor's degree in architecture in 1951. Wold studied at Harvard University and then returned to Minneapolis to join Milton Bergstedt's firm about 1955. The firm was renamed Bergstedt, Hirsch, Wahlberg and Wold in 1957. Wold left the partnership in 1968 to form Wold Archi-

tects and Engineers, later renamed The Wold Association. Twenty years later, he sold the practice to three associates and retired about 1990. The firm continues to operate as Wold Architects and Engineers in St. Paul.

Wold died in St. Paul on June 5, 1995.

Notable Buildings

ATTRIBUTED TO THE WOLD ASSOCIATION
Osborn Building (now Ecolab), 370 Wabasha Street, St. Paul (1968)
Ramsey County Adult Detention Center, 12–14 Kellogg Boulevard W., St. Paul (1980)
Hill City School, Hill City (1984)
Hidden Valley Elementary School, Burnsville (1987)

Kindy Wright (1893–1976)
Kindy C. Wright was born in Minnesota on March 27, 1893. Much of his life and career remains unknown, but he practiced architecture in the Twin Cities area for many years. In 1920, he was listed in the U.S. Census as vice president of a bank building company; ten years later he was an architect. In the mid-1940s he designed at least two significant structures at the Minnesota State Fairgrounds: the Agricultural-Horticultural Building and the Hippodrome, both in association with Wesley Wells. From about 1951 to 1960 he was the official architect for the State Fair.

Wright died in St. Paul on November 19, 1976.

Notable Buildings
Agricultural Horticultural Building, Minnesota State Fairgrounds, St. Paul (1945)
Hippodrome, Minnesota State Fairgrounds, St. Paul (1947)

Myrtus Wright (1881–1960)
Myrtus A. Wright was born in 1881 in Wisconsin. He began working as an elevator operator in St. Paul and enrolled in a correspondence course for architec-

Agricultural Horticultural Building, Minnesota State Fairgrounds, St. Paul, 1945 (Kindy Wright). *Photograph 1947 by* Minneapolis Star-Journal. *Courtesy of Minnesota Historical Society.*

Grandview Theater, St. Paul, 1933 (Myrtus Wright). *Photograph 1980 by Henry B. Hall. Courtesy of Minnesota Historical Society.*

tural training. He was in private practice from 1917 to the early 1920s, before partnering with Charles Hausler for a short time. From 1925 to 1929 Wright was an employee of the Omaha Railroad, and then resumed private practice from 1929 to 1935. He returned to work for the Omaha Railroad in 1936, his practice probably a victim of the Depression. He remained with the railroad until 1949, when he transferred to Chicago to work for the Chicago & Northwestern Railroad. It is not known when he retired or when he returned to St. Paul.

Wright died of pneumonia in St. Paul on October 26, 1960.

Notable Buildings
George Alverdes residence, 633 Holly Avenue, St. Paul (1919)
Grandview Theater, 1830 Grand Avenue, St. Paul (1933)
Highland Theater, 760 Cleveland Avenue, St. Paul (1939)

Phelps Wyman (1870–1947)
Alanson Phelps Wyman was born in Manchester Center, Vermont, on April 13, 1870. He received his bachelor's degree in agriculture at Cornell University in 1897, and studied architecture and landscape architecture at the Massachusetts Institute of Technology (1902–04). He worked as a draftsman for Ossie C. Simonds in Chicago (1897–98), Daniel W. Langdon, New York (1898), Olmsted Brothers, New York (1899–1902), and Charles Platt, New York (summers of 1902 and 1903).

Wyman opened an office in Chicago in 1905 and practiced there while also teaching at the University of Illinois, before moving to Minneapolis in 1911, where he maintained a practice, combining architecture and landscape architecture, until 1924. At the same time, he served on the Minneapolis Park Board (1916–24), the U.S. Housing Corporation, Washington, DC (1918), and the Minneapolis Planning Commission (1921–24). He was elected a fellow of the American Society of Landscape Architects in 1912.

In 1924, he moved to Milwaukee, Wisconsin, to assume the position of landscape architect for the Milwaukee County Regional Planning Commission. He resigned in 1926 and opened his own practice. He remained in business in Milwaukee for the remainder of his career. From 1929 to 1932, he was a consultant to the Park Board of Neenah, Wisconsin.

Wyman died in Milwaukee on November 16, 1947.

Notable Buildings

LANDSCAPE DESIGNS
E. L. King residence, Homer (1912) (razed 1987)
South Dakota State Capitol grounds, Pierre, South Dakota (ca. 1913)
Game Lodge, Custer State Park, South Dakota (1922)
Doty and Washington Parks, Neenah, Wisconsin (1929–32)

Albert Zschocke (1859–1892)
Albert Zschocke was born in Zwickau, Saxony, on May 10, 1859. He graduated from an architectural school in Germany at an undetermined date and came to the United States in 1882. He settled for a short time in Wisconsin, and then moved to St. Paul in 1883. He worked for a succession of architects, including George Wirth and William Willcox, before setting up his own office in 1885. He designed numerous residences, apartment houses, and schools.

Zschocke died in St. Paul on November 3, 1892, of typhoid at the young age of thirty-three, leaving a wife and five young children.

Notable Buildings
John Minea residence, 382 S. Winslow, St. Paul (1886)
Lucy Miller Double house, 156–158 North Farrington Street, St. Paul (1888)
George Hosmer residence, 808 Ohio Street, St. Paul (1889)
Farrington Place, 312–316 University Avenue W., St. Paul (1889)
Peter Giesen residence, 827 Mound Street, St. Paul (1891)

Alan K. Lathrop is professor emeritus and former curator of the Manuscripts Division at the University of Minnesota Libraries. He is the author of *Churches of Minnesota* (Minnesota, 2003), and his work has been published in *South Dakota History*, *Minnesota History*, *Journal of Southeast Asian Studies*, *Historic Preservation*, and *The American Archivist*.